S0-ARO-093

SPAM WARS

Our Last Best Chance to Defeat Spammers, Scammers, and Hackers

DANNY GOODMAN

SelectBooks, Inc.

Spam Wars: Our Last Best Chance to Defeat Spammers, Scammers, and Hackers
Copyright ©2004 by Danny Goodman
All rights reserved.
This edition published by SelectBooks, Inc., New York, New York

First Edition
1-59079-063-4

Library of Congress Cataloging-in-Publication Data

Goodman, Danny.
  Spam wars : our last best chance to defeat spammers, scammers, and hackers / Danny Goodman.-- 1st ed.
      p. cm.
  Includes bibliographical references and index.
  ISBN 1-59079-063-4 (hardcover : alk. paper)
1. Electronic mail systems. 2. Unsolicited electronic mail messages. 3. Computer networks--Security measures. I. Title.
TK5105.73.G66 2004
004.692--dc22

                            2004010099

Manufactured in the United States of America

                10 9 8 7 6 5 4 3 2 1

To Sidney Finortny

SPAM WARS

ACKNOWLEDGMENTS

Usually when I tell inquiring friends and family about the book I'm working on, I receive a mixture of polite smiles and blank stares, as the gibberish computer subject escapes their comprehension. Such was *not* the case with this book. Instead, everyone wanted to know more about it, especially how soon it would be ready to read. That universal interest added fuel to my personal motivation for writing this book.

I also had a lot of help along the way from friends and colleagues who sacrificed their time and energy to offer expertise, critiques, and suggestions that made me write a much better book. Fellow author Molly Holzschlag's response to an early draft of a few chapters convinced me to take a liberating step in the creation process: throwing everything out and starting over. Linda Racine schooled me in the ways of the direct mail industry. Anne P. Mitchell was kind enough to supply recordings of the 2004 Spam and the Law conference by the Institute for Spam and Internet Public Policy. Thank you also to Luis von Ahn, Manuel Blum, Nicholas Hopper, and John Langford of The CAPTCHA Project at Carnegie Mellon University for their assistance.

After nearly a year of researching and writing, I had a new draft that needed a good scrubbing for technical accuracy and overall readability. To the rescue came my friends Carl and Becky Malamud, who provided voluminous, insightful, and invaluable notes. Carl may be the only person on the planet equally adept at DNS (Domain Name Service) and CMS (*Chicago Manual of Style*). Another old friend, Dan Shafer, also offered feedback on several chapters. Joe Hutsko's contagious energy provided a welcome morale boost in the final stretch.

Publishing a book on a timely subject requires special talents in compressing schedules, exploiting new technologies, and inventing new conventional wisdom. It is therefore a thrill for me to work with Kenzi Sugihara of SelectBooks to publish this title. Kenzi published my best-selling books at Bantam and Random House in the late 1980s and early 1990s, and I've treasured his friendship and support since the "old days." He brought into this project additional experts who have helped immensely, including attorney Jessica Friedman and editor Janice Borzendowski. I also wish to thank Al Gross for his contribution of the spamwars.com and spamwars.net Internet domains to this effort.

Contents

INTRODUCTION

I've been using email on a regular basis since 1981. Although thousands of pioneers were emailing each other before then, in the early 1980s there was still no publicly accessible Internet. If I wanted to exchange mail with someone on CompuServe, I needed my own CompuServe account because no other service could get mail into CompuServe; nor could CompuServe users send mail to users at The Source or local systems, such as The Well. At one point, my business card had three email addresses on it—a badge of geek pride.

Yeah, I know it sounds like the 30-miles-to-school-through-the-snow story that grandparents like to tell. But back then, we didn't know how crude it was. Within our own little islands, we explored primitive notions of virtual community, often among fellow users who weren't necessarily computer nerds. We were simply early adopters who weren't afraid of modem squeals or typing commands into text screens. And 300 baud was fast enough.

As primitive as they were in retrospect, those ultrasimple email systems spoiled us with an amazing amount of reliability. Nearly every email message in our inboxes really counted because it came either from an individual we wanted to communicate with or from an automated mailing list that we had signed up for. Lots of signal, very little noise.

Fast-forward to the mid-1990s, when the signal began losing ground to the noise. The noise came primarily from advertising pitches for which we may or may not have been suitable customers. Perhaps we had grown accustomed to receiving targeted marketing in our postal mailboxes, but the waves of email ads seemed to completely ignore our personal preferences — and, at times, our genders. In short order, an America Online (AOL) account of mine attracted so much unwanted garbage that I abandoned it.

In 1995, I launched my own Web site and domain (dannyg.com), initially to experiment with a new Web browser technology called JavaScript, and to support the technical books that I was writing on the subject. At the same time I was an active participant in public forums where others interested in JavaScript (and some of my hobbies) hung out and helped each other. With my email address readily available on most pages of my Web site, and exhibited plainly in archived forum messages, it gradually became embedded within lists of addresses that were passed around among senders of bulk email.

I was screwed.

Within a few years, the situation was growing grim, but I hung in there, deleting the junk as it arrived in my computer's inbox. I knew that I'd have to implement email filtering of some kind eventually, but the pain of learning about email servers was more than I was willing to bear—until, that is, the vicious Sircam virus hit in July 2001. Messages both with the virus and warning of the virus flooded my server, literally overloading my allowed space. I had to perform some sweaty-palmed manual recovery to get to a point where the server would allow my personal computer to download email again. That was the last straw for me.

After researching tools that would work with my email server, I implemented a filtering system, which I continue to tweak and use to this day. The system was doing such a good job that I didn't take the time to quantify how well it worked until the Klez worm struck in 2002. In an attempt to head off potential complaints from users who received Klez copies with my spoofed email address as the sender, I posted an analysis of my mail server logs to demonstrate how much junk was cluttering up my system, too. In one 24-hour period, I had received 343 unwanted messages.

While I was glad that a majority of the junk was being silently eliminated at the server, I wasn't thrilled that my Internet domain had become a junk magnet (eventually attracting more than 2,000 garbage emails per day by April 2004). Unwanted mail that wasn't summarily trashed was diverted to a server directory of "suspects," which I scanned periodically. I was appalled at the amount of deception employed in these messages. Much of it seemed particularly crafted to fool unsuspecting and gullible email newbies.

But as I looked into the matter further, I discovered that inexperienced newcomers weren't the only ones falling for the tricks. Public forum discussions all across the Internet revealed that those whom I thought would know better failed to recognize when they were being conned. They held mistaken notions about how basic systems worked and were unaware how their own behaviors put their privacy and computers in harm's way.

Individual and corporate complaints were rising. The email system was beginning to crack. That prompted me to begin nearly a year of in-depth research into the email field to try to fully understand the situation. Studying Web sites, documents, speeches, legislation, and court records, I found that professional technologists, marketers, and legal types focused only on their own areas of expertise and used jargon understood only by those in the know.

Thus, everyday email users would be hopelessly lost in piecing together the true nature of the threats and possible solutions.

My job in this book is to translate the gobbledygook spouted by all sides of the email wars into language that any email user can understand. My main goal is to snap email users out of their passive roles, waiting for others to solve the "email problem." The real power, it turns out, lies in all of our hands.

I also want you to become as enraged as I am by the way hustlers, weasels, and outright thieves literally steal their way into email inboxes and computers. They are not only wrecking a valuable Internet service, but doing everything in their power to rip off your identity, privacy, and even the processing cycles of your PC.

If you receive only a handful of unwanted messages a day, you may wonder what all the fuss is about. I hope that by the time you see what the attackers are really doing to the rest of the Internet, you'll want to be on your guard. It's also likely that you have been attacked, and you're not even aware of the damage being done to your computer.

This is intentionally not a detailed how-to book with steps for installing filters or choosing the right software. The products and technologies that fight those battles change so quickly that the Web provides the best up-to-date information (I'll have some pointers for you).

You won't see some other things in this book that you might expect. First of all, I don't believe most statistics I read in news reports, especially those released by spammers and antispam product companies. I keep seeing the same numbers bandied about until they become almost a mantra in report after report. Repeating them here would only propagate the propaganda. Not everyone receives the same junk messages or the same amount of junk at the same time. Some users might claim they've experienced a spam-free day, while others were inundated with more than usual. Quantifying spam or viral activity across the Internet is a dangerous game.

I must also be careful about displaying email content generated by others. As you will learn, the folks who send unwanted mail can be a litigious lot. The only individuals or companies I mention by name are those listed as defendants in a New York state lawsuit. I maintain all of the original messages that I quote throughout the book, but where addresses that reveal either the true sender, true advertiser, or valid address that might belong to an innocent bystander, I blank out those characters, replacing them with a uniform sequence of characters: \x\ .

Because I tend to think on a global scale, I want to make sure that readers outside of my own country, the United States, are not confused by potential ambiguities. Currency amounts are in U.S. dollars. Large numbers represented in billions are in units of 1,000,000,000 (known in some parts of the world as a thousand million).

Finally, I intentionally am not building a large Web presence around this book. There is a Web site to read about updates (spamwars.com), but there is little sense in setting up yet another spam news site, when several sites I mention already do a good job of it. Instead, I'm taking this topic to other media, where I hope the word will spread to a wider audience faster. It's a far greater challenge to use these media, but I believe it will be worth the effort.

Learn and enjoy!

SPAM WARS

Email Predators, Guardians, and Victims

Electronic mail—email—is under attack. I'm not talking just about your own email inbox, but the entire concept of email as a reliable, desirable, and speedy communications medium. Important mail you want to receive—if you receive it at all—is often buried among piles of unwanted email messages that do the following:

- Clog your inbox with offers for products you don't want (or wouldn't use even if you had the necessary body parts).

- Lure you to buy products that never come (and that might kill you if they did arrive).

- Trick you into infecting your computer with viruses and worms ("Check this out, Dude!").

- Dupe you into divulging personal identifying numbers to outright thieves ("Please re-enter your account details with our security department or we will terminate your account.").

- Embarrass or disgust you or your children with blatantly pornographic images ([blush]).

To defend inboxes from nonconsensual contact, you or your email provider may feel compelled to apply email filtering that blocks or quarantines spam and viruses. But aggressive filters are quite capable of inadvertently refusing or discarding messages you want, all without your knowledge. Less draconian filtering may instead divert suspect messages into a separate folder, whose contents must be scanned with a human eye to make sure no "ham" gets tossed out with the spam—as if scanning through junk mail in batches were any less annoying or time-consuming than having it in your inbox.

Even if spam filtering were perfect, messages that appear to be from people you trust (and thus glide right past computer and human barriers) may actually be virus- or worm-laden, sent unknowingly from a computer owned by your best friend. If you then open the email attachment, you've just performed the computerized equivalent of exposing yourself, in one dramatic swoosh of your trench coat, in Times, Red, and Tiananmen Squares at the same time.

So we're now stuck with a broken system in which email you want to receive may never reach you, email appearing to be "from" people you know may be data-deadly, and tons of unwanted crap still comes through unless you use a service that literally blocks anyone you don't already know. Worse, you pay the "postage" for every piece of email that arrives at your inbox, just as if you were required to pay postage due on physical mail addressed to you.

I ask you: Is this any way to run a post office?

As much as my rant up to now sounds like a description of a traditional conflict between good and evil, the decay of the email system is not attributable to only two clearly defined sides. Numerous participants play vital roles in the drama, roles that fall into four main groups I've identified:

- **Originators**, who send the stuff
- **Facilitators**, who help Originators accomplish their goals
- **Guardians**, who try to protect us
- **Victims**, who suffer the most

Unfortunately, the systems and individuals throughout the email world have competing agendas and use different terminology relating to the problems and potential solutions. Some players even regard the solutions *as* the problems. That's why trying to clarify the issues surrounding email spam, scammers, and hackers is such a freakin' mess.

To help make sense of that mess, let me introduce you to the players, the *dramatis personae,* of the email tragedy.[1] These are the constituencies who wage wars—in tones ranging from inaudible whispers to violent rages—for their email causes. In all honesty, my sympathies lie with very few of these characters. You'll probably figure that out as we go along and as I discuss them in more detail throughout the book.

---

[1] *Dramatis personae* is Latin for "masks of the drama," otherwise known as the cast of characters. The primary meaning of *persona* is a full head mask, as worn by players of Greek and Roman (and probably other ancient) dramas. (See, I knew my college degrees in Latin and Greek were not in vain.)

Dramatis Personae

Originators

Spammy Spammers Accused of being responsible for the majority of spam emails on the Internet, expend substantial effort to send massive amounts of mail to people who don't want it, using techniques such as deceptive From: and Subject: message lines and relaying their tonnage through email systems owned by spam-friendly providers around the world or hijacked from unsuspecting computer owners. Firmly believe they do no wrong. When threatened, can lash out with vicious email and other Internet attacks against the opposition.

Spamvertisers Companies that offer products or services for sale online but hire Spammy Spammers to perform the mailings to attract orders or sales leads for still other companies. The email messages typically include links to the Spamvertiser's Web site, which is physically unrelated to the Spammy Spammer's email spewing machines.

Deceptive Email Marketers Companies that present a slick Web site offering their email lists and mailing services to legitimate companies that don't know any better. Despite claims of offering only opt-in email address-es to their customers, they commonly acquire unqualified addresses from other sources and injure the reputations of their mailing customers when spam reports start flooding in after a mailing. Constantly exploit loopholes in laws and thus claim the legal high ground.

Honest Email Marketers Companies that present a slick Web presence to offer their email lists and mailing services to legitimate companies that have done their homework. Have collected genuine opt-in names with the name owners' permission through completely consensual means. Impossible to dif-ferentiate from Deceptive Email Marketers except through performance results.

Online Product/Service Sellers To reach as wide an audience as possible as cheaply as possible, frequently employ one or more Email Marketer char-acters to supply addresses and do the mailing. Rarely have the expertise or perform the due diligence to distinguish between Deceptive and Honest varieties because they look alike, and there are far more of the former than the latter. May find their Web sites turned off abruptly and without recourse when their Internet service provider (ISP) gets too many reports about their spamvertised site.

Direct Marketing Organization Members Bulk email senders who proudly display a trade group logo on their Web sites and email messages to "prove" that they adhere to all of the organization's guidelines and codes of conduct. They've done *their* job.

Scammer Spammers Broadcast messages in large quantities (sometimes using Spammy Spammers, or assuming the role themselves) to bilk recipients gullible enough to order a product or service from the email offer or spamvertised Web site. Consist of unrepentant criminals in far away places who engage in credit card fraud, identity theft, and advance-fee ("419") activity. Presumed to be the most financially successful characters in the drama.

Affiliate Spammers Commonly use tools provided by Spam Software Suppliers to send partially disguised and unsolicited email on behalf of Spammy Spammers, Spamvertisers, and Scammer Spammers, earning a commission for each click-through and/or order placed as a result of following a coded link in the email message. Probably got started by responding to a "work from home" spam message, and won't be in it for long.

Virus/Worm Writers Largely hidden individuals of all age ranges who devise and propagate rogue programs that exploit security holes in existing operating systems or software products, as well as human gullibility. Attempt to use "social engineering" tricks to get unsuspecting users to open email attachments containing programs that not only spread the infection, but also open up computers to be hijacked by remote control to capture passwords and relay spam.

Facilitators

Spam Software Suppliers Sell relatively inexpensive software that can harvest email addresses from the Internet, locate computers that can be used as unsuspecting relays or proxies for untraceable spamming, and pump high volumes of mail through another character, the Bulletproof ISP. Group also includes purveyors of get-rich-quick schemes offering cheap email list compilations on CD-ROM, along with bulk mailing software for any PC, feeding an already overdiluted pyramid scheme.

Direct Marketing Organizations Act as political lobbyists on behalf of direct marketers, working hard (and frequently succeeding) to weaken pending legislation that would prevent mailers from sending unsolicited messages to the public. Publish guidelines and codes of conduct that favor the mailer at the expense of the recipient.

Unresponsive Outgoing ISPs Ignore reports of spam activity emanating from or pointing back to their customers. Their abuse desks may be overwhelmed or they simply don't give a damn. Their Acceptable Use Policy (AUP) may specifically outlaw spam activity, but so what? Known among Antispam Activists as "black-hat ISPs."

Bulletproof Outgoing ISPs Providers that cater to Spammy Spammers, pornography sites, and spam wannabes by ignoring all abuse complaints. Have arrangements with their own providers (called "upstream providers") to ignore complaints about the bulletproof ISP. Commonly located in Russia, China, and Brazil, but host predominantly U.S-based spammers.

Internet Backbone The infrastructure that facilitates the transmission of email and all other Internet traffic around the world. Owned by numerous companies and government entities, accounting for tens of billions of dollars in bandwidth costs each year. Most Internet users take it for granted. Like oxygen.

Administrators of Improperly Configured Mail Servers Through careless security management (employing loose default settings and/or passwords), unknowingly hand control of their mail servers to Spammy Spammers, disguising the true source of Spammy Spammer messages. Also allow their Web servers to host, or redirect to, Spamvertisers' and Scammer Spammers' Web pages. Usually haven't a clue about what's going on inside their servers.

Owners of Zombie PCs Typically, owners of computers running Microsoft Windows operating systems who have not updated their machines with the latest security patches from Microsoft. Nor do they employ up-to-date antivirus software. Their computers are usually connected to the Internet at all times via DSL, cable modem, or their employer's unsecure network, hence become zombie slaves used to forward huge quantities of spam, thus disguising the true source. Have opened virus-laden email attachments or allowed "spyware" to be installed on their PCs. Oblivious participants in potentially massive Internet terror attacks.

Proprietary Email List Renters Offer one-time "marketing partner" rental email addresses collected from their online registrations and subscriptions, by applying the direct (postal) mail customer list rental model. Frequently control entire mailing process to prevent their addresses from escaping, charging $.30 or more per demographically targeted address.

Guardians

Responsive Outgoing ISPs Upon receiving reports of spam emanating from their customers, spamvertised Web sites hosted on their networks, or one of their customer email addresses being used as a destination for spam replies, act promptly to terminate the account of any customer who violates the ISP's AUP provisions against spam activity. Known among Antispam Activists as "white-hat ISPs."

Incoming ISPs Bear the primary brunt of high-volume email onslaughts by being the initial recipients of all messages aimed at their customers. May use a variety of spam-blocking and -filtering technologies to prevent unwanted messages from reaching their intended targets. High-volume, consumer-friendly services (such as AOL, MSN, and Earthlink) expend substantial money and energy to fend off spam and virus attacks.

Incoming Independent Mail Server Administrators Act as Incoming ISPs for corporations or universities, and thus become the first recipients of all mail directed to the organization's domains. Administrators are generally under pressure to block or filter spam and virus-laden email to prevent it from reaching employees' inboxes—if they want to keep their jobs.

Antivirus Software Makers Companies offering commercial software that attempts to block activity on mail servers and personal computers bearing the hallmarks of virus or worm activity. During vicious worm attacks, are responsible for tons of worthless spam-looking messages that accuse your computer of virus infection, even though the infected machine spoofed the From: address with your address (plucked from the infected machine's email address book or mail archive).

Antispam Services/Software Makers Companies that offer commercial software, subscriptions, and outside services to block and/or filter spam from the flow of incoming messages. Comprise firms boasting numerous competing technologies that definitely work better than others on some customers' systems. *You* figure it out.

Antispam Activists (Blocklist Providers) Networks of mostly volunteers who collect spam reports to trace the sources of spam messages, and provide blocklists (aka blacklists and blackhole lists) to mail administrators who wish to use those lists as guidelines to block or filter incoming spam messages. Not infrequently list large address blocks belonging to Unresponsive Outgoing ISPs, affecting the ISP's non-spamming Innocent Bystanders. Uh-oh.

Antispam Activists (Mail Administrators) Incoming ISPs and Independent Mail Server Administrators who use a combination of blocklists, antispam software, and other technologies on the incoming mail server to block or filter spam from incoming email.

Antispam Activists (Chorus) Participants of a variety of newsgroups, mailing lists, and organization Web sites who exchange spam-fighting tactics and antispam vitriol with (and sometimes at) each other. Have developed a colorful vocabulary about the activities of spammers and spam fighters. Subject to high burnout rate, leaving numerous antispam Web site carcasses in their wakes.

Legislators Government representatives who have heard the roar from their constituents to "do something" about spam. Generally do too little of anything to protect the consumer. U.S. legislators have to word their laws carefully out of respect for a little document called the Constitution, while also being strong-armed by well-funded direct marketers.

Lawyers and Courts In lieu of sufficiently powerful antispam laws, participate in individual cases when one party feels it has been wronged by the spamming or spam-blocking actions of another. Apply their own centuries-old vocabulary and concepts to a twenty-first-century activity.

Prosecutors Painstakingly research evidence against violations of weak antispam laws. Generally underfunded and understaffed, requiring them to focus on a limited number of alleged violators within their jurisdictions. Assemble cases much too slowly in the eyes of Antispam Activists and Spam and Scam Victims.

Antispam Book Authors An as-yet very small group of writers who want to be your friend. Many simply provide treatments for symptoms; the bravest of the brave actually try to explain what the hell is going on.

Victims

Innocent Bystanders Customers of Unresponsive Outgoing ISPs who find their emails refused by systems that use public blocklists containing groups of the ISP's addresses. Become outraged when they learn about indiscriminate blocklist persecutions, especially if they do not send bulk email. Antispam Activists (who promote blocklists as an ISP pressure tactic) offer little sympathy.

Spam and Scam Victims The largest email war constituency who, but for lack of organization, awareness, and a little technical expertise, could rid the Internet of most garbage email within two years with no new technologies or laws. Currently the weakest, but potentially the most powerful, link in the chain between the recipient and the spammer-scammer-hacker trinity. Cumulatively have more money than all other players combined, and are thus rich targets for all other players. For most readers, see: the nearest mirror.

It's clear that this epic saga has a cast of thousands—well over 100 million, actually. The story is loaded with liars, virtuous do-gooders, bullies, scamps, earnest workaday folks, serial white-collar criminals, gullible chumps, and, thanks to the legislative angle, no shortage of participants in political intrigue.

A lot of money is at stake, too. The spammers aren't sending billions of messages for the fun of it. Some direct marketers (and their advocacy groups) see dollar signs in email addresses of unwitting (and unwilling) prospects. Antivirus and antispam software makers present a sizable industry on their own. Unscrupulous ISPs charge extra for turning a deaf ear to complaints. On the other end, ISPs that deal responsibly with spam and viruses (incoming and outgoing) must throw additional personnel, software, and equipment dollars at the problem—dollars that ultimately come from their customers. That's out of your pocket and mine.

At the risk of sounding trite and too good to be true, my biases throughout this book are for the common email user, especially those who might not yet understand how serious is the threat to email as a viable medium. These folks are at the greatest risk of losing money and privacy to the worst of the predators. They also can put the rest of us in great peril by allowing themselves to be bullied, tricked, and lied to—making reprehensible tactics pay off for criminals or hackers and encouraging the vandals to increase their attacks.

It is only by understanding who the characters are in this drama, and by comprehending their motivations—to extend the theatrical metaphor—that we will be able to behave rationally in the face of this scourge. In the remaining chapters, you will get to know more about our players. To that end, I'll also introduce you to the lingo of marketers, legislators, the American legal system, and antispam activists. To understand the players' debates, you must know their languages.

And so we start with a word that everyday email users think is easy to define, but turns out isn't so easy to pin down: *spam*.

CHAPTER 2

Grasping Spam (not SPAM®)

You can't accuse someone of sending it, you can't compose a law to limit or ban it, you can't issue a complaint about receiving it, and you can't sue someone for screwing up your system with it, unless you can precisely define what "it" is. And, because human languages tend to be imprecise (what with connotations, innuendos, and lies), the likelihood of all email constituencies voluntarily agreeing on a single, unambiguous definition of "spam" is zero.

This situation isn't anything new. I mean, take murder. You'd think that taking another human's life was murder, plain and simple. But it's not always either plain or simple. For example, depending on the circumstances and motivation of the killer, the offense may be treated as first-degree murder, second-degree murder, voluntary manslaughter, or involuntary manslaughter. Killing in self-defense or in an act of war (among other situations) disappears from the murder radar entirely, and is called justifiable homicide. And the French have this whole *crime passionnel* thing.

A suitable definition of spam usually starts out simple, but then becomes complicated with the addition of several conditions and subclauses to address human nature and the imprecision of language. If you try to keep the definition simple, then high-volume email senders will slither through loopholes and swear on a stack of Bibles that they do not spam.

Before I get to defining spam, it's worth looking into where the term originated. My love of Latin and Greek etymology doesn't help us here, because that one-syllable word didn't exist in the English language until New Year's Eve in the hours leading up to the year 1937. By the end of 1936, George A. Hormel & Company had 45 years' experience producing, packaging, and

9

selling pork and other meat products. Although the company had been sell-ing canned hams since 1926, it developed a new product made from pork shoulder, other pork meat, and spices, all contained in an unrefrigerated tin can. The product was to be released in 1937, originally with the name Hormel Spiced Ham.

But the name didn't have quite the marketing zing a new product need-ed in the depths of the Depression, so Jay Hormel, second-generation presi-dent of the company, held a "contest" at his New Year's party to see if any of his guests could come up with a better name. I don't know what this party was like, but I have this vision in my head derived from 1930's movies, in which the wealthy classes who had managed to avoid the worst of the Depression motored around in Stutz Bearcats and lit cigars with $100 bills. The world existed only in shades of gray.

Attending this party was one Kenneth Daigneau, a Broadway actor and (nudge, nudge, wink, wink) the brother of one of the company's executives. Without too much wit, in my opinion, he compressed "spiced" and "ham" into "spam," winning himself a quick hundred bucks from Jay Hormel and eventual immortality on the Internet.[1]

The product, trademarked in all uppercase letters as SPAM, hit the market in the 1937. World War II, despite its ravages in many parts of the world, turned out to be a bonanza for Hormel and its new product. In the United States, meat was rationed and difficult to obtain. SPAM was not (not because it didn't contain meat, so put down your joke-making machine), and thus became a staple at home during wartime. It was available in Britain, as well. Former Prime Minister Margaret Thatcher once reminisced about how SPAM was, in her words, a "war-time delicacy" (poor sods). That the meat didn't require refrigeration was a boon to the military supply lines, which managed to keep the boys on the Allied front lines (western and eastern fronts, according to testimonials from Dwight Eisenhower and Nikita Khrushchev) supplied with SPAM. And SPAM. And more SPAM. Which brings us to the true start of the connection between the meat and email.

Hormel shipped its two billionth can of SPAM in 1970, and in December of that year, the BBC first aired the twenty-fifth episode of a popular televi-sion show called *Monty Python's Flying Circus.* The program, an homage to farce, poked fun at every sacred cow it could find, seemingly taking especial glee in both lampooning and glorifying the British working classes in the same breath. A sketch at the end of episode 25 takes place in (as we learn

---

[1] Daigneau's connection with the naming of SPAM outshines his legacy as a Broadway actor. The Internet Broadway Database (www.ibdb.com) lists him appearing in only three productions between 1923 and 1937. (Sometimes I wonder if using Google can lead to Attention Deficit Disorder.)

later) the Green Midget Café in Bromley. As the scene opens, most tables are occupied by men dressed in full Viking warrior regalia (logic was often the first casualty of any *Python* sketch). Mr. and Mrs. Bun enter the café—not the usual way, but floating into their seats from overhead wires.

Mrs. Bun and the Waitress are played by Graham Chapman and Terry Jones, respectively, speaking in shrill and forced women's voices that could shatter glass. Mr. Bun (played by Eric Idle) inquires about the menu, and the Waitress replies:

> *Well there's egg and bacon; egg sausage and bacon; egg and spam[2]; egg, bacon and spam; egg, bacon, sausage and spam; spam, bacon, sausage and spam; spam, egg, spam, spam, bacon and spam; spam, spam, spam, egg and spam; spam, spam, spam, spam, spam, spam, baked beans, spam, spam, spam and spam.*

Upon hearing that, Mrs. Bun innocently asks if they serve anything without SPAM in it because she doesn't want any SPAM. After more back-and-forth, it becomes clear that everything on the menu has at least some SPAM in it, to which Mrs. Bun shrilly replies:

> *I don't like spam.*

Suddenly the Vikings start singing a song with the words:

> *spam, spam, spam, spam, spam ... spam, spam, spam, spam ... lovely spam, wonderful spam ...*

To quiet the Vikings, the Waitress yells "Shut up! Shut up! Shut up!" This exchange continues for awhile, each time the menu items revealing more and more SPAM, at which point the Vikings start up their song again, and the Waitress ends it all with "Shut up! Shut up!"

The routine goes on for just a bit more, but if I try to describe the Hungarian tourist and ensuing nonsequiturs, you'll think I'm one of the escaped and lobotomized mental patients that frequently appear in the program. The lasting impression most viewers got from this sketch was an ever-increasing presence of SPAM mindlessly overtaking everything.

Although *Monty Python* was originally a BBC program, it soon found a following in the United States with the help of local Public Broadcasting Service (PBS) stations, which were accustomed to importing programming from the United Kingdom to fill their commercial-free broadcast hours. In the 1970s and into the 1980s, there was scarcely a PBS station that didn't run the *Python* episodes year after year. The program developed a genuine cult

---

[2] The published script uses the nontrademarked version of the word "spam," but the meaning is clearly for SPAM. The full script text can be found in *The Complete Monty Python's Flying Circus, All the Words*, Volume 2, Pantheon Books 1989.

following, consisting of a high percentage of computer geeks who could recite dialog from the funniest skits by heart (whether or not you wanted to hear them). They all knew what "naughty bits" were.

At this point in the SPAM-to-spam story, the trail runs cool. Brad Templeton, chairman of the board of the Electronic Frontier Foundation (eff.org), researched the first instance of the term in computerdom, and found a few possible leads. His best guess, supported by a variety of remembrances, is that it occurred in the mid- or late-1980s in a community on the Internet called Multi-User Dungeons (MUDs). This was back in the days when computer role-playing games were carried out exclusively by typing commands on a text-only terminal. There may have been an instance in which one of the participants wrote a little program that made it appear to others in the community that someone was sitting at a keyboard and continually typing "spam, spam, spam,..." in imitation of the most annoying (and hilarious) lines voiced by the *Python* sketch's Waitress and Vikings.

Brad unearthed what he believes is the first instance of specifically labeling rampant message transmission as "spam." By the early 1990s, public discussion forums—USENET newsgroups—had begun to be hit with obnoxious levels of cross-postings, where the same message would be sent to numerous groups (which could then generate all kinds of extra traffic when members of each group responded to the message, spawning a thread that would show up in the other groups, and on and on (Shut up! Shut up!). A USENET system administrator named Richard Depew wrote a program that would remove excessively cross-posted messages from unmoderated groups (a radical, censorship-laden idea that still doesn't sit too well with some). Unfortunately, on March 30, 1993, a bug in his program caused a couple hundred identical messages to spew to the news.admin.policy newsgroup, the very nucleus of USENET movers and shakers (and troublemakers).

Although there was a lot of good-natured ribbing expressed in return, not everyone was amused, especially those who had to pay for the privilege of receiving the redundant messages by metered connect time. On March 31, 1993, at 11:32:10 A.M. Pacific Standard Time, a participant of the group, Joel Furr, posted a message to the news.admin.policy newsgroup with a sarcastic definition of the program that Depew had written. The definition states in part (emphasis mine):

> Transformed by programming ineptitude into a monster of Frankenstein proportions, it broke loose on the night of March 31 [sic], 1993 and proceeded **to spam** news.admin.policy with something on the order of 200 messages in which it attempted, and failed, to cancel its own messages.

This message, still in the USENET archives online, shows sufficient comfort with the word to use it in this context, expecting others (many of whom were perhaps MUD-aware) to either know what it means or figure it out by their familiarity with the *Python* sketch.[3]

Although this possible first occurrence of spam originated from a technical mistake, it didn't take long for others to begin exploiting USENET to flood that world with commercial offers. One of the earliest and certainly most notorious cross-posting was launched by a Phoenix, Arizona, law firm named Canter & Siegel. The firm's USENET spam message, offering information about an upcoming Green Card lottery taking place in the United States, marked the beginning of no-longer-funny spamming. In fact, the attorneys, despite the difficulties they originally experienced in having their Internet access cut off, went on to become spam artists, first on USENET and eventually email.

SPAM may have continued to stay in the can, but spam was out of the bottle. Today, Hormel has sold over 6 billion cans of SPAM, while the incoming email servers of the world block or filter over 6 billion spam messages every day.[4]

So much for the origin of the word. But how does one define spam?

This is where the dust starts to rise as a variety of interests—competing and complementary—squabble over viewpoints and interpretations. I'll cover four constituencies: legislators, anti-spam advocates, a powerful direct marketing trade association, and spam victims.

Legislative Spam

By the end of 2003, 36 U.S. states had enacted laws that restricted email messages in one way or another. Unfortunately, all of the individual state laws were subsequently superseded by U.S. federal law: Controlling the Assault of Non-Solicited Pornography and Marketing Act of 2003 (CAN-SPAM), which was enacted at the end of the year. Even so, it's instructive to see how state legislators attempted to define spam.

---

3 You can read the full text of the message by visiting the following contorted URL: http://groups.google.com/groups?hl=en&lr=lang_en&ie=UTF-8&selm=1993Mar31.192731.3167%40mnemosyne.cs.du.edu.

4 This figure is an extrapolation of hard data provided by Bill Gates in a *Wall Street Journal* editorial he penned in July 2003. He claimed (and he oughta know) that his MSN and Hotmail servers filtered 2.4 billion messages per day. To that figure I added guesstimates about similar blockages by other free email systems (like Yahoo!), plus AOL, Earthlink, and other high-volume spam magnets—and more than 2,000 a day at my own server.

The language among the state laws, as you might expect, is all over the place, depending upon the technical sophistication of the laws' sponsors and the extent to which marketing organization lobbyists had been able to weaken the bills before they were enacted. Virtually all of the legislative language used to describe email issues include the words "unsolicited" and "email," joined by either "commercial" or "bulk." This in no way passes judgment on the legality or morality of this stuff; it's just a way to define what the laws intended to cover.

California's comparatively tough law, titled Restrictions on Unsolicited Commercial E-mail Advertisers (California Business and Professions Code, Division 7, Part 3, Chapter 1, Article 1.8), went to great lengths to itemize the components of a legal definition. The law starts the ball rolling with this general tidbit about what constitutes commercial email (solicited or otherwise):

> "Commercial e-mail advertisement" means any electronic mail message initiated for the purpose of advertising or promoting the lease, sale, rental, gift offer, or other disposition of any property, goods, services, or extension of credit. [§17529.1(c)]

Before the law reaches the payoff definition (unsolicited commercial email), it has to cover some other ground, notably definitions of "direct consent" and "preexisting or current business relationship," which are scenic points on the way to the final destination:

> "Direct consent" means that the recipient has expressly consented to receive e-mail advertisements from the advertiser, either in response to a clear and conspicuous request for the consent or at the recipient's own initiative. [§17529.1(d)]

Translation: Displaying a contact email address on your own Web site's home page and posting a message to a newsgroup do not mean you invite unsolicited email.

> "Preexisting or current business relationship," as used in connection with the sending of a commercial e-mail advertisement, means that the recipient has made an inquiry and has provided his or her e-mail address, or has made an application, purchase, or transaction, with or without consideration, regarding products or services offered by the advertiser. [§17529.1(l)]

Translation: The intended recipient either explicitly registered or transacted business with the advertiser.

It's a long way to go, I know, but with these definitions in mind, we come to the crux of the law's definition:

"Unsolicited commercial e-mail advertisement" means a commercial e-mail advertisement sent to a recipient who meets both of the following criteria:

(1) The recipient has not provided direct consent to receive advertisements from the advertiser.

(2) The recipient does not have a preexisting or current business relationship, as defined in subdivision (l), with the advertiser promoting the lease, sale, rental, gift offer, or other disposition of any property, goods, services, or extension of credit. [§17529.1(o)]

Translation: Most of the garbage in your inbox.

The reason the California law was so explicit is that it was one of only two state laws (Delaware's was the other) that placed an outright ban on sending unsolicited commercial email. Other states tended to apply similar definitions, but then proceeded to let senders spam away as long as they were truthful about their identities, labeled their message subjects in an easily recognizable way, and provided a way to "opt out" of future mailings. A lot like the U.S. CAN-SPAM law.

Antispam Spam

Let me now turn to definitions proposed by another constituency in the email world: antispam advocates. Here you'll find two terms that have a subtle, if perhaps cultural difference: *unsolicited commercial email* (UCE) and *unsolicited bulk email* (UBE). What's the difference between the two?

Spam definers in the United States are sometimes squeamish about labeling noncommercial emails as spam. The U.S. Constitution protects political speech, leaving one to wonder if anyone could successfully defend against a prohibition against, say, a bulk mailing to U.S. citizens on behalf of a political candidate or party. As you'll read in Chapter 7, one political campaign decided not to pick that fight. Because most bulk email is selling some product or service—anything to separate a recipient from his or her money—most spam easily falls under UCE. Even so, I prefer the broader UBE moniker, as I'll explain shortly.

The problem with any simple definition of spam is that spammers find loopholes through which they try to defend their practices. That forces a more complex definition that defines (or provides examples of) what "consent" really means. The Spamhaus Project (www.spamhaus.org), a highly visible volunteer effort that tracks spam activity around the world, publishes a definition that attempts to fill some of the loopholes:

The word "Spam" as applied to Email means Unsolicited Bulk Email ("UBE").

Unsolicited means that the Recipient has not granted verifiable permission for the message to be sent. Bulk means that the message is sent as part of a larger collection of messages, all having substantively identical content.

To be Spam, a message must be sent Unsolicited AND Bulk. Unsolicited Email is normal email (first contact enquiries, job enquiries, sales enquiries, etc.), Bulk Email is normal email (newsletters, discussion lists, etc.). ONLY the combination of Unsolicited AND Bulk is Spam.

Technical Definition: An electronic message is "spam" IF: (1) the recipient's personal identity and context are irrelevant because the message is equally applicable to many other potential recipients; AND (2) the recipient has not verifiably granted deliberate, explicit, and still-revocable permission for it to be sent; AND (3) the transmission and reception of the message appears to the recipient to give a disproportionate benefit to the sender.

The Technical Definition section is copied from another antispam activist organization called Mail Abuse Prevention System, L.L.C. (MAPS at mail-abuse.org). This extra wording is the result of spammers' tactics and attitudes toward the email they send. For instance, a spammer would insert computer-generated "personalizations" and random words into each message and claim (with a weasely straight face) that the messages weren't strictly "bulk" email.

But even antispam activists do not see eye-to-eye. It's not uncommon for heated debates to arise on various email abuse forums about whether automated spews of virus-laden emails are spam; or whether email delivery failure notifications (*bounce* messages) that result from spam messages containing unsuspecting victims' email addresses in the From: message field should be considered spam. These are important issues for spam reporting organizations (such as SpamCop) because they need to define what constitutes a message worth reporting to ISPs as spam.

It's not a straightforward topic. For example, in August and September of 2003, the Internet was flooded with an extremely virulent round of worm-laden emails (the Sobig worm). Like most worms that had been born in the year and half prior, Sobig dug through the email address book and other files of an infected PC to search for anything that looked like an email address (that is, somebody@someplace.whatever). The worm included its own outgoing mail server software that retransmitted the worm software to all of the email addresses it could find, and using one of those addresses in the From: field of the message. And that's where things really got out of hand.

Many incoming email servers had already been equipped with virus detection software, largely in response to earlier email-borne virus plagues. Unfortunately, most of the anti-virus software was configured by default to send an email message back to the apparent sender (the address in the From: field) to warn that the message contained a virus. But the message did not originate in a computer of the From: address. Nevertheless, these virus warning messages flooded the inboxes of users who simply had the misfortune of being listed somewhere on another user's computer hard drive.

The question then arose among antispam activists (and others) who were being deluged with these messages: Weren't these automated responses spam? Shouldn't they be reported so that the antivirus software could be reconfigured to avoid sending virus bounce messages for infections known to use forged From: addresses? To the dismay of some avid antispammers, spam reporting systems responded with a firm no. It's true that bounce messages were annoying, frustrating, and even damaging (mail boxes unattended over a weekend could fill up and reject valid incoming email); and it wasn't uncommon for the messages to encourage the users to buy the latest version of antivirus software for their PCs ("Aha, commerce!"). But the messages were not the result of a deliberate bulk email campaign. Bounced email messages are treated as *epistulae non grata* in the spam-reporting community.[5]

Despite occasional disagreements about borderline spam, the antispam community has a clear view of unsolicited bulk email being spam. Loopholes are not tolerated.

Direct Marketing Association Spam

Founded in 1917, the Direct Marketing Association (DMA) is an advocacy group for businesses and organizations that communicate directly with their target audiences. As stated on the DMA Web site (the-dma.org), the goal of direct marketing is to elicit a response: an order, an information request, or a visit to a store. Although the DMA's roots are in postal mail and telemarketing, it recognizes that its members use the Internet for some of their

---

[5] Latin for "unwelcome letters." If Latin were still spoken today, I wonder whether an electronic letter would be called an *e-epistula*.

direct marketing activity. As a result, the organization was eager to be heard during the evolution of the federal law covering email marketing. With the start date for the restrictive California antispam law looming, the pressure to encourage passage of a weaker federal law must have been intense.

The U.S. law, CAN-SPAM, spells out unlawful activity with respect to commercial email. Wording in earlier drafts of the law, like the state laws, included definitions of unsolicited commercial email. But by the time the bill reached President George W. Bush's desk for signature, the definitions were gone. In the new law, email is email unless it hides the identity of the sender, misleads the recipient, or arrives via hijacked computers. In other words, the law permits sending properly labeled and truthfully identified unsolicited commercial email as long as the message contains a valid way to opt out of future mailings.

Thus spake the U.S. Congress, handing the DMA and similar organizations a definition of what was legal. The DMA gets off the hook by not having to define "spam" and potentially alienating its members and consumers. Instead, it can hide behind the law it helped weaken and offer a simple message to its members: Follow our legal guidelines and you can claim you're not spamming.

Victim's Spam

This is my book, so I get to have the final say on the matter of a spam definition in these pages. First, I believe it's important not to talk about unsolicited mail as being commercial in nature. To me that connotes the significance of the content of the message. While I don't appreciate receiving messages that promote products and services that I don't like (or that might gross me out), that is not my issue with spam. The biggest problem with spam is that recipients are forced to pay the bill (in money and time) to receive this garbage. Strictly speaking, if a potential recipient does not give explicit (not just implied) consent to a sender, the sender should not have the right to use the recipient's resources (money and time).

But that's blatantly unfair to some senders. Using explicit consent by itself is hazardous where laws and spam reporting might be concerned. While I may welcome and eagerly solicit email messages from readers who agree with me and think I'm the best writer on Earth, I'm not as eager to get messages from readers who think I'm full of crap. But you know what? It would be unconscionable to use the consent issue against the full-of-crapper as long as the message were composed and sent by a human, in a one-on-one earnest communication. If a public Web site invites contact, then it implies consent for an initial one-on-one personal communication from anyone.

Continuing an exchange after that would require the mutual consent of both parties, and is thus removed from the spam debate entirely.

To eliminate the consent issue with one-on-one communication, I include a "bulk" or "automated" component in my definition of spam. Merely personalizing an automated message with my name ("Dear dannyg40") does not make it a one-on-one communication. Messages sent to masses of email addresses eliciting all recipients to respond with similar actions (click to visit a certain Web site, call this number, order, donate, forward, opt out, and so on) is a "bulk" or "automated" message. Therefore, my definition of spam is on the simple side: *Any bulk or automated message sent to me without my prior explicit consent is spam.* Content is irrelevant. My definition includes commercial, political, religious, and any other category you'd like to add. Just because political speech is protected in my country doesn't mean that a candidate has the right to enter my home and place a bumper sticker on my dining room table without my permission. Consent. Consent. Consent.

By the same token, if you give consent to a sender, you must assume the responsibility it entails. You cannot in good conscience sign up for a newsletter today and report it as spam next week because you disagree with the editorial policy, had a fight with your boss, or forgot you had subscribed. Consent is a two-way street.

Despite the U.S. loosey-goosey definition of "legal" unsolicited email, the law does not force anyone to receive it. In fact, the law explicitly gives ISPs and recipients the ability to block and filter any mail they want. Spam is, indeed, in the eye of the beholder, and even the most U.S.-legal, DMA-appropriate unsolicited commercial message will be blocked, bounced, filtered, and deleted unread by those who believe the junk has no place in their mail servers or inboxes. To most spam fighters, consent means:

1. I initiated contact with a potential sender and requested to receive automated mail from that sender only.
2. The sender verified my request with a message that required my explicit confirmation.
3. I confirmed my request.
4. At my request at any time, the sender will remove my address from its automated mailing list promptly.
5. As a current or former recipient of automated email from a sender, my email address will not be sold, rented, leased, traded, or given to another sender without my explicit permission.

Any other kind of automated bulk email is spam. Simple.

CHAPTER 3

How We Got into This Mess

I'd like to nominate the worldwide email system as a legitimate contender for ranking as a wonder of the modern world. A handful of geeks established standards that today allow Amy in Cleveland to send a picture of her school project to Dad traveling in Hong Kong in a matter of seconds for a tiny fraction of a penny. Any email-equipped computer can exchange messages with any other email-equipped computer. All this in a world in which you can sometimes cross the border into a neighboring country and fail to find a compatible power outlet for an electric hair dryer.

Unfortunately, the same standardization that makes email so amazing (which, remember, was developed in a simpler time among a small community of technical users who respected each other and the integrity of the system) makes today's worst spam and virus assaults possible and frequently difficult to trace. To begin to understand how the technology came back to bite us, we need a brief history lesson about the origins of email.

In the early 1960s, computers were generally room-sized behemoths that few "regular" people saw, except perhaps through a wall of glass that designated the boundaries of the computer room at some large corporation, government department, or university. The notion of anyone other than a trained engineer even touching such a machine was many years away. Each giant computer was a "closed machine," operating as an island unto itself. An engineer could communicate with the computer by typing esoteric sequences of codes at a keyboard. Only the most advanced computer labs would have a text-only video terminal, while others used clickety-clackety teletype machines or specially

21

adapted electric typewriters as terminals. The computer could store simple text files, and each engineer typically had a private directory. As a point of reference, computer storage was rather precious in those days. In 1963, IBM introduced the first removable disk pack drive (model 1311), which was the size of a washing machine, while the disk packs held a whopping 2 megabytes of data each. Put 15,000 of those babies together and you have the storage of the 30-gigabyte iPod music player in my shirt pocket.

Although perhaps not intended for the purpose, computing systems provided places where users could log on to the system and either read or write text files openly in a shared area. If you wanted to send a message to Fred, you might save the file with the name "forfred" and hope that Fred would notice it the next time he scanned the shared list of files. There was about as much privacy as a public bulletin board in a laundromat. But it was a way to use a computer to convey a message to another human, who could retrieve the message at a later time. As related by computing pioneer and then MIT student Tom Van Vleck, this is how the first messaging worked with a computing system called Compatible Time-Sharing System (CTSS), which was installed at Massachusetts Institute of Technology (MIT) in 1961. Users of the system could even communicate with the CTSS system from another location if they had a terminal and a telephone modem.

In 1965, Tom and colleague Noel Morris took it upon themselves to write the first mail program for CTSS. The program gave the machine special powers to write the contents of a new message to a specially-named file located in the recipient's personal and private directory space in the computer's storage system. Whenever the user logged in to the system from a terminal, and the special file had anything in it, the terminal would display the message

YOU HAVE MAIL BOX

This was decades before America Online users would hear a disembodied voice blab "You've got mail!" each time they dialed into their AOL accounts.

There were no electronic email address books back then. There wasn't even a command to reply and send an answer back to the original sender. If you wanted to respond, you created a brand-new message, manually addressing it. Copy and paste was pure science fiction then. If you wanted to refer to something from the original message, you retyped it into your new message.

It was also a time prior to the concept of network etiquette ("netiquette"), yet the gentlemen and (exceedingly few) ladies with computer access respected each other's private space and the integrity of the entire system. Mail software writers even worried that by calling the command that generated a new message MAIL, they would aggravate the United States Post Office Department, which might insist that a user purchase and physically destroy a five-cent first-class postage stamp for each message originated in the system. Such fears seem quaint in light of the abandon of today's users, who see nothing wrong with downloading music free, even though it may be from copyrighted recordings.

Other closed computing systems existed at this time, and it is likely that similar—and similarly crude—mail systems were in use within the organization by the mid-1960s. Like the nature of the computing systems themselves, the messages went no further than the systems on which they were born. This continued to be true well into the 1980s, even when massive computing systems owned and operated by companies eventually known as CompuServe Information Services, The Source (my first e-hangout), and others opened their services to geeky consumers who were beginning to dabble in personal computing. The only way to send a message to a friend on CompuServe was to have a CompuServe account of your own. There was no email interchange outside any of the closed systems.

MIT proved to be fertile ground for other early thinking and activity that led to the notion of connecting otherwise isolated computing systems to facilitate communication between humans. A landmark paper by J.C.R. Licklider and Wesley Clark (not the U.S. Army general) published in 1962 described a worldwide network of computers that allowed an individual, logged in to one computer, to access applications and data at any other computer—at the time a radical idea, for which neither the technology nor infrastructure existed.[1]

By the middle of that decade, experiments proved the concept of connecting computers to each other across a linkup originally using a regular telephone line. With much funding help through the U.S. Defense Department's Advanced Research Projects Agency (ARPA), several universities and a few private corporations worked toward the goal of connecting multiple systems to allow researchers from one facility to run applications and access data at another facility in collaboration. In 1969, the network built with ARPA funding, called ARPANET, successfully connected the first two, and then four, computers at different locations around the western United States (Los Angeles, Santa Barbara, and Palo Alto, California, and Salt Lake City, Utah).

---

[1] The article was titled "On-Line Man-Computer Communication," published in the *Proceedings of the Spring Joint Computer Conference,* 1963.

The first public demonstration of the ARPANET didn't occur until 1972. And, by "public," I mean to other computer engineers outside the approximately two dozen organizations connected to the network at the time.

Even the earliest connectivity experiments revealed a limitation in the way information flowed through standard telephone lines. Two computers could "talk" to each other across the line, but that was about it. If multiple systems were going to communicate among themselves across a shared line, there had to be a way to enable data to flow from its source to destination without colliding with other data flowing on the wire.

In the mid-1960s, scientists in the United Kingdom and United States (initially working separately) devised an idea for allowing data to flow collision-free between computers on a shared network. The concept was to chop the data into little identified pieces, called *packets*, which would then be reassembled electronically at the receiving end. This was a remarkable idea that remains today the foundation for data moving through the Internet. To demonstrate how packets work, imagine that you ordered a printed set of encyclopedias from a publisher. Rather than shipping you one giant, groin-injury-inducing box containing all 20 volumes, the publisher sends you one volume per day via registered mail over the course of four weeks. Each volume is enclosed in its own padded envelope, with the addresses of the sender and recipient on the outside. You must sign for each volume as it arrives to confirm that it reached the correct destination.

If one of the volumes goes astray and the publisher doesn't receive the acknowledgment of your receipt, it sends a replacement copy. Or if one of the volumes arrives damaged, you know which volume number it is, and request a replacement be sent. Of course, you never know how the mail will pass along each envelope, so the volumes don't necessarily arrive in the order in which they were sent. But no problem, because the volumes are numbered, enabling you to assemble the set in the correct order on your shelf.

The lights you see flickering on your modem while you surf the Web or exchange email represent the packets of data flowing between your personal computer and the computer you are communicating with at that instant. Your computer may be downloading a Web page and sending an email message at the same time, but the packet-handling facilities inside your computer and on the network keep the packets for each transaction organized so that packets coming from the Web site are sent to your Web browser program and assembled into the page you eventually see; at the same time, your outgoing email message's packets flow in the other direction to your provider's email processing computer. All of these packets share the same "wire," whether it be a telephone line, cable connection, or wireless linkup. Each packet includes what is called a *header*, which conveys all addressing and sequence information to help your computer, the network, and computers at the other end keep everything straight.

By the early 1970s, email within isolated computer systems was a common activity among those privileged users who had access to computers. However, the mail software was still a long way from user-friendly. A user might have to run one program to send a message and run another program to read awaiting messages—all by typing commands in a text-only terminal or mechanical teletype machine whose readable output was printed on a continuous roll of paper. Because participants were all sharing the same machine, email addresses consisted of nothing more than the unique user name that the system administrator had assigned to each user account on the system.

In 1971, an engineer named Ray Tomlinson was working for an engineering consulting company called Bolt Beranek and Newman (BBN) in Cambridge, Massachusetts (founded in 1948 by two MIT professors). BBN was instrumental in configuring parts of the computing systems that allowed the first ARPANET systems to communicate with each other in 1969. Tomlinson had developed the email software running locally on computers at not only BBN but many other systems on the ARPANET. This email system operated by appending an incoming message to the recipient's private email text file: one file that held all incoming messages for that user. At that time, however, there were no email interconnections between computers on the ARPANET.

Driven by little more than an adventurous spirit, Tomlinson experimented with two Digital PDP-10 computers located at BBN facilities. Even though the two machines, creatively named BBNA and BBNB, sat side by side, they were connected to each other through the ARPANET. Tomlinson soon poked his way through the systems to force his mail software to work across the ARPANET. (At this time, the term "hacking" was used universally in a positive way, meaning that someone had found a way to perform some useful action on the system in a way not intended by the original designers.) Tomlinson described this early networked email experiment— which slightly extended the way the system was designed to allow one user to transfer files to another user on another computer—as a "clever hack."

One piece of unfinished business was how to handle addresses. While user names might be unique within a closed system, this certainly wouldn't be the case when connecting multiple systems. Therefore, a giant, universal lookup directory of user names would not help the systems forward a message to a particular user's mail file. Tomlinson knew that an address would have to include both the user name and an identifier for the computer on the network (each computer was called a *host).* He needed to come up with a character from the limited teletype keyboard, but one that would not conflict with those that were allowed for user names or host names. After a quick scan of his teletype keyboard, and recalling that the @ symbol stood for the English word "at," he chose that symbol as the divider (known as a *delimiter* in the trade) between user and host names in an address. By early 1972, the modified software including his network email "hack" was distributed to other hosts around the ARPANET that used the same system software.

The development of email on the ARPANET was unplanned, but it rapidly became the most widely used application across the network. A study the following year reported that email was the source of roughly 75 percent of all ARPANET traffic.

But it wasn't exactly smooth sailing after that.

As often happens in the formative stages of a new technology in the hands of computer engineers, one email program (or suite of programs) would not suit everyone. As the number of host computers on the ARPANET increased, so did the number of software systems running the host machines (I hesitate to call them operating systems, but they served similar basic purposes). New email programs popped up as programmers either hand-built software for the new systems or improved on what had come before. Many of the improvements made by early email developers were breakthroughs at the time. For instance, as mail software evolved from 1972 to the mid-1970s, programs began to allow users to view individual messages without reading the entire file that contained all incoming messages, and then to reply to a specific message without having to reenter the address of the person sending the original message. The ability to organize messages into the equivalent of folders amazed the world back then.

Not all of these email programs worked flawlessly with others. Just because Ray Tomlinson was the first to choose the @ symbol as a delimiter for email addresses on his system didn't make it the unanimous choice among others on the ARPANET. In fact, some other systems, including another fairly popular system called Multics, used that character as an editing command that deleted all characters on a text line before that symbol. Thus, Multics users had to incorporate a different delimiter character when addressing mail to external systems, which non-Multics systems wouldn't understand.

As the sophistication of the network and mail messages in general increased, further technological battles ensued over the way messages should carry and specify important information such as the subject, date, and addresses of both sender and recipient. Mail programs were becoming more powerful, and could do more with this so-called header information. (A header gets its name by acting as a series of text directives at the very top, or head, of the message.)

Header formats began to be formally codified with the publication in September 1973 of a document called RFC 561.[2] Much of what is included in email message headers today was standardized in RFC 733 (November 1977). Some extensions were added in later documents (notably RFC 822 from August 1982), culminating in the current standard spelled out in RFC 2822 of April 2001. All of this effort was directed at how an email message was to be formatted so that email software on any computer could manage messages for users. By standardizing on a way to identify the address of the sender, the subject, and date of the message, all email software programs could extract that data and display it anyway they wanted, such as in lists of incoming messages or as a nicely formatted opening to a displayed message.

Apart from the message content, another standard was needed to make sure a message could navigate from the sender's host to the recipient's host computer. That's what a *mail transfer protocol* does. Wouldn't it be great, too, if that transfer protocol could be *simple?*

When a host computer has an outgoing mail message in its queue, it attempts to move it to the recipient host computer by way of a brief electronic "conversation" between the two machines. The conversation consists of some shortcut commands from the sending host and brief responses from the receiving host (a code number and plain-language descriptions, such as 250 OK). If there is a problem (perhaps an invalid address, or the receiving system is temporarily on the fritz), the receiving host sends a different response code, advising the sending computer about the error. The sending computer might then report to the human sender that the message couldn't be sent.

If the sending machine gets the okay from the receiver, it sends the text of the message, including all header information. After the last character of the message, the sending computer sends a single period on a line by itself— a special character signifying the end of the message. The two computers then exchange a few parting "words" before moving onto other activities.

---

2 RFC stands for Request for Comments, a formal mechanism for publishing ideas among interested parties. Begun in 1969, Internet RFCs frequently acted as living laboratories for ideas about topics such as formats and how ARPANET (and eventually Internet) technologies would work together. The groups that manage the RFC process elevate some RFCs to Internet Standard status. Today's email formatting guidelines are specified in Internet Standards published as RFC documents.

Specifics of the conversation between the two computers are spelled out in an RFC document titled "Simple Mail Transfer Protocol" (first published with that name in RFC 788, in 1981). If you have set up the configuration of the email software running on your personal computer, you may have encountered a setting for what is called an SMTP or outgoing email server. This server operates at your Internet service provider or corporate computing center. It's the server that initiates the conversation with a recipient's mail system when your PC pushes an outgoing message to the Net.

The "simple" part of the protocol is based on the fact that the conversation is in so-called plain text and is kept to a minimum so as not to burden the network with more than is needed to complete the transaction. Although the SMTP protocol has been enhanced over the years to facilitate email attachments of various types, the fundamental way it works has not changed for over 20 years.

As an agency of the U.S. Department of Defense, ARPA and its network were intended for noncommercial research purposes only. That didn't stop some users, as early as the 1970s, from stretching this charter to convey personal messages that didn't specifically apply to an ARPA project. One of the first documented instances of a blanket spamlike email message occurred on the ARPANET in 1978, sent by an overzealous marketing executive at Digital Equipment Corporation (DEC), announcing a commercial product.[3]

In 1989, the Department of Defense transferred management of the network infrastructure of the ARPANET to the National Science Foundation (NSF), another research group funded by the U.S. government. By that time, several commercial networks were already in operation, providing greater public access to the network (at least to more educational institutions) and other services (such as public newsgroups). Although it was slightly dicey to allow these commercial networks to use the government-funded network infrastructure (the so-called backbone) to carry their users' traffic for nonresearch purposes, no one was ever thrown into jail for attempting commercial use of the network. But long-time users were displeased with the perceived impurities that threatened the ARPANET.

An additional effort was underway to put Internet technologies into the hands of nonengineers. The concept of *domain names* was also spreading far and wide around the Internet in the late 1980s. Prior to the deployment of the Domain Name System (DNS), addresses of nodes on the Internet were

---

[3] For details about this proto-spam, including the full text of the message and the difficulties the sender had to endure in those days before automated messaging, visit Brad Templeton's page on the subject at www.templetons.com/brad/spamreact.html.

strictly numeric, using the same style of Internet Protocol (IP) address you see from time to time, such as network control panel configuration fields (e.g., 192.168.1.100). A domain name is the somewhat plain-language name for a network node, and DNS allows computers to find the IP address that corresponds to a domain name. Thus, whereas we humans know the amazon.com address, the Internet refers to it as 207.171.166.48.

Email systems that openly courted the public, such as CompuServe, Prodigy, America Online, and others, were still largely unconnected private networks. The first major mail system to allow its customers to connect to the Internet was MCIMail in 1989. Anyone on the Internet could send a message to an MCIMail customer by addressing the message to the user name followed by @mcimail. It would be several more years before other consumer-oriented services allowed their customers to be reached via the Internet. New to the whole "Internet thing," it wasn't uncommon in the early 1990s for consumer services to charge an extra "Internet gateway" fee to send a message to an Internet address.

By the mid-1990s, the NSF no longer controlled the Internet infrastructure, as existing telecommunications companies had assumed the mantle. It became easier for the consumer online services, and then a flood of Internet service providers, to offer a direct Internet connection to their customers. Email flowed easily along the same paths and via the same protocols that are used to this day.

It was this simple mail transfer standard that allowed the Internet email system to grow so large so quickly, reaching nearly every corner of the planet. But as you'll learn in the next chapter, it was also the "simple" part that enabled jerks to begin to deceive and confuse recipients about the spam or virus-infected mail arriving in mailboxes every minute of every day. Preventing this kind of trickery and deceit might be possible with a technical update to the SMTP standards, but the amount of change needed to build a high level of accountability and traceability, while acknowledging the occasionally valid need for anonymity, would require a massive overhaul of the entire mail system.

The last time a change of this magnitude occurred, the connected world was teeny tiny. It was a superimportant change that brought the term "Internet"—a connection between networks—into the geek's lexicon. To make all the computer networks on ARPANET move packets to their correct destinations, the community agreed on an electronic signaling protocol that computers on the network use to talk to each other. The change to the Internet Protocol occurred in one massive move on January 1, 1983. After that date, your system either used IP or it couldn't connect to ARPANET without some difficulty. The ARPANET community was still small enough and sufficiently in sync to make such a dramatic technological shift all at once—perhaps the last time such a radical change would ever be possible. The current protocols for basic Internet traffic and email are so widespread that improvements enter circulation very gradually and with care not to break existing systems or cut off current branches of the Internet.[4]

In an ideal world, the fundamental SMTP standard in use today could continue for decades. But it's clear that greedy malcontents prefer to abuse the privileges afforded us by SMTP's pioneers. We are at a precarious moment in the evolution of email, with no clear path ahead of us.

---

[4] This is how an effort called IPv6 is evolving, as it works toward implementing an enhanced Internet addressing scheme that will head off an eventual depletion of available IP numbering combinations.

Behind the Curtain: How Email Works

Nerd Alert! Nerd Alert! We're going to get bits under our fingernails in this chapter.

It may be true that one does not need to know how an internal combustion engine works to be a successful automobile driver. But if someone threatens to steal one of your car's spark plugs or contaminate the gas in the fuel tank, you might want to know more about how the thing works so you can spot potential trouble before you end up with a two-ton paperweight. In the same way, I believe it's helpful to have a basic understanding of how the email system works to the predator's advantage, because so many email senders "out there" abuse the system to cause you potential grief. It's the same battleground on which guardians fend off attacks on your inbox. Along the way, I'll explain some of the gobbledygook buried in every email message you receive. If I've done my job by the end of this chapter, you'll treat every unexpected message as if it were an unattended parcel in an airport terminal.

To most nontechnical email users, it's a mystery how the characters typed into one computer find their way to another computer perhaps halfway around the world. At least with regular postal mail, we can imagine what happens to a letter we drop into the mailbox. Our letter may be bundled, bagged, transported, and sorted along the way by people and machines we don't ever see, but the physicality of the envelope lets us visualize it making its way from the mail drop slot to the recipient's mailbox (at least most of the time). If it's an important letter or parcel traveling a great distance, we may even create a mental picture of the piece of mail riding in the cargo hold of a jet plane racing above the ocean.

It's quite a different story with an electronic missive. The mail drop slot is a button on the computer screen labeled Send. At the recipient's end, a button labeled something like Get Mail brings the message to a personal computer screen where it can be read. But no people handle the message en route; the message isn't stuffed into a sack with tons of other mail pieces and thrown into a truck for its trip to the next point on its journey. So, how does Aunt Flo's invitation to an upcoming family reunion make its journey from her computer to yours? It takes the power of several unseen computers along the way, plus some normally invisible modifications to the message before you ever see the message.

For any message to find its way from sender to recipient, the message must contain an address of the recipient. That's no different from sending a message by postal mail. An email address performs the same job as the printed address on a physical envelope: It provides the mail system with enough information to forward the piece to its destination.

An Internet email address consists of at least two, and sometimes more, pieces of information. The basic format, though, is the same as Ray Tomlinson's first "Internet" email message in 1971.

The address starts with the *name* of the recipient's mailbox, usually the same as the recipient's account *login name*. Login names don't allow spaces or most punctuation symbols. That's why you typically see computer user names combining first and last names or initials into a one-word amalgam. Thus, John Doe may be assigned the login name of jdoe or johnd. On any given computing system, no two users can share the same login name or mailbox name. If the combination has already been claimed by another user, the system may choose to add the next available number in sequence, and stick it onto the end of the letters-only part of the name (such as johnd2, johnd3, and so on, as more John Ds join the system). This happens a lot at popular online services with millions of subscribers past and present.

After the mailbox name comes the @ symbol. Every Internet email address has one and only one @ sign separating the mailbox name on the left from the destination computing system on the right.

The most common designation to the right of the @ sign is a simple *domain name.* A domain name consists of at least two parts, each part separated by a period ("dot"). For example, the domain msn.com (belonging to Microsoft's MSN service) is one domain within a group of domains sharing the .com (dot-com) top-level domain (TLD). The TLD portion of a domain name is always the rightmost part of the domain address.

Until recently, the powers that ruled the Internet naming schemes sanctioned only a handful of *generic* top-level domains (gTLD), each theoretically dedicated to a particular kind of Internet activity. A domain bearing the .com top-level domain was intended for commercial purposes. The .edu TLD was for educational institutions, particularly universities, while .net usually indicated that the owner was involved with the Internet infrastructure. Any individual or organization could register for a domain name at most of the available generic top-level domains without much in the way of credentials (a few gTLDs, notably .gov, .mil. and .edu, had more rigorous requirements). New generic top-level domains, such as .museum, .biz, and .info, are now available.

A domain name to the left of the dot could be reused with other TLDs without conflict. There might be consumer conflict and confusion between, say, amazon.com and amazon.net, but in the Internet's "eyes" (and the eyes of domain name registrars), the two domains are very separate entities. Because of the potential for confusion, some scammers attempt to play name games in the hope that unsuspecting users won't read the TLD part of the email or Web address, enabling them to trick recipients into believing that they are communicating with a company or organization that has built up a good reputation over the years.

A domain name can have more than one dot in it, depending on its location around the world. By industry agreement, a two-letter code identifies each country. For example, in the United Kingdom, a commercial entity's domain might end in co.uk. The "co" part indicates a commercial organization, while the "uk" part stands for United Kingdom. For instance, to visit Amazon's British Web site, use the address www.amazon.co.uk. The formal name for this kind of TLD is Country-Code TLD (ccTLD). The following table shows several examples.

ccTLD	Country
.ar	Argentina
.au	Australia
.br	Brazil
.ca	Canada
.cn	China
.de	Germany (Deutschland)
.fr	France
.jp	Japan
.mx	Mexico
.ru	Russia
.za	South Africa

Not many countries have the three-stage domain system as in the United Kingdom. For example, eBay's German address simply uses the domain ebay.de.

A generic TLD is open to the world, meaning that whoever fills out the domain registration form for a gTLD name can be from any country. Unfortunately, domain registrars perform precious little verification of an application before granting use of a domain name to an applicant. And it is rather common among the more elusive criminal spammers to use deliberately false information in their domain registrations.

Sometimes an email address domain may include one additional piece of information, coming immediately after the @ sign and before the domain name used to route the message around the Internet. Some organizations create *subdomains,* distinctly named divisions that have meaning only within the confines of the company's computing system. The Internet's job is to get all mail to the primary domain; from there, the organization's computer "sorts" mail according to subdomain. For example, if a corporate entity uses the example.com domain, but has divisions that manufactures widgets and gizmos, and uses those names for its division host computers, the addresses jsmith@widgets.example.com and jsmith@gizmos.example.com would belong to two different people, and their email messages would never collide.

Let's say that your Aunt Flo is a customer of popular Internet service provider Earthlink, and that you use your office computer to receive your personal email (I won't tell the boss). Flo types her message on her computer at home, using email software—probably Outlook Express because it came with the computer. She has your email address in her Outlook address book, and chooses your name for the To: text box of the message. If she accesses Earthlink via a telephone dial-up account but is not connected to the Internet at the time she writes the message, she may save it in Outlook's Outbox on her computer.

Unbeknownst to Auntie Flo, Outlook has performed some preliminary actions that will assist the message in reaching you. Information that she entered in the New message window (your address and subject), her return address (pulled from Outlook's preferences), and some other normally hidden information about the message's origination is formatted into the *header* portion of the message. The header information is placed at the top of the message's content, waiting in the Outbox.

The next time her modem dials into Earthlink, she sends all mail accumulated in her Outbox. As the configuration preferences in her Outlook program specify, the message first goes to the Earthlink SMTP server. The SMTP server is the computer that actually sends the message out into the Internet on behalf of all Earthlink users (although for a service the size of

Earthlink, the duty is shared among numerous physical SMTP servers, all doing the same job).

An SMTP server has a lot of work to do before it actually sends the message anywhere. One of its first jobs is to insert a kind of postmark into the message header. The postmark indicates the source of the message (Flo's computer), the address of the SMTP server that received it for further processing, and the date and time. Each SMTP server involved in the exchange of an email message—including the sending server—adds information about its handling to the header of the message. This is very much like the olden days of postal mail, whereby each post office handling a letter might stamp a dated postmark on the envelope.

Before it can begin the transfer, the SMTP server scans the header for the sender and recipient addresses to help it create what is called an *envelope*. Just as an envelope of a piece of "snail mail" contains necessary information for routing the letter to its destination, so does the email envelope. Envelope data is used later as the message wends its way across the Internet. If the message is going to multiple recipients, the SMTP server creates an envelope for each copy with one recipient's address listed as the destination.

Next, the sending SMTP server reads the address of the recipient from the envelope in preparation for a two-stage lookup (via the Internet) at the Domain Name Service (DNS). DNS is a global system of continually updated collections of domain routing information. The first query asks DNS for the domain name where all mail for the addressee's domain is to go. This actual destination domain is called a mail exchanger (MX), and is not always the same as the addressee's domain.[1] Armed with the MX record domain, the outgoing SMTP server then queries DNS once more, this time to retrieve the numeric IP address equivalent of the MX record's domain. Your Web browser does the same type of query whenever you enter a Web address to navigate to a site (or choose a bookmark) because the inner workings of the Internet use only those numeric IP addresses to signify locations around the world. When the SMTP server gets the numeric versions of the address back from DNS, it then attempts to communicate with the incoming SMTP server at that address.

It's not uncommon for an incoming email server's IP address to be the same as the Web server for that domain. But by industry agreement, SMTP servers communicate with each other through a particular "port" at the IP address. Perhaps the best way to describe this port business is to think about a factory building. The building has one street address, but many different

---

[1] A large system may list multiple MX records to give the sending server alternate choices, in case one of the incoming servers is overloaded or down. An organization with multiple domains may also have MX records for all domains point to a single SMTP server.

kinds of doors for a variety of purposes. The front door is for management and staff; a side door is for factory personnel; one set of doors in the rear provides access for delivery trucks that bring in raw materials, while another set of doors are for loading trucks with finished goods to be delivered to customers. It's all one street address, but each door (port) has a well-defined purpose in the plan. For SMTP servers, port number 25 is the one dedicated for mail delivery.[2]

If the sending SMTP server is able to connect to the recipient's incoming mail computer, the two machines carry on a brief conversation. It is literally a back-and-forth discussion during which the sending SMTP server sends a series of commands, some of which convey information from the envelope. The receiving computer responds to each command (with a numeric code and short plain-text response) and can either advise that the mailbox is available or that it is not (perhaps it doesn't exist because the account closed, or the mailbox is overstuffed with too much unread mail).

Earthlink's mail server begins sending the message header and the message content that Flo wrote on her computer. As part of the transaction between the two SMTP computers, the receiving machine inserts its own postmark details of the transaction to the message's header.

After the complete message has been sent, the sending server sends a carriage return (like pressing the Enter key), a period, and another carriage return to signify the end of the message. If all went as planned, the receiving machine sends a code number to the sending machine to indicate that the message was received and is being passed to the recipient's mail file. The sending server, having completed its task, tosses the envelope in the trash.

If your employer's email system uses the common Post Office Protocol (POP for short), then all of your incoming mail is placed in a single file in a reserved place on the company's server. The file is nothing fancy: a simple text file that appends the latest incoming message (along with its header) at the end of the file.

When you use the email software on your own desktop or laptop computer to read incoming mail from your account, a click of the Read Mail or Get Mail button uses your stored account name (the name of your mailbox) and password to log on and read the mail file in your private area of the corporate computer.

---

[2] The format for specifying a port number in an IP address is to append a colon and the port number. For example, the usual port number to a Web server is 80. The notation looks like this: 192.168.1.100:80. The SMTP server at that same address would be 192.168.1.100:25. I show this because you will see this notation occasionally inside spam messages and even in your Web browser's Address field. Now you know what it means.

Thanks to the RFC standards established for email message headers, your PC's email software program can download a copy of the single mail file from the company computer, and divide it into individual messages that appear in your inbox. Information about the sender, date, and subject immediately appears in the list of unread messages in your local inbox. With typical email program settings, after your PC downloads the single mail file, it deletes the contents of the file on the server, preparing it to receive the next incoming messages.

When you double-click the message in the list, your software reads more of the header to show you the precise details of the message. Depending on how the POP server is configured, some envelope data, including the "postmark" stamps of the message's routing path, are preserved with the message, but are visible only if you choose to view the source code of the message (easier to do in some email programs than others).

It took a lot of words to describe the process of getting a simple message from sender to recipient, in contrast to the actual process, which very likely took place within a stretch of five or ten seconds, even if Flo were on the other side of the planet. All of those address lookups, two-way server conversations, message header modifications, and the actual message transfer itself occur nearly in the blink of an eye under normal conditions.

This description of sending and receiving email didn't, however, take into account some more recent advances in the email process. I didn't describe here any antispam filtering that may be employed at the receiving SMTP server or in your PC's email software. This scenario also assumed that the message was from a legitimate sender (you do want to hear from Aunt Flo, don't you?) who wasn't trying to hack the email system. Unfortunately, the system is easily twisted to allow spammers, scammers, and hackers to disguise themselves and their locations to make it difficult to track them down or block their efforts. Specifically, it is the system's reliance on mail envelopes and message headers that enables a great deal of deception. To begin to understand that, we'll look more closely at an email message's header information.

For the uninitiated, the header portion of an email message looks mighty intimidating. Lots of strange words, numbers, and symbols. Some of it makes sense, such as the From:, To:, and Subject: labels at the start of some lines; but there's a lot of stuff there that you rarely, if ever, need to know. That's why modern email software programs running on personal computers hide the header from you during normal operation, though most programs provide a menu or deeply nested option to view the header. It's also the email headers and the incredibly easy way they can be forged that have a lot to do with how spammers get away with disguising their identities. To understand that, it helps to know what a few key components of an email header can reveal to anyone who bothers to look at it.

To serve as an illustration of a typical email message and header, the following represents the entire source code listing for an email message that was sent from a colleague to my primary email address (long ago compromised among spammers, so I might as well continue to use it in public here). Other parties, computer names, and IP addresses are disguised to protect their innocence. I also add line numbers to make it easier to point to specific places in the header and message. These line numbers do not appear in the actual message source code, nor is the order of most fields bound by any rules.

```
(1)  From freddiej@example.com Thu 7 Aug 2003 16:15:54
(2)  Received: from smtp.example.com
     (jimbo.example.com [192.168.1.101]) by dannyg.com
     (8.12.9) id h77MFrGx025158 for
     <dannyg@dannyg.com>; Thu, 7 Aug 2003 16:15:54 -
     0600 (MDT)
(3)  Received: from freddiej (dhcp-172-24-30-
     238.north.example.com [172.24.30.238]) by
     smtp.example.com (8.11.2/8.11.2) with SMTP id
     h77MFm326503 for <dannyg@dannyg.com>; Thu, 7 Aug
     2003 15:15:48 -0700 (PDT)
(4)  Message-ID:
     <004d01c35d30$ff50bac0$ee1e18ac@north.example.com
     >
(5)  From: "Freddie J Muggs" <freddiej@example.com>
(6)  To: <dannyg@dannyg.com>
(7)  Subject: Available for lunch next week?
(8)  Date: Thu, 7 Aug 2003 15:12:31 -0700
(9)  Organization: Examples, Ltd.
(10)   MIME-Version: 1.0
(11)   Content-Type: text/plain; charset="iso-8859-1"
(12)   X-Priority: 3
(13)   X-Mailer: Microsoft Outlook Express
     5.00.2314.1300
(14)   X-UIDL: a<!#!Od~"!+A~"!YAe!!
(15)
(16)   Hey Danny,
(17)   Just got back from a week in Bermuda. Let's
     get together next week so I can show you the
     photos.
(18)   Freddie
(19)
```

For the purposes of understanding how an email message makes the journey from sender to receiver, we have to focus on only a handful of header lines: 1, 2, 3, 5, and 6. For details on all of the others, see Appendix A.

Line 1 may not be visible in your email program's header display, but incoming mail servers tend to record this information (sometimes with the Return-Path: label). The address here is copied from the message's envelope, which, as I said above, gets destroyed once the message is received. By recording this information, the incoming email server knows where to send bounce messages if a problem should develop in getting the message to the intended recipient. Most of the time, this address and the From: address (Line 5) are the same, but there is no requirement for that to be the case. The originating mail server can put any return address it wants on the envelope.

Spam hunters direct most of their attention to the Received: header fields (Lines 2 and 3), which record trace information. A message may have as few as one or many Received: lines. Each time an SMTP server receives a message to be passed along, the server adds the current trace information to the top of the list. Therefore, the most recent transfer line is the one that your own receiving email server made.[3]

A Received: header line written by a properly configured server reveals the identity of the most recent sending server (the "from" part), the receiving server's identity (the "by" part), and other relevant data, such as time and date of the transaction. A legitimate email message should contain an unbroken series of handoffs between the original sender and your email server. You can work the sequence backward by reading the Received: headers from top to bottom. In the example above, dannyg.com received the message from smtp.example.com; before that, smtp.example.com received the message from a computer identifying itself as freddiej.

Upon receiving the message from smtp.example.com, the dannyg.com mail server recorded the IP address of the sender and placed it into the Received: header inside square brackets. This information is very important in spam research because, except in very rare cases, this IP address is not forged. The dannyg.com server also performed a reverse IP lookup on that address to report the identity of the server associated with that IP address (jimbo.example.com in this example). Note that the reverse IP lookup revealed a slightly different identity of the sending server, although both are from the same domain (usually a good sign). The identity that appears after "from" is supplied by the sending server. That identity is not

---

3 Additional Received: lines may be added by firewalls, spam filters, and transfers between internal mail servers. Appendix B provides tips on finding the most significant Received: line.

validated anywhere, and it's quite common for deceptive spam to use an identity wildly different from the true identity.

Line 3 in the example is simply the previous exchange between Freddie's computer and his ISP. The IP address and reverse IP lookup recorded by smtp.example.com reveals that Freddie is likely an example.com customer, and appears to connect via DSL or cable modem (the "dhcp" marker means that his IP address is handed out dynamically by the ISP).

Be aware that the only Received: header data that you can always trust is the stuff entered by your own email server. All other Received: data—including whole Received: lines—could be forged. The bogus information is inserted into the message by the spammer's outgoing SMTP server, including the servers (zombies) secretly installed on consumer PCs by email viral infections. The same is true for the From: and To: fields (Lines 5 and 6). With a normal email message, the sender's email program dutifully fills out those header fields from information supplied by the sender. But there is no authentication of this information at any point. Nor does your address even have to appear in the To: field for the message to reach you: It need be inserted only in the server-controlled envelope.

Now that you know perhaps more than you ever thought you would about an email message and its header, you may have an appreciation for how fragile the whole email system is if someone wants to play games with messages. The specifications for how the system works were developed at a time when the number of individuals and computers connected to the ARPANET was the tiniest fraction of the number of emailers on today's Internet. In the early days, the online community was small enough to largely police itself through social pressure. If someone needed a dash of anonymity for any purpose (e.g., blowing the whistle on improper activity), it was anonymity for a good cause. It's a different world today.

While sufficient reasons for occasional anonymity on the Net may exist, the ability to hide one's identity is one of the technical loopholes through which the most egregious spammers, scammers, and hackers operate. Their ultimate desire is to be untraceable so that complaints about spam to their ISPs don't get them cut off from the Net entirely, or a traced virus won't land them in prison. Although all spam messages include some kind of contact point—a Web address, a phone number, or a reply-to email address—those contact points are rarely the same as the actual sender. The sender tries to stay hidden in the shadows.

A simple email transfer mechanism that helped email grow into a mainstream application worldwide is easily abused by Bad Guys. An even simpler way of formatting email message headers invites liars and thieves to play mind games with both spam trackers and unsuspecting recipients.

The bottom line about email today is that you cannot trust everything you read. Headers are easily forged, and deception is rampant. Even a message and attachment appearing to be from a person you know and trust may not be what it seems. That's why you have to be smart with every email message that finds its way into your inbox. Don't let a spammer, scammer, or hacker get the better of you.

CHAPTER 5

It's the Spanonomy, Stupid![1]

Spam would disappear from the Internet almost overnight if the economic incentive for spamming disappeared. The notion of a spam economy, or *spamonomy* as I like to call it, encompasses far more than just the $49.95 (plus shipping and handling) some spam recipients pay for $2 worth of an extremity extension elixir. The spamonomy trades in other currencies: our stolen email addresses, "click-through" visits to spamvertised Web sites, and others. Eventually, spamming predators convert these noncash assets into real money for themselves without paying us a commission for the privilege.

If that weren't enough, the spam problem has spawned a profit-seeking antispam industry. This industry—especially those segments responsible to shareholders and investors—thrives on the woe caused by spam to ISPs, mail server administrators, and individuals. When I try to create a mental picture of this system in my mind—antispam companies that need spam to justify selling us products to stop spam—all I come up with is an M.C. Escher illustration. You know, the ones where you enter an up staircase only to exit upside down on the floor below.

Let's look first at the more visible parts of the spamonomy, parts that are actually under our control, but for lack of knowledge and other human weaknesses (insecurity, vanity, and greed, to name a few). Whereas my definition of spam from Chapter 2 is all about *consent*, the spamonomy is all

---

[1] The title of this chapter is inspired by signs reportedly taped to the walls of campaign offices during Bill Clinton's 1992 presidential race: "It's the Economy, Stupid!" The sign encouraged strategists to focus on a major issue. There's a good lesson there.

43

about *content:* getting that content in front of our eyes and convincing us to act in response to it by doing something other than just hitting the Delete key.

Even if you commonly delete messages that are obviously spam—based on the email message's subject line that appears in your inbox list—some subject lines are written in order to trick you into opening the mail. Others appear to represent genuine offers for products or services that you might be interested in. Each of these email messages—sent to you (and perhaps millions of others) by an automated system—has two goals:

1. Get you to open and read the email message.

2. Entice you to take further action, such as make a phone call or click a link to visit a Web site in your Web browser.

You don't even have to open the message to start contributing to the spamonomy if the email software on your personal computer is set up to display a preview of the message when you simply click on the message listing in your inbox. In Chapter 12, I'll show you a spammer trick, called a *Web beacon* or *Web bug,* that automatically confirms your email address as being active when the image appears on your email program's Preview pane. A verified email address is an incredibly important asset in the spamming community. Because email addresses are more fluid than home mailing addresses or phone numbers, a freshly confirmed live address is worth a lot to spammers and list sellers (and list resellers and re-resellers). Your precious address becomes both a currency that spammers use to trade among themselves and a valuable piece of data that is sold or rented for real money to other spammers. The "address merchant" sells your address, and all you get in return is more spam, whose "postage due" comes out of your pocket.

Even if the email message does not contain an explicit beacon, it is equally easy for the spammer to code a beacon in the message's clickable links that opens a page in your Web browser. In other words, by clicking on the link and visiting the page, you may inadvertently be confirming your email address to the site's computers without your knowledge or permission. Addresses of recipients who click through to advertised sites are even more valuable on the resale market.

A simple visit to the spamvertised Web site can also contribute to the spam economy if the advertiser pays the spam-sending service for "hits" (visits) or "click-throughs" to the Web site. Therefore, while no immediate funds have left your pocket, your valuable email address may have been added to the saleable list of valid addresses, and the spam's sender may receive a payment as a result of your visit to the advertiser's site.

The mother lode of the spam economy, of course, is The Order, that magical moment when a spam destination extracts funds from the spam message recipient. And some of these sites do provide the product or service that is being advertised on the site. The spammer receives a commission for the sale, frequently a very large percentage of the sale (as much as $10 to $20 per order for products that sell for less than $100). Because of the extremely low cost of sending out hundreds of thousands or millions of spam messages, the breakeven point for the spammer can be fewer than ten orders from 1 million spam messages. It doesn't take many orders for the spammer to profit enough to encourage continued spamming.

The biggest money, of course, is in the *complete scam.* Tales of outright fraud could fill this book on their own. Work-at-home schemes, herbal and diet remedies, and tons of other promises too good to be true bilk tens of thousands of email recipients out of hard-earned cash all year long. In a rare case of the crook getting caught, an email scammer who promised to deliver a program that enabled participants to earn money at home by stuffing envelopes, pled guilty in 2003 after allegedly receiving $2 million from an estimated 50,000 fortune hunters—and delivering little or nothing in return.[2] Typically, few victims complain when their $30 or $40 disappears into the ether (only 400 complained about the envelope-stuffing rip-off), while the crooks get all that money before moving onto their next scheme. Even when a crook is caught and convicted, victims are lucky to get any of their money back—and then only after the hassle of filing claims with documentary evidence years later. In the envelope-stuffer's case, the court ordered repayment of less than $225,000.

How do spammers get you to open their email messages in the first place? Some go about it the straightforward way, by labeling the subject line of the message (which you see in the list of messages waiting in your inbox) with an attractive offer for the product or service they're selling. Here are some examples from one day's spam traffic:[3]

```
Subject:  Refinance Now at 4.25% and Save
Subject:  Incredible - world's smallest camera -
          digital
```

---

[2] The Federal Trade Commission's investigation found 16,000 Visa credit card charges for nearly $700,000 over an eight-month period. The FTC total figure extrapolates the number of charges on other cards, the known electronic checks, and unknown quantity of postal checks received at the defendant's post office boxes *(FTC v. stuffingforcash.com, et al.).*

[3] All subject lines, headers, and messages shown throughout this book are from real spam received at my email server. Spelling and grammatical errors are left unedited.

```
Subject:  Pro Kitchenware - up to 80% Off
Subject:  Viagra, Phentermine & more prescription
          medications available
```

Just because the subject line appears to state clearly what the message is about does not guarantee that these are legitimate (or even legal) offers, nor does a polished, artful look to the spamvertisers' Web sites. More than likely, you won't recognize the seller's name (or URL). You have no way of knowing (until it's too late) whether the "company" that takes your credit card information is interested only in your money or your credit card number. Moreover, how secure would you feel about submitting your credit card number to a Web site hosted on a different continent?

More commonly, however, spam messages come in a number of disguises. Subject lines are tested and tailored for a variety of audiences. For example, young people send a lot of informal messages to each other, so the messages try to look like they come from a friend or a friend of a friend:

```
Subject:  contact me back asap
Subject:  Dannyg, I saw your profile
Subject:  What are you doing?
Subject:  See my newest movie
Subject:  How are you doing!
Subject:  Don't be silly
Subject:  Re: party
Subject:  Did you hear?
Subject:  Have you heard the story about Kirk
Subject:  you owe me big time
Subject:  im back, are you?
Subject:  You're not going to believe this!
Subject:  You missed this Instant Message...
```

Then there are potential recipients who can be enticed because they're cheap and/or greedy:

```
Subject:  Get 4 Harry Potter Books, Pay Only
          Shipping!
Subject:  Pending Transfer to Your Account-
          Response Requested
Subject:  Unclaimed Inheritance
Subject:  Your name came up a winner!
```

Subject: Create Perfect Copies of DVDs and PS2 Games

Subject: Get Your Free Product Samples!

The gullible:

Subject: Congratulations!

Subject: Sensitive materials for Danny Goodman. Delete after opening

Subject: Scheduled PC Maintenance

Subject: Make money processing FedEx & UPS refunds!

The lonely:

Subject: Re: You Have Been Selected

Subject: We Have Been Trying To Reach You

Subject: re: Hey - I have been searching for you!

Subject: You Have One New Message Waiting...

The older, polite generation that doesn't want to offend:

Subject: Please Respond!

Subject: Trace Goodman Family Tree For Free!

Subject: You left your umbrella

Subject: One last question

Subject: Is this your email?

And those who can be intimidated by technology or a seemingly personal message:

Subject: Be careful of downloading music files

Subject: Why your computer is running so slow

Subject: Danny, Vice President Cheney has sent you a message.

Subject: Regarding Your Prescription

Subject: You forgot to respond

Subject: Your PC may have already been infected with a virus.

Subject: FW: Dannyg, Protect your email box from spam, trojans and viruses

Subject: Your Cell Phone Account

```
Subject:  Delete all spyware/adware/pop-ups/
          surfing history - offer ends soon
Subject:  Credit Card Cancelled
Subject:  RE: Your Account
```

Embedded among all of the message subject lines shown above are numerous techniques that spammers use to add to their deceits, and which are all part of a tactic called *social engineering*. The most common approach is to make the message appear to be in response to something you sent earlier (starting with "Re:"). Another is embedding part of your name or email address prefix in the subject. If the spammer harvested your email address from a public bulletin board or Web log posting, your name may become part of the spammer's address database, and portions such as your first or last name can be easily inserted into placeholders of their message templates. That's how you receive the "personalized" subjects that are supposed to make you believe a human sent the message.

A familiar spammer technique is to create a subject line or message that is intended to elicit an emotional response from the recipient. For example, a subject may indicate that "your order is ready," when you know that you didn't order anything. The message probably includes an order number. The goal, of course, is to irritate you enough to visit the linked Web site and cancel the order, supplying your valid and active email address in the process. Had you ignored the spam message, no order would have been shipped or charged to you, and you would not have verified your address as being actively read.

A lot of messages append extensive disclaimers about how the message adheres to various antispam laws. The following is one of my favorites. It appeared in a December 2003 message addressed to a corrupted and garbled address at my domain, citing a proposed (but never enacted) law from the year 2000:

```
=== Spam Disclaimer ===

IMPORTANT...This is not SPAM... IMPORTANT

* antiSPAM Policy Disclaimer: Under Bill s.1618
Title III passed by the 105th U. S. Congress,
mail cannot be considered spam as long as we
include contact information and a remove link
for removal from this mailing list. If this e-
mail is unsolicited, please accept our apologies.
Per the proposed H.R. 3113 Unsolicited Commercial
Electronic Mail Act of 2000, further transmis-
sions to you by the sender may be stopped at NO
COST to you!
```

One thing is certain: the more strident the claim, the less likely the sender cares one whit about the law. Moreover, just because an unsolicited message complies with a weak law doesn't mean that you must accept it as anything but spam.

Spammers know how to infuriate unsuspecting recipients. False claims about you having opted in to their mailing list directly or through some mysterious partner Web site can drive you to distraction. If the message provides instructions to remove yourself from their mailing list, most of the time those instructions lead to dead ends: nonexistent email addresses or Web sites. But even when the instructions link you to a real location, your request is rarely honored. Quite the opposite in most cases. Getting angry and demanding to be removed from the list is another way you have validated your email address to the spammer's database. Expect the spam to continue…and grow. The whole game reminds me of those science fiction plots wherein the hero smashes the attacking alien to pieces, only to have each piece immediately reformulate into a new alien.

It greatly troubles me to advise you not to remove yourself from spam lists because there are some mass mailers (both spammers and true opt-in mailers) who not only honor your request, but don't then turn around and resell your address to others as a hot prospect. In my experience, the firms that do the best jobs of handling removal requests are those that also market through direct mail catalogs, as well as senders of genuine opt-in mailings. These organizations tend to understand the importance of being a responsible mailer to prevent making permanent enemies. Therefore, you have to exercise well-considered judgment, and even do some research, before electing to remove yourself from an email list. My advice: *Never* unsubscribe from a list you didn't explicitly subscribe to in the first place.

Spam continues to grow for purely economic reasons because clever spamming is profitable. If it's at the expense of others, the spammer doesn't care as long as the cash rolls in. Spam recipients who actively react and respond to spam contribute the most to the spamonomy. But even those who hate spam can unwittingly contribute to the spamonomy if they're not careful.

Crushing the spamonomy is the most effective means under our immediate control to wipe out spam. Let me get the ball rolling by whispering two words into your ear: *zero response.*

In the meantime, if you ever wondered how spammers learn about your address, that's where the next chapter picks up the story.

CHAPTER 6

How Spammers Get Your Email Address

An email address is a funny thing. Not funny ha-ha. Funny strange.

On the one hand, most of us willingly display our email addresses on Web sites, in public forum messages, and on our business cards. The goal of such exposure is to make ourselves accessible to others—including strangers—who share our interests and wish to engage in one-on-one personal communication about topics dear to our hearts. On the other hand, most of us treat our email addresses as something private. It is a globally unique identifier, yet (thankfully) no global master email address directory exists. Someone who wants to send a message to your address must know that magic combination of letters and numbers.

The trouble with spammers is that they misinterpret the boundaries between the public and private spheres of an email address. Does including your email address on your Web page with a link that says "Email me!" mean that you invite anyone to send you mail about anything? Many spammers would answer a resounding yes! But your original intention was to be courteous on the Web, and perhaps to hear from others who want to contribute to your site. Too bad. You may think of your email address as being private property, but once it's "out there," you can never reel it back in.

There it is: a sequence of several characters with an @ sign and a dot or two that, once exposed, can be traded, rented, and sold for real money (in the spamonomy) without your permission or knowledge; a character sequence that allows strangers to use up your bandwidth, mail server disk space, PC disk space, and time without your permission; a sequence that, no matter how much sanctity you ascribe to it, will be desecrated by spammers who couldn't care less.

51

The subject of how spammers get your address is a potentially scary one, because you may be doing things on the Internet that would seem, to the nontechnical user, innocent enough, if not even considerate behavior. Yet it is this innocence and good manners that can put your email address into the widest distribution among spammers. And as is well documented, you don't even have to be all that active on the Internet for your address to become a destination for spam.

No, that's not paranoia: *spammers really are after you.*

I'll describe the five most common ways your email address becomes spam fodder. Two of them, *harvesting* and *dictionary attacks,* don't require much action on your part; two more, *Web site registration* and *e-commerce,* involve you or someone else submitting your address to a Web site such that the address ultimately reaches a spammer's database; the fifth and most insidious way is completely beyond your control.

Huge quantities of valid email addresses are exposed in plain view on the Internet. In the public archives sit millions of messages posted through the years in more than 30,000 USENET newsgroups worldwide.[1] A lot of those messages have valid email addresses either listed in the From: field or buried within the message bodies. All it takes is a computer program that knows how to navigate through the archives (such a program is easy for any server programmer to write) and scan the messages for the telltale @ sign, the text before it, and the text (including at least one dot) to the right. Automate navigation from site to site, and you'll soon be the proud owner of a database of *harvested* email addresses.

Take that same thought and apply it to the tens of millions of Web pages that have email addresses on them. The addresses are most commonly in the form of clickable links that facilitate a site visitor contacting the owner of the Web site to ask questions, place orders, or comment about the site.[2] Web site body content may also convey email addresses. For instance, a community organization may list its officers, along with their email addresses in case visitors wish to communicate with them directly. These Web-published addresses are the low-hanging fruit for computerized email address harvesting.

Web page email address harvesting is an incredibly easy technical feat to pull off. If you're not a programmer, you can buy off-the-shelf software from spam merchants for well under $200. Another, more expensive prod-

---

[1] The archive is stored at http://groups.google.com. You can also post messages there, or from most email programs, provided you have Internet access to a newsgroup server.

[2] Such links include a URL that begins with `mailto:`, such as `mailto:dannyg@dannyg.com`. A click on that link switches to the local email program and starts a new message with the To: field already filled in.

uct boasts that, if connected through a typical home DSL or cable modem, it can scrape 75,000 email addresses from the Web per hour (300,000 per hour through a faster T1 data line). Experienced, high-volume spammers have their own harvesting operations running to collect large databases of addresses that they can then market to other spammers. Because harvesting relies on existing Web search engines to find pages bearing mail addresses, creators of both the harvesting software packages and the professional harvesting operations talk about how they can "target" pages that bear certain keywords. I suppose they want their customers to believe that if they wanted to mail to, say, people interested in cats, the search criteria would focus on the appearance of the words "cat," "kitten," "kitty," and other feline-related words. In the harvester's mind, the owner of the `mailto:` address on such pages would be dying to receive spam with products for cats. Of course, the list would also contain addresses from Web sites about "hep cat" beatniks, the pop vocal group Atomic Kitten, and poker (as in feeding the kitty). But harvesting does not have to run in "target" mode. Untargeted harvesting is faster—and would probably gather the same percentage of cat lovers as the "targeted" harvest. A Google search for "mailto:" yields nearly 9 million pages, a good enough place for a harvester to start.

Sadly, the most prolific spammers and spam merchants (those who sell or rent lists to other spammers) have this bizarre belief that if your email address is located anywhere in the open, and it can be harvested, then you have *opted in* to receiving mail. In other words, when you receive the spam that states unequivocally that you are receiving the message because you opted in to receiving it (either from this particular vendor or one of its "partners"), it may be saying that you opted in because your email address was harvestable from a Web page or a newsgroup posting. Who but a spammer would define "opt in" in such a fashion?

Do you have a friend whose email address user name is something like jason2 or jennyd? Spammers know that most email account names generally include somebody's name, most commonly the first name and perhaps an initial of the last name or a serial number because others with the same name are on the system. If you have ever signed up for a free email account, you may have requested an easy-to-remember address, but it is likely already taken by someone else. In response, the email registration system suggests a variety of possible addresses, usually comprised of your first and last names, plus a number.

I recently signed up for a Hotmail account. The mailbox name I originally chose was taken (surprise, surprise!), so the system recommended four variations with my name and numbers: Danny_Goodman1, DannyGoodman_5, Danny_Goodman_630, and Danny_Goodman482. I elected not to use their suggestions—or any variation that included any or all of my names—but it's a safe bet that lots of folks sign up using one of the suggested addresses once they've exhausted the ones they'd like to use.

It's child's play for a computer program to use a database of common names (or valid user names from other domains) to start sending massive barrages of blank messages to domains that likely have large numbers of users to find which ones bounce and which ones don't. Addresses of messages that find a mailbox on the server are deemed active email addresses; the bounced addresses are not added to the final database of active addresses. This is one type of technique known as a *dictionary attack*. Names and numbers aren't the only components of mailbox names. There is evidence that some dictionary attacks use other words (hence, "dictionary") and even seemingly random characters. Pity the poor incoming email server that has to process all of these invalid addresses. Or, rather, pity the poor systems administrator who has to try to fend off these attacks while keeping the system running for legitimate traffic. For instance, in one 24-hour period in June 2004, my server refused connections for more than 7,000 messages directed to nonexistent mailbox addresses at my domain.

Not long ago, server software programs commonly shipped with default settings that left them wide open to public snooping. Back when "hacker" meant a techie who might poke around another computer system but do no damage, a few not-so-secret commands could potentially yield a gold mine of email addresses. While more software these days ships with such holes plugged, numerous old mailing lists and corporate directories are still left wide open. And now, the hacker (more accurately, "cracker") is after valuable booty—and your address could be part of the treasure.

Perhaps you have to be of a "certain age" to remember when products, such as appliances or other items covered by a warranty, included a warranty card that you had to fill out and mail back to the manufacturer. The company might state on the card that your warranty wouldn't be valid unless you provided information requested on the card, specifically your name, mailing address, and little bits of information about you and your household. Oh, yes, and the serial number of the product, too.

The threat of an invalid warranty was a scam to get you to part with some valuable information.[3] What the company really wanted was your name and address, along with a modicum of demographic information to assist with its marketing research. The mailing address was valuable. A name and address

---

[3] U.S. consumer protection law (specifically the Magnuson-Moss Warranty Act of 1975) automatically gives a purchaser the warranty coverage stated in the product's printed warranty. Warranty coverage is activated at time of purchase. Just be sure to keep your receipts.

of a product purchaser is at the top of the pecking order when it comes to compiled mailing lists. It means you have money, are comfortable parting with it from time to time, and perhaps even make the purchasing decisions in your household. The manufacturer will be interested in contacting you again when it comes out with some new gizmos, or runs a promotion to save you 5 percent on your next purchase. Your name will also be valuable to the manufacturer as an asset to rent or sell to other marketers of related products, including catalog companies that sell the type of product you bought.

This kind of market research and address collection had been going on for decades before the world found the Internet and email. These days, however, you are more likely to find instructions on the warranty card urging you to register your product at the company's Web site. Web site registration is extremely common, not only for product registration and downloading "free" software, but even to be granted access to deeper portions of some sites. You are also often invited to enter your email address into a form to receive periodic mailings from the site.

If you enter your own address into one of these forms and submit it, you are opting into the list. Plain and simple. The more reputable outfits will then send you at least a confirmation message to provide more details about the mailing policies of the firm, as well as provide legitimate ways to remove yourself from the list. In addition to the email confirmation, the most reputable outfits also ask you to confirm the subscription request. In theory, this should prevent someone else from signing you up for mailings.

That said, you should be very careful about where you sign up for anything or submit your email address in *any* registration process. There are plenty of email marketing firms on the Web that portray themselves as information providers for various technology, professional, entertainment, and hobby interests. They hope you will sign up to receive their newsletters about whatever their special areas claim to be. You may even receive the said bulletins as promised. But you may have also put yourself into the spam cauldron by granting permission to the address collector for indiscriminate distribution of your address to heaven knows who.

Most sites that include a registration form (which may be nothing more than a field in which you enter your email address, along with a Submit button) now also include a link to a privacy policy page or user agreement. Despite the legal mumbo jumbo in these e-documents, you should read them carefully before entering your email address anywhere. In particular, watch out for provisions that state your registration automatically gives the site the right to reuse your address as it pleases. For example, one site's privacy policy—after a bunch of phraseology that makes you want to trust it— includes the following line:

```
We may share this information with third parties
to enable them to provide you with additional
products and service opportunities.
```

In other words, sign up with this outfit, and your address will spread like wildfire across the great spam plains. It was necessary to agree to these terms or you could not proceed into the site or retrieve the downloaded goodies. Jeepers!

The problem with privacy policies, including those that show one or more logos of services that supposedly endorse the completeness of the policy, is that they may simply be false, and you won't know it until it's too late (even if you could attribute a submitted address leak to one particular site). Firms producing heavy email promotions with data gathered from their own registrations and lists acquired through "partners" seem to find it hard to distinguish their own addresses from those gathered by their partners under less-than-reputable conditions (e.g., harvesting). If a marketer promises to follow genuine opt-in procedures for its own list, but then one of its partners supplies a list containing harvested names (the partner may have lied—oh my!), the marketer is immediately suspect.

In the emailing list databases of the world, rarely is there an audit trail associated with your email address that indicates where it entered the system or how it got there. Whenever I see one of those spam disclaimers that I'm receiving the message because I opted into the mailer's list or a list of one of its partners, I want to scream "Prove it!" But I know that they can't prove it. Worse, I have seen disclaimers that claim I opted in from a particular IP address (one of those xxx.xxx.xxx.xxx numbers) at a certain date and time—hoping that I wouldn't know what the numbers mean. But I *do* know what they mean, and the IP address comes from some computer in China. Either someone in China signed up to an unconfirmed opt-in list with my address (not bloody likely), or the sender is pulling information out of thin air (very likely).

Disreputable email address list marketers tell so many lies to spam recipients and to each other that they have destroyed the credibility of email offers from firms that obtain proper consent. After awhile, you stop to think each time you are asked to register with your email address. In today's environment, that's a *very* wise practice.

You may wonder whether it's safe to register anywhere. It is, but there is no hard-and-fast rule, and you have to make some educated guesses. I tend to put more faith in Web sites associated with companies that have a well-known presence outside of the Internet and that don't ask for too much information. That goes for publications and retailers. High-visibility online presences may also be reliable places *if* their privacy policies confirm that belief. The reason I place more trust in these companies is that they are trying to build brand awareness on the Internet, and can't afford to be called on the carpet by privacy advocates who accuse them of betraying their customers' trust. Such firms also tend to use an opt-in confirmation system, with legitimate ways of turning off the mail when you want it off.

But even some big names have it all wrong. I will not, for instance, sign up to the *Los Angeles Times* Web site because it demands too much information, and its privacy policy provides no guarantee of keeping that information within its own organization. It's a paradox, because the organization is up front about its disrespect for my privacy, and because of its reputation, I believe them. Boy, this is goofy. (I could also lie about the information they request, but I don't like to do this. First of all, there is enough lying occurring on the Internet that I don't need to contribute any more. Second, no matter how much I dislike what they're doing, any poison I add to their data would be too diluted to serve as a silent protest. Besides, because they demand some kind of geographical reference, I could wind up receiving spam tailored to whatever bogus city, state, or country I submit. A lie is just one more thing to have to remember. No thanks!)

So when you see a registration form asking for your email address, you must trust your instincts. Along the way, you'll get burned because some site looks very professional, flashy, and consumer friendly, but it turns out to be a mask fronting an address-gathering machine that can now confidently place your address in its opt-in bin, and then the bins of other mailers until Time, itself, ceases.

You always have the option of creating a free email account at services such as Hotmail, Yahoo, and others to experiment with a particular registration site. Consider the address(es) you create at these free sites as "throwaway" addresses. Don't become attached to them (which means don't waste your time trying to be too clever in devising a mailbox name). Register in one or two places to receive their opt-in mailings. Then wait a few weeks (a month or more would be better) to see if offers from other mailers start flowing in to that address. If so, then you know you don't want to give up your workaday email address to them. But if they seem to be living up to the word of their privacy policy, then unsubscribe from your free email account and re-register with your primary account.

You can also try email address disguise services, such as sneakemail.com. This service (offered in both free and paid versions) lets you register at sites with an address from the sneakemail.com domain. Mail sent to that address is automatically forwarded to your real address without revealing your true address to the sender. If the sneakemail address is compromised, you can either use the service's filters to keep out the junk, or simply discard the address and create a new one.

The unconfirmed opt-in registration is a potential nightmare, especially if the system is set up to activate an account or subscription simply by receiving an email message. During one of the worm attacks that spread rapidly across the Internet in 2003, numerous mailing list and newsletter owners received messages that originated from infected machines. One of the characteristics of these worms is that they harvest email addresses from address books, Web page caches, and any other readable text file on the infected machine's hard drive; then they propagate the worm by sending copies of itself to harvested addresses, using one of the harvested addresses in the From: field of the message header. If the infected machine contains the address of any one of these unconfirmed opt-in subscriptions, then the poor sap—me—who was unlucky enough to be inserted as the From: address receives an automatic (and automated) subscription to the newsletter.

Yes, I received a confirmation of the subscription, but it was an opt-out type of confirmation: Further issues would come unless I opted out. Some of these were addressed to dummy addresses that readers of my Web programming books use in a few online examples. Therefore, somewhere along the line, a reader of one of my books was also a subscriber to, or had visited the Web page of, some investment "guru." The worm randomly connected those dots and sent itself to the guru's automated subscription address that was sooo intelligent it added to its subscriber list the address of a worm-laden mail message bearing an inane subject and body.

It gets worse.

Because I couldn't tell whether the newsletter in the confirmation was legit or some spam marketing ploy, I dared not unsubscribe from it. Spammers are known to send out bogus confirmations in the hope that an opt-out request will confirm an address. I didn't want to take that chance ("they" may be after me). Fortunately for me (I control my own mail server), I could delete every issue before it ever reached my inbox. Thus, Mr. Newsletter Publisher thinks he has one more subscriber than really gives a hoot about his latest advice.

In another case of opt-out registration run amok, a few years ago some stranger claiming to be Danny Gonzales signed up with a Web site that offers a high school reunion service. He did so with a bogus mailbox name from my domain. Spam started flowing not only from that site but plenty of others. I couldn't unsubscribe because the registration was password-protected. Sure, it's easy for me to reject all mail directed to that mailbox, but it points out that there are many places for unconfirmed registration of your email address to start you down the road to spam hell. And if there really is a Danny Gonzales out there, I'd like to flick your forehead.

Each time you make an e-commerce purchase on the Internet, you generally must supply an email address for the order to be accepted. Of course the vendor won't do much to validate the address other than to make sure it contains an @ symbol and at least one period plus a valid top-level domain (like ".com"). But there is usually good reason to supply a working address, even if it is a throw-away address from a free service.

E-commerce sites use the email address typically to send a confirmation of the order, and sometimes a notice when the order ships, along with tracking information. An order confirmation is good information to have, especially if you forgot to print or write down the finished order form on the Web site that contains an order number. If you need to contact the company about the order before it arrives (or if it got lost), you'll likely need that order number to get the information you expect.

But for every order form you fill out with an e-commerce vendor, you should first read the company's privacy policy, if it exists. Also pay very close attention to every square inch of the order form—or each page of the form if you are led you through multiple screens in the order process. If you find any radio buttons or checkboxes, look at them and their labels closely. They may be providing you a way to opt in or opt out of further mailings, not only from the vendor you're buying from but further distribution of your email address to other companies.

If you like the company and its products, you may, indeed, wish to be on its mailing list to receive further offers emailed to its customers. You can sometimes obtain good deals on closeouts of limited quantities that firms offer to their e-commerce customers. But don't get click-happy with the checkboxes if you don't want to get mail offers from others. Even if you trust the e-commerce vendor, giving permission to distribute your address could mean it will wind up in places you don't want. As much as the vendor may try to protect its customer lists, it may be fooled by one of its partners along the way. Once your address is abused through deceit somewhere in the marketing chain, you're screwed for the life of that address. And if in five years after you've cancelled an email address someone should be granted the same address, he or she will immediately receive spam without having done a thing on the Internet.

Pay special attention to the way checkbox or radio button labels are worded. Although the practice may be on the wane due to the efforts of privacy advocates, the typical default settings give all the power to the vendor. They count on you being so concerned with the products you're ordering and getting your credit card number into the form correctly that you'll skip over the boxes. Some of the wording in the boxes can also be confusing, filled with double negatives that would take a trained logician to figure out. Spend the time to decipher the meaning if it's not clear. I've even seen examples where the form tries the double-psych: the default setting has checkmarks unchecked, but in the roundabout wording, you need to check the boxes to keep your address out of the distributed lists.

```
Check this box if you don't want to be removed
from our weekly mailings of special offers and
exciting announcements from our marketing part-
ners.
```

Huh? Take nothing for granted in these forms. Study them closely.

Also be on the lookout when working your way through the product selection and order process. It is not uncommon, especially for small firms, to hire other, more experienced firms to handle the shopping cart and ordering process for the vendor. You frequently see logos or other indications in non-obvious places on the page that the shopping cart is "powered by" some other firm. The shopping cart firm may be legit, but there are many ways by which this kind of system can easily abuse your email address and other information without you, or the vendor whose products you're buying, realizing it. If the shopping cart outfit is also in the email marketing business, it is very likely pulling your order information, including your shipping address and phone number, into its database, which may then be sold or rented to other marketers. The fact that the shopping cart company and the product vendor have different privacy policies may easily escape even the wary consumer. Besides, can you fully trust the privacy policy of a firm you don't know, even if it is associated with one you do? Not really. And that's a crying shame.

The linkage between your email address and your physical address can lead to some creepy spam messages. If one marketer has these two pieces of information available for sale, then any other email database owners can quickly (through a technique known in the list business as *appending*) add that information to their database, as well. Mortgage loan and other real estate offers magically know which town you live in. This can sometimes lead to incredible spam claims, like one I received recently that revealed there was a mortgage lender in my town with incredibly low rates. Except that my tiny unincorporated town barely has a post office and a general store. The latter serves hardware and ice cream, but not mortgages of any flavor. Some messages may even mail-merge your street address into the messages, raising one's paranoia level a few notches.

It's unfortunate that you practically have to be a computer detective to know whether what you see on the screen is true. Expecting every user to be technically equipped to recognize potential avenues for abuse is out of the question. That there is no reliable way to know who is lying or telling the truth only complicates the matter further. Each time a new site asks for your email address, think first about how much you trust the site or how much you are willing to risk revealing your address to the site.

I come to one more possibility of how spammers can obtain your email address, even if you are the most careful Internet user on the planet. Given the alarmingly high rate of (primarily Windows) personal computer virus/worm infections by Trojan horse programs that load spam-related programs in the background, your email address in any of your correspondents' electronic address books or in any undeleted message you sent to a friend's or colleague's infected machine is at grave risk for being collected by spam thugs.

Technical studies of these worms suggest that they may be written in such a way as to be able to communicate with each other to relay information around the network without the users of those computers knowing a thing about it. Conceivably, the same method of harvesting PC addresses used by worm programs could be used to gather addresses of the infected machines and direct them to collecting points around the globe.

How dangerous is this? Let's say that you don't use your address to register with Web sites, nor do you post to message boards, public or private. You use email strictly to communicate with your corporate colleagues. One day a colleague asks you to send a message both to her corporate account and to a home email address. You send the message, and it arrives in the inbox of the home computer, which is shared by the rest of her family and is not necessarily updated with the latest Windows software patches. One of the kids downloads a cool screensaver from a site recommended by his best friend. A Trojan horse program arrives with the download, and gets installed lickety-split. Embedded in the download is another hidden program that scans the PC's hard disk for email addresses, finding yours among the pile. Off it goes to…who knows where?

Any collection of valid email addresses, even if gathered legitimately and kept entirely within the database owner's control, is subject to theft by various means. For instance, disgruntled employees have been known to steal lists. In June 2004, an America Online engineer was charged with selling the company's complete list of 92 million screen names to a spammer (who then resold portions of it to other spammers). But that's not the only way theft can occur. A friend of mine has anecdotal evidence that an address he used only once to register with a popular travel industry Web site was either lifted by an insider or was perhaps grabbed from the company's newsletter mailings using a computer network tactic known as "packet sniffing." If a hacker (in this case, a genuine cracker) could gain sufficient access to a server system through which the newsletter mailings are routed (not necessarily easy, but certainly not impossible), it then becomes a simple task to monitor the flow of characters to capture thousands of pre-qualified addresses as the traffic shoots by.

Except for the alleged AOL heist, it's difficult to quantify how much of these kinds of high-tech thefts occur. They're all technically feasible, and I don't think I've given spammer-hackers ideas they haven't already had. The point is: all email addresses are at risk for being collected, sold, rented, and traded by spammers. Then, once your address gets into spammer databases, you cannot remove it universally. The spam will keep coming, no matter how many times you sit in the *Monty Python*-esque Green Midget Café in Bromley and yell with a shrill voice, "I don't like spam!"

C H A P T E R   7

Meet the Spammers and the Scammers

There is no single profile of a spammer. In fact, the description of a spammer varies with how much you know about spamming and email in general—not to mention your definition of "spam."

Also, the volume of unwanted mail you receive has a direct bearing on your reaction to spam as a problem. If you get very little spam, then you might not even believe that spamming exists or is a problem about which so many others appear to be up in arms. (I don't know who you are—is your modem connected?) But if you are deluged with spam and have bothered to look at any of it, then you may have unconsciously defined several categories of spammers based on the kinds of messages they send and the tactics they use. Let me paint some broad strokes with a spammer brush to describe my categories.

The Earnest Do-It-Yourself Vendor

How many businesses are there in the world? I'm not just talking about companies with offices, factories, and warehouses. Lots of business are built around services. Untold numbers of regularly employed people have sidelines that they use to generate extra income to help house, clothe, and feed themselves and their families. It's all part of an economy, whether you live in an aboriginal village in the outback of Australia or jet between condominiums in the financial centers of the world.

The most challenging job of these millions of enterprises is finding customers for their products and services. Reaching potential customers, though, can be a costly and time-consuming enterprise. Just because you're a gifted inventor, a skilled artisan, or, um, writer, doesn't mean you have equal skills in getting your product or service in front of people who might want what you have to offer.

Traditional advertising routes, such as direct mail, print advertising, and radio or television advertising, can be very expensive. You must pay not only for the delivery of the message, but also for the creation of a professional-looking message that will be seen or heard above the already-high background noise of life in the twenty-first century. Making a memorable impact on the audience is extraordinarily difficult. (Quick, tell me the brand names that were advertised in the most recent half-hour program you watched on commercial television! I didn't think so.)

Enter the promise of conveying a message to millions of people at a cost per message that is so low—between one-hundredth to one-thousandth of a cent—the entrepreneur figures, "Why not give it a try?" A spam message advertising inexpensive CDs with tens of millions of email addresses and software that sends bulk email is too much to resist.

Perhaps cognizant of local laws about commercial email, the emailer-to-be tries to obey the letter of the law by correctly identifying itself as the sender, and provides a way for recipients to be removed from future mailings. After composing the message and getting computers set up and ready to go, a click of an on-screen button starts the flood of outgoing messages.

That's when trouble starts for the unwary entrepreneur.

Depending on the ISP he uses, the ISP may begin blocking the outgoing messages before the message count gets very high, suspecting that the sender is a spammer. Many of the messages that do go out will likely be blocked by incoming spam filters at the larger Internet providers that battle two or more billion spam messages each day. Some of these providers may then add the sender to blocklists that prevent future traffic from that address (or domain) from being allowed into their systems, including a genuine one-on-one message, until evidence of spamming ceases. The offense will also be reported to the sender's ISP, who will likely suspend or close down the account of the sender. If the message includes a link to the sender's Web site, the hosting service for that site (if it has an explicit "no-spam" policy in its user agreements) will also likely be warned about the spamming, and the host will disconnect the site.

The small percentage of messages that actually get through to recipients will certainly anger many. Any goodwill that could have accrued to the entrepreneur is immediately destroyed by those who don't want to receive the offer. Finally, a tiny handful may respond to the offer. If the offer Web site manages to stay active (perhaps after frantically moving the domain hosting to another provider following the first shut-down), the entrepreneur will manage to snag a few orders.

In the meantime, the entrepreneur has generated a lot of wrath on the Internet. The more militant of the antispammers may even try to launch cyberattacks on the sender's Web site and email servers. In response to warnings and account cancellations from the sender's hosts and providers, the entrepreneur has to dig around the Internet to find a new way to connect to the Internet and host his Web site.

At this point, the sour experience can direct the earnest do-it-yourselfer down one of two paths. One path leads to being dissuaded from using automated mailing as a way to look for new customers. This would make the mailing a one-time occurrence, and spam emanating from that domain will never happen again.

Unfortunately, because of the irritation caused by his first outing (not to mention the personal abuse he had to take from spam fighters), the more likely path the entrepreneur takes will be to find ways to prevent the problems encountered the first time out, but still trolling the Internet for prospects. That will turn the earnest do-it-yourselfer into one of the other categories described below. Things will get ugly.

"Nudge-Nudge, Wink-Wink" Marketers

Even large companies with brand names you'd easily recognize face the challenge of acquiring new customers. The more competitive the industry, the more desperate participants are to reach prospects. The more lucrative the business segment, the more companies are willing to pay to pull in just one new customer.[1] A complete sub-industry called *lead generation* supports numerous industries by using various marketing methods to uncover potential customers. Lead generation is particularly popular in financial service business: mortgage and car loans, credit repair services, and credit card issuers. These tend to be exceptionally high profit margin business segments, making it economical for such services to hire companies that specialize in locating prospects. Anyone who fills out a form—even to receive a free gift of dubious value—is considered a fresh email lead. In an email message produced as evidence in a deceptive spam prosecution in New York, an accused bulk email master calls these leads "freshies."

---

[1] Did you know that the first order you place with a company through a direct mail catalog usually loses money for the catalog company? The high cost of acquiring you as a customer outweighs the profit the company makes from your first purchase. It won't make a cent from you until you place subsequent orders from the same or future catalogs.

The problem is that the companies that receive the leads don't always know where the leads come from or precisely what tactics were used to acquire the leads. It's not uncommon for a supplier of email addresses to have acquired those addresses from yet other sources.[2] Some of these outfits charge outrageous fees for one-time use of the lists, usually to trick newcomer sellers who falsely associate a high price with quality. Even if the companies that hire the lists claim to have a strict policy against using spam to fish for customers, they have no idea whether or not the lead generation companies are using unsolicited bulk mail to reach prospects. Even if the mailer is familiar with the lead generation company, there is a high likelihood that the definitions of "spam" and "opt-in" used by the lead generation company are not the same as in the mailer's public policy. To the lead generation company, the fact that someone eventually responds to a purely spam mail means that the user has opted into the system, although the original mailing was anything but opt-in. Some would call that lying; others would call it a difference in interpretation.

The point is, plenty of legitimate companies employ others to find leads, but the legitimacy or truthfulness of the third-party lead generators may be doubtful. Too many lead-generating spam messages were addressed to my spam "trap" addresses, which could only have been harvested. The companies that hire the lead generators are also too busy raking in the business to dig too deeply into actual practices. They know that they'd have to spend a lot more money to find new customers if it weren't for third-party spammers doing the dirty work for them. They must believe it's okay to look the other way, while deploring the very tactics that are responsible for their business.

Companies hiring lead generators of questionable operation in the United States hide behind the "independent contractor" status of the spam-, I mean, lead-generating outfits. If you complain to the company that contacts you as result of your return to a lead generator (perhaps it illegally forged message headers), the company says it can't control the actions of an independent contractor, and is not accountable for any bad behavior on the contractor's part. When you consider that lead generators frequently hire affiliate email senders to do even more of their dirty work, the distance between the actual spam sender and the company at the other end of the line stretches still further. Or, as the mortgage broker might say, in a Bart Simpson voice, "I didn't do it."

---

2   To experience the frustration of trying to get a satisfactory answer from a spammer about the sources of their leads, you can read an email exchange between a spam recipient and a credit counseling firm that initiated the spam. The URL is unwieldy, but it lets you read a newsgroup message with all of the details: http://groups.google.com/groups?selm= yof%25a.1932%24kK4.691%40nwrddc02.gnilink.net.

Unsolicited automated email is not an acceptable way to prospect for customers. Companies must find ways other than via email to attract new buyers for their products and services. As long as legitimate businesses hire spammers to do their dirty work, the spammers will continue to spend our time and our money on sending their messages to us.

Email "Marketing" Services

Anyone who wants to send out a bulk email campaign doesn't have to look too far to find hundreds of email marketing services on the Web. There are probably thousands if you include all the people who have purchased software and email lists from others so as to "cash in" on the "email marketing explosion."

A precious few of these outfits may be legitimate in one way or another, but the well is poisoned by throngs of those who put up a professional face to the world, while lying right through their privacy policy statements. One spam message I received noted in plain language that it was sent through an email marketing company. Out of curiosity, I visited the Web site of the outfit. It was extremely professional-looking. Nice graphics. Easy navigation through the site. It was easy to see and understand the range of services the company provided.

The original message I received said that I received it because I had opted in to either its list, or through a list of one of its marketing partners. The offer was for a product category in which I have no interest, so if the idea was to target the message at recipients interested in these kinds of offers, based on my activity elsewhere on the Web, the marketing service failed.

Following another link on the site, I studied the rather elaborate privacy policy statement. As a mailing service, the company appeared to recognize the extra responsibility it has to describe how it treats its own lists that its customers might use for mailings. There was plenty of language in the policy that I didn't like, particularly how the marketing service isn't responsible for abuses by its customers (nudge-nudge, wink-wink). But the one point that really caught my eye was the promise to mailers and recipients alike that the email addresses it collects are absolutely opt-in addresses, derived from its own registration forms and those of others with which it has business relationships.

Lies.

The mail message I received had been sent to an address that I use only on one page of my Web site, to let me know when a user is sending me a message about the content of that page. I have never used that address to sign up at any Web site. It is not in any of my personal computer address books. Despite the claims to the contrary by the service, the firm emailed to an address that had been harvested from my Web site. Thus, I had a slick-looking and established email marketing firm plainly lying about the way it does business. Even if the firm wasn't doing the harvesting itself, it was acquiring lists from other sources that had harvested the addresses. Most likely, the marketing outfits believed the lies of the other sources about their opt-in leanings. The chain of lies they tell each other and their customers is unbreakable.

Simply put, no one should believe the opt-in-ness of any email address list acquired from another source. This nonsense about obtaining opt-in addresses from "partners" must stop.

Even organizations that should know better get stuck from time to time. In August 2003, Vermont governor Howard Dean's presidential election campaign organization hired two established email marketing firms to send email to gain supporters for the governor. Unfortunately for the Dean camp, the two firms—despite their claims to be opt-in firms—sent messages to recipients who had not necessarily opted in to receive campaign emails. For instance, a Web log author (www.tnl.net/blog) received one of the messages at an address he claims to have used only for a product registration form. Complaints ran so high so quickly that the Dean campaign not only had to immediately cancel its association with the firms, but representatives from the campaign made public apologies to spam activist forums around the Internet. Despite a candidate and campaign that showed more signs than most of being "Net savvy," they got caught in an embarrassing and potentially damaging situation caused by believing the marketing malarkey of professional email firms. A cautionary tale, indeed.

To their credit, some email marketing firms operate in the open, without disguising the source of their messages. They operate in accordance with most of the incredibly weak laws that govern email, thus standing on their legal ground to do what they do in the open. They find Internet connectivity points that tolerate massive amounts of outgoing mail, spam or otherwise. Yet these firms genuinely seem to be interested in removing invalid addresses from their databases—to a degree. Their addresses contain a working Reply-To: or Errors-To: header field, where an incoming server can report the message as being addressed to a mailbox no longer active (such return addresses typically include the word "bounce" or "errors" as part of the server address to which invalid addresses are directed).

Removing an invalid address from their databases is not necessarily the same as honoring a request to be removed from a database. A dead address is completely useless to them, while a known active address that requests deletion is a valuable asset, regardless of the desire of the recipient not to receive unsolicited automated mailings. While it's true that individual removal requests sometimes are honored by established email marketing firms, you cannot automatically trust that your address won't then be consolidated into another list that gets sold or rented to other mailers as being an active (albeit disinterested) email address owner.

One more problem with these operators that mail in the open: they aren't always really operating in the open. Often there is still some kind of indirection taking place. They own dozens, if not hundreds, of Internet domain names. Domain names are cheap to register (as low as $5 each per year), and they enable the sender to make it seem as though dozens of domains are mailing a million messages, rather than one domain mailing dozens of millions of messages. Their messages include pleasant-sounding verbiage about the name of their service—names that might include words such as dealz, 4u, offers, offerz, optin, and buyz—implying they are doing you a favor by letting you know of their product offers. Even if the firm removes your address from one of these domains (each domain being treated as a distinct "business unit," despite being owned by one registrant and headquartered in the same office), you will not likely be removed from mailings issued by the other domains.

High-Volume Spam Mills

The creepiest of the creepy in my opinion are the high-volume spammers who gladly boast about how many millions of messages they and their associates blast through the Internet in any given hour of the day. Can you trust statistics from someone who lies and steals his way into your inbox? I treat these tales of spew, which get quoted in the occasional spammer interview or governmental hearing, just like the one-that-got-away fish stories told around the cracker barrel.

It's not clear how many of these mills exist. One antispam activist group, called The Spamhaus Project, claims to have identified approximately 200 spammers who are responsible for 90 percent of the spam on the Net in North America and Europe.[3] It may not be so easy to pin so much spam on so few operators these days. It is simply too easy to find spam-friendly hosting services (frequently in Asia and South America), unprotected mail

---

[3] Spamhaus (www.spamhaus.org) is a volunteer organization that helps identify major spam offenders, and assists ISPs with identifying spam sources. One list published at the organization's site, the Register of Known Spam Operations (ROKSO) is a database of spammers who have been booted from the Internet for violating an Internet provider's antispam service agreement at least three times in a row. For each entry, you can read as much data as Spamhaus has gathered from the public domain about the spammer, frequently citing media reports of criminal records or convictions of the offenders.

servers, and zombie personal computers around the planet that permit disguised relays of vast quantities of mail. Finding the true source of these messages—the ones being paid to cause these messages to be sent in the first place—is an arduous, costly, and sometimes technically impossible task, and one of international scope.

On the other hand, it doesn't really matter how many or how few master spammers there are. As long as they break no laws on the books, or enforcement of the laws they break stops at jurisdictional boundaries, they toil assiduously to stay one step ahead of spam-fighting forces around the world. The financial incentive to keep pumping out spam is strong, even if it means moving connectivity and Web sites from ISP to ISP to stay ahead of antispam activists.

Spam mills are hired by all kinds of companies selling products with extraordinarily high profit margins so that the spammers can collect a comfortable commission from every sale that results from the spam mailing. Even if the response rate is as low as 10 for every million messages, the spammer can break even for doing a minimum of computer work in preparation for clicking the buttons that unleash the volleys of messages to the world.

To ramp up their spam output even more, high-volume spammers use spam to attract affiliate mailers who will use their own computers to send the high-volume spammer's messages to more recipients by way of more open email servers.[4] For the primary spammer, it's just paying a small fee to increase the volume of spam being transmitted in any hour.

Affiliate usage isn't all that difficult to see for yourself. In the links within the email message that lead the recipient to a Web site, you can frequently, and clearly, see add-ons to the link, signifying that it originated from an affiliate (that word appears in the add-on code), along with an ID number so the Web site can credit the affiliate (and the affiliate's parent) with the Web site hit and sale.

High-volume spammers have no conscience about the offers contained in the messages they send, much less any sensitivity about the recipients. If questioned by the press, they immediately deny sending anything having to do with pornography. This denial is merely a legal dodge because of the ramifications surrounding the dissemination or promotion of pornographic materials when the recipients may be underage. There is no way to know from an email address whether the recipient is in grade school or retired. It is better to deny any asso-

---

4 For less than $100 (another contribution to the spamonomy), anyone can buy a Windows software program that trolls the Internet in search of what are called open mail proxy servers. This kind of server lets any spammer relay untold quantities of messages in such a way that the destination server knows only where the proxy is on the Internet, but not where the email originated.

ciation with pornography than to invite The Law to investigate the situation. But the quantity of pornographic spam and potential profits are too great to be left to small-time operators. Some of the big guys must be sending it—their definition of "porn" is probably as slippery as their definition of "spam."

Scammers

If high-volume spammers are creepy, the scammers are the very bottom of the barrel. They prey on the technology-challenged, the unsuspecting, the gullible, the lonely. Even if you are the most alert, savvy, and skeptical spam fighter on the Internet, many of your friends and family are likely at serious risk of being taken for their money, credit card data, and privacy.

Most of the scams taking place through email are simply updated versions of the same scams that have been duping people for decades, if not centuries. The Internet and its spam-friendly technologies simply make it easier and quicker for more scammers to target more potential victims at greater distances. You can also be sure that some of the high-volume spammers mentioned earlier are also in on scam enterprises. The lines of distinction among spammer categories blur easily.

A scammer is interested in extracting something of value from you by gaining your confidence—hence the *con game*. The two easiest high-value assets to lift from the unwitting target these days are money and credit card numbers. Scammers are out for your money and financial information, so you must be especially alert.

You can divide major scams into three basic categories:

- Outright thieves, who steal your money or identity

- Subtle crooks, who sell you worthless crap

- Advance-fee (419) scammers

Each group has its own subgroups of tricks and techniques to carry out their nefarious enterprises. Let's look at some of them.

Outright Identity Thieves—Gone Phishing

Millions of email users continue to receive messages that purport to originate from legitimate companies with which the email recipient may (or may not) have an existing relationship. Senders of these bogus messages want the recipient to believe the messages come from legitimate places such as eBay, Paypal, CitiBank, Earthlink, and dozens of other companies, where lots of email users may have an account of one kind or another. The opening message contains an "important" alert that either their account will be closed or the company is performing some kind of security audit on personal information, requiring that the recipient click the email message's link to a form where they can "verify" their information.

The forms in both the email and phony Web pages use art directly from the real companies' Web servers; and other wording on the page, such as copyright notices and privacy policies, are copied verbatim from the original, honest sites. The goal of this trickery is to get unsuspecting recipients to believe a highly plausible story about security precautions, and enter their account numbers, passwords, and sometimes more detailed financial data into the form. But the page at the other end of the email message link is not to the site whose art appears on the page. Instead it goes to another Internet destination, sometimes on another continent, where thieves can then do all kinds of damage to the accounts and assets of the victims.

Antispam activists (who have quite a lexicon of jargon all their own) call this kind of activity "phishing." Using "ph" for "f" in the name of less-than-honest activities goes back at least to the 1970s when telephone system hackers used handheld audio generator boxes to trick phone system computers into providing free international long distance calls. This activity was called "phone phreaking." Apple cofounders Steve Wozniak and Steve Jobs were members of the phone phreak community. But I doubt they ever stole a credit card number.

The eBay variant of identity phishing has a potentially extra nasty touch to it. Once the phisher has a sucker's eBay account user ID and password in hand (the first fields of the bogus form), the crook changes the password and email address to the eBay account so that only he can operate it. With luck, the account is one that has been established for a couple of years and has dozens or hundreds of positive feedback rating points. A long-time eBay membership and a high feedback rating is generally a sign of stability and reliability, giving bidders high confidence in the seller. But now the crook has taken over the account. He studies the existing or recent auctions for high-priced goods—auctions bringing a frenzy of activity that yield a closing auction price in the thousands of dollars. That means there are plenty of willing bidders out there with money to spend on whatever the thingamajig was.

The crook then copies the images (or links to the images) and item description into a brand-new auction under the hijacked account name. With so many disappointed bidders from the previous auction for this item, the auction is sure to attract bidders of the same caliber. Payment terms may be different for this second auction, however: usually an untraceable method, such as money order or bank transfer (to an account that closes immediately after the money arrives and is too costly to trace).

Fortunately for the eBay world, many times these schemes are carried out very stupidly. Bidders for rare and high-priced items know their favorite categories in eBay very well and watch the auctions like hawks. When a rare item suddenly appears that had recently been in another auction, the auction watchers immediately recognize the wording and photos as being from an earlier, legitimate auction. Surprisingly, I've seen this scam done many times on one-of-a-kind items and numbered, limited-edition items, where the scammer's description uses the identical serial or limited-edition number in the second auction. They must hope to catch the novices in the category who would be thrilled to pick up a "bargain." If the auction is listed with a "Buy It Now" price, anyone can jump in to claim the item and close the auction immediately. This is the best hope for the scam artist, who will get his money quickly, before the category watchers report the suspicious activity to eBay. In short order, the eBay newbie is screwed out of thousands of dollars, probably cursing eBay all the way, when it was really a combination of faults on three other parties: the victim who yielded his or her eBay account and password to the phisher, the scammer, and the greedy bidder who was getting a deal too good to be true (because it was).

The eBay scam isn't the only way you can lose money (fast!) on the Internet. In fact, it's one of the more elaborate and time-consuming ways to separate unsuspecting dupes from their money. Far easier is the spam that directs you to a Web site for an amazing deal on a product or service that you'll never receive, even though you've filled out the order form with your name, physical address, email address, telephone number, and credit card information.

Over a decade ago, when the Internet was still a very "new thing" to the public, and plenty of jokes flew around about how people would disguise who they were in chat rooms, a rather prescient cartoon appeared in *The New Yorker* (July 15, 1993). One dog, sitting on a desk chair in front of a computer, says to another dog on the floor, "On the Internet, nobody knows you're a dog." It's truer today than ever. Not only do you not know who's spamming you to con you out of your cash and information, but you don't necessarily know where on the planet the scammer might be. Unless you have evidence to the contrary—and taking the Web site's word for it is *not* sufficient evidence—a Web site you reach from a link in a spam email message should not be trusted without further research. Just because the email or Web site says the company or product is the one "as seen on TV" doesn't mean that the TV program endorses either. An investigative exposé about a scam artist ripping off thousands of victims may be "seen on TV," but you obviously don't want to do business with that guy.

A lot of victims who send money but receive nothing in return do little or nothing to complain. If payment was by credit card, they can at least usually get their money back from the credit card company. But a lot of scam offers require payment by check or money order, which, once cashed, is money down the toilet. There are a few reasons why only a minority of scam victims complain. If the scam artist doesn't respond to complaints (the scammer may have moved his operation), then the victim is frequently at a loss about where a complaint should be directed. The days of the Better Business Bureau (BBB) acting as a registry of good and bad guys are long gone when it comes to Internet businesses—even if you know where the scammer is located.[5]

More commonly, the scammer has taken the victim for a not-big amount of money. How much aggravation is it worth to try to recover $30 or $40 for some undelivered miracle product? Do you even want to admit to yourself or others that you allowed yourself to be duped? Many victims feel great personal shame for allowing themselves to be taken. Would you call the state attorney general to complain that you didn't receive the magic pills that promised to increase or decrease the dimensions of a part of your body? Probably not, and that's what the scam artist is counting on.

You'll also get offers for attractive-sounding deals (sweepstakes or prize winnings, free trips, other goodies you dream about) that ask you to phone what appears to be a toll-free telephone number. What you don't know is that the phone number—even those within the real toll-free prefixes—illegally redirects the call to non-toll-free numbers (frequently to the Caribbean) that end up appearing as charges on your next phone bill.[6] The charge for the call can easily run into the $100 range. You don't know this, of course, until your next phone bill arrives. Then you have the pleasure of going through an incredible hassle with the phone company to complain about the charge and get it removed from your bill. Lots o' luck.

Remember: the "con" in "con artist" does not stand for "conscience." A scammer has none.

Purveyors of Worthless (or Dangerous) Junk

Despite the raft of scam artists who have no intention of sending you any-

---

5 The BBBOnline program (bbbonline.org) lists only companies that are members of their local Better Business Bureau and have registered to be in the BBBOnline Reliability Program. The site does not list complaint or compliance data about program members. Information about non-members is non-existent.

6 As incredible as this claim sounds, the problem is prevalent enough for the Federal Trade Commission to issue a formal warning (www.ftc.gov/bcp/conline/pubs/tmarkg/toll free.htm).

thing in return for your hard-earned cash, there are even more outfits out there that use spam to sell their worthless wares to a gullible public. A lot of the merchandise is, indeed, shown "on TV," when the products show up in the news, as part of reports on the investigations of the U.S. Food and Drug Administration (FDA), the Federal Trade Commission (FTC), and various states' attorneys general, regarding false product claims and medicine contaminations. I guess the advertiser forgot the "as evidence" part.

The once valuable promise of a "money-back guarantee" is now used so cavalierly that it holds little meaning from a company you know nothing about. You might be able to get your money back if you go through the trouble of packing up and mailing the unused portion of the product (at your expense) back to the company. More than likely, however, you'll just forget about it, and chalk up the loss to your education—until the next time you're taken in by another gimmickmeister.

In the meantime, you have fattened the wallet of the seller. Many of the medicinal products offered via spam cost their sellers only a few dollars, but they turn around and charge you $20 to $90. Each sale has to generate enough revenue to pay commissions to any spammers or affiliate spammers that lured you to the Web site in the first place.

The spam for cheap junk really starts flying around gift-giving times. The latest fad products are hawked unabashedly, claiming that the thing is so hot that you have to order it via the Internet or you won't find it. During the 2002 Christmas selling season, the "hot ticket" was the tiny radio-controlled (RC) car. The messages said they were impossible to find, and they had a supply, but it would cost you $30 (plus shipping and handling). Of course, my local Radio Shack store had stacks of them left over on Christmas Eve at less than $20.

Plenty of spam messages offer products and services that are either counterfeit or illegal to use. A well-known commercial software product that sells in real software stores for $199 is not the same as the counterfeit copy for $25 (if, that is, you actually receive the package). Using a cable descrambler (if it works on your cable system) or DVD copier is illegal. When the seller gets busted, the first thing law enforcement does is confiscate the customer lists to pursue the buyers. You don't want to be on any of those lists.

Then there are the emails that promise to let you buy brand-name prescription medicines without prescriptions. You're free to gamble with your own life, but you should also know that the worldwide market for counterfeit brand-name drugs is huge. The packaging looks just like the real thing, yet the drugs are anything but. Yes, it's a crime that consumers, especially in the United States, have to pay a premium for the latest drugs. But unless you know what you're buying, and from whom, you are playing a very dangerous game.[7]

A lot of the caution I've been promoting in the last few pages is nothing more than *caveat emptor* common sense for consumers. I believe one of the serious problems is that a spam email can include a professional-looking image, and even a clever HTML layout, making it look like a legitimate offer from a reliable source. A link to a Web site with the same characteristics might lead someone to further trust in the tales woven by the mail and Web site. A fancy layout or a pretty graphic (the latter available from spam art collections hosted around the world) can give the spammer and scammer a level of credibility he doesn't deserve.

I'm reminded of my high school physics teacher, who was a real hoot. Countless times he blurted out the old adage, "Seeing is believing!" Then he'd demonstrate an optical illusion to prove just the opposite. To many recipients of spam, seeing a snazzy presentation is believing the presentation. But more than likely, there is some optical illusion trick behind the pretty message, and we must all be alert to the possibility. Seeing is believing!

Advance Fee (419) Frauds

To those of us who have received thousands of these messages over the years, it's hard to imagine that anyone would fall for the advance fee scam. But people do—in droves. While there are many variations on the stories that are told in the introductory spam messages, they all involve some large amount of money supposedly tucked away in a bank vault, chest, or diplomatic parcel in a foreign land that can be freed with your help. In return you are to earn a sizable commission, somewhere around 20 percent of the millions you're going to help get out of the country. What they don't tell you (aside from there not being any money stashed anywhere) is that you'll have to come up with thousands of dollars ($1.6 million in perhaps the sorriest case of a German victim in 2003) to temporarily cover bribes and other expenses...until the money clears, and you'll be reimbursed. Yah!

The primarily West African gangs that run these scams have elaborate scripts and props that they use. If the scammer successfully entices you to visit his country, you may be shown a chest full of blackened paper stacks,

---

7 A growing problem these days is the ease with which people addicted to painkillers and other prescription drugs can get them online without prescription. This trade is largely responsible for the high percentage of medication-related spam and a significant portion of what the U.S. Food and Drug Administration estimates to be 5 million consumer shipments from offshore drug sources each year.

purportedly bundles of cash that were dyed to disguise their true nature from authorities. Your contact and his friends will produce what they claim is a very expensive chemical and wash the black off one note as a demonstration. After pulling a simple magician's replacement trick, they show you a clean Ben Franklin. Your eyes bug out as you feel you are within steps of your big payday. But then they tell you that they don't have enough of the chemical to wash all the notes, and need you to supply them many more thousands of dollars to acquire the stuff. And on it goes. Over a period of a year and a half, an Ormond Beach, Florida, retiree was taken for over $300,000, most of it borrowed or mortgaged. He traveled to Dubai and was shown a suitcase of blackened "money." Despite being warned by law enforcement back home, he still believed that the people he worked with were honorable friends—a testament to the cleverness of these scam artists in winning over their victims with politeness, flattery, and even an appeal to a faith in God.

A lot of advance-fee scam messages emanate from Nigeria, where this scam seems to have become very popular decades ago (pre-Internet). The large number of such offers coming from Nigeria—and the unfortunately high number of people from North America and Europe who fell prey to them over the years—led the Nigerian government to pass a law against the practice. The number of the Nigerian criminal code section covering the crime, 419, has now become synonymous with the scam technique, regardless of the location.[8]

Email has made it so easy for traditional 419 letters from Africa, the Middle East, and Asia to flood inboxes in recent years, it's surprising to me that they keep coming. That said, if the United Kingdom's National Criminal Intelligence Service (NCIS) estimates 419 scammers defraud British folks out of £200 million ($315 million) each year, it's no wonder the mails keep coming. Even more troubling are the variations on the 419 scam that pull the same trick but with entirely different themes. These could catch unsuspecting recipients unaware of the 419 technique in other guises.

One such message started appearing in the summer of 2003, targeted specifically to email addresses pulled from the Web sites of non-profit organizations. Given the economic conditions of the time, charities were suffering a substantial sag in donations and grants. Thus, when an email suddenly appeared from someone wishing to donate $20,000 to a cause, it got the attention of small, cash-starved nonprofit organizations. Here is the text of the email as forwarded to an email abuse newsgroup by a recipient:

---

[8] A terrific online resource of news reports connected with 419 fraud prosecutions can be found at the Web site of The 419 Coalition (http://home.rica.net/alphae/419coal).

```
Hello,

My name is Joshua Williams, i am a business man
based in  Holland Netherland.

I read about your organisation over the inter-
net, and i was so moved with the effort you are
putting together to make a better living for
others.

Therefore i have decided in my mind to donate
towards this programme and fund your organisa-
tion.

I need you send me an email of the name and the
address to appear on a cheque,TAKE NOTE please
makesure you send me A TELEPHONE NUMBER WITH
FULL CONTACT ADDRESS NOT A P.O. BOX because the
cheque will be send by fedex courier and fedex
does not deliver to a p.o.box address.

But to make thing more easier and faster,  I am
especting the sum of $96,000.00 from my stock
company in US,i will ask the company to send you
the cheque after clearing of the cheque in your
bank account you will deduct $20,000.00 as a
donation and tansfer $76,000.00 to my account in
Europe.

  I HAVE MADE UP MY MIND TO DONATE $20,000.00
and you will wire the rest of the money to my
account in Europe. If this is ok, let me know so
that i can ask them to forward you the cheque
immediatly.

Best Regards

J.Williams.

Holland.

Netherland.
```

I don't know if this would lead to a true 419 scam, because it could follow another route that has been used recently, where a bogus high-value
check is issued to the victim. After depositing the check into his or her
account, the victim is then supposed to issue a check from his or her
account for the majority of the original check's amount, ostensibly keeping
the rest. Out goes the victim's money to the scammer; but, eventually, the

big check fails to clear, and the victim's bank holds the victim accountable for all funds.

Regardless of the specific path or outcome, that a scammer would target struggling nonprofit organizations, with perhaps the goal of cleaning out their bank accounts, is beyond reprehensible. But then I remind myself of the lack of a con's conscience.[9]

Other advance-fee spams include those that alert you that you've won some worldwide lottery or other prize, worth tens of thousands of dollars or more. By the time they're through bilking you for a variety of upfront fees and taxes (and no lottery payoff), you'll be much poorer than you were when you read the spam in the first place.

Pornography Vendors

There are times when I don't believe my eyes when viewing a list of subject lines that my spam filtering has sent directly to the server trash. There are even times when I feel I have to wash my eyes with soap and water to cleanse them of the explicitly pornographic verbiage in the occasional message that slips through the filter.[10] You wouldn't believe some of the domain names that the mails link to. Domain registration computers neither blush nor wince.

I'd be nearly the last one to cast judgment on what is defined as pornographic, as far as consenting adults go. But, you know, there are simply things I don't like knowing are being sent my way, even if I never see the details. The explicit nature of the subjects and messages leave nothing to the imagination, and frequently refer to acts of bestiality and borderline child pornography (things supposedly involving teens can't all be dedicated to eighteen- and nineteen-year olds).

Sex and pornography tend to play roles in most new media-oriented technologies. They drove the early days of the home videocassette recorder, helping drive down the cost of the machines as the volume increased for players

---

[9] Some adventurous (or foolish, as the case may be) folks practice the potentially dangerous art of scam-baiting 419 hucksters. The baiters lead the scammers to the brink of making a deal without actually carrying through. The goal is to get the scammer to part with even the tiniest bit of cash, or do crazy things that get documented in a digital photo. There have even been cases where the baiters enlist friends in the 419er's country to take photos of the scammers, who are waiting at the airport for the arrival of the intended victim (who isn't on the plane).

[10] And this from someone who wrote numerous articles about electronics for *Playboy* magazine in the 1980s, and who finds the crude, sophomoric humor and foul-mouthed fourth graders of *South Park* to be hilarious.

and tapes. Companies are even researching ways of communicating tactile sensations through high-bandwidth Internet connections. But I digress.

When these spams land indiscriminately in email recipients' inboxes, I wonder how others with lower tolerance levels respond. What must a relative newcomer to the Internet think about the online world when one of these blatant spams suddenly appears in the mail? Some of these messages even include explicit images to lure the curious to their Web sites for more. It has to be quite a shock for Aunt Flo to see this stuff in her mailbox some morning.

More troubling, still, is when these messages, with or without the images, arrive at the mailboxes of children. As stated earlier, an email address is rarely correlated against demographic data of its owner. Pornographic spammers, despite their protestations to the contrary to stay out of legal hot water, aren't concerned where the mail lands, as long as it leads to a click-through or, better still, an order or phone call to the advertised service. Unless parents permit their children email access through child-friendly, restrictive services that provide adult-supervised email blocking (more specifically, mail is allowed only from known senders), the raunchiest of messages will find their way to kids. Their curiosity may lead them to the Web sites, where they'll be exposed to material unsuitable for minors—if not most majors.

I could highlight lots of common threads that link all of these spammers and scammers together, but let me focus on two in particular: disrespect for the recipient's email system and greed.

First, by my definition of spam (Chapter 2), and given an ideal world in which spam were not only outlawed, but a sender would be instantly fried with a bolt of lightning, I should receive no email from most of the sources discussed in this chapter. Spammers and the infrastructure surrounding them rob me of the sanctity or privacy of my email address. No matter how hard I try, I cannot control who has permission to address a message to me. Yes, I can block lots of it, but I shouldn't have to. Nor should I have to keep my blocking activity up to date as the spammers try to work around blocking systems.

Second, greed plays an enormous role in the spamonomy. If someone has something of value, then another person wants it and may do illegal or amoral things to take it away. Spammers harvest your email address for free, without your permission, then earn money from the crop. Spam offers for work-at-home schemes and Internet multilevel marketing "systems" goad suckers into thinking they'll become Internet millionaires, when, in truth, it's the spammers who sold them a crock that make most of the money. In search of saving money, some spam recipients willingly give up personal information to thieves. On the promise of winning a worldwide lottery or conning a backward country out of a multi-million- dollar hidden treasure, scam targets send hundreds or thousands of dollars to strangers in foreign lands.

With spammers having zero respect for the sanctity of our addresses, and scammers successfully playing on human greed, it's no wonder we're in such an email mess.

CHAPTER 8

The Spammer's View of the World

Unless you've been napping and turning the pages in a trance, you should be fully aware that I don't like spam invading my space. Or anyone's space. The question I mutter to the perpetrators while I waste time managing my spam is, "What gives you the right to send this to me?" This chapter attempts to supply the answers that the mail senders would provide.

I really want to understand how spammers justify what they do. They and I must have different values on one or more levels. The likelihood that we'll ever agree is nil. I accept that. They are not the target audience of this book. Of course, if they're reading here to look for loopholes in the antispam argument, that's okay too. Howdy! How ya doin'? May a power surge fry your address databases.

In my efforts to understand spammer lingo, I find that even the term "email" has a different meaning depending on a particular spammer's mindset and/or context. Throughout this book I've been using email (the noun) to describe the entire electronic email system. When I refer to an address or a message within that system, I use "email" as an adjective: email address or email message. In spammer-speak, however, email (the noun) can also mean an email address and/or an email message. When some spammers talk about selling, renting, or trading email addresses, they frequently just call those addresses "emails," as in, "I got me 30 million emails on this here CD-ROM." In other words, your address is an "email" to spammers.

You'll also hear spammers talk about email as a particular message that is sent in bulk to a large number of targets. Spammers who act as tutors to other

83

spammers advise "testing emails," that is, writing up a few variations on a product offer and, based on coding in the spamvertised link URL, recording how well each variation performs. The technique of testing different offers is nothing new to direct marketing (catalog mailers commonly print two or more sets of covers for the same catalog), but in this case, "testing email" refers not to one message, but rather one format that may go out to millions.

My advice when listening to spammers spouting about their businesses: Pay close attention to context whenever the word "email" is mentioned.

Before I get to spammers, I want to address those bulk emailers who acquire their address lists through true opt-in confirmations. These mailers regularly suffer from the fallout from the spam plague, caused by clueless opt-in recipients. Let me explain.

A lot of companies that sell to consumers and businesses (originally through direct mail catalogs) use email to send the equivalent of flyers to their customer lists on a regular basis. I have signed up to many of these mailings through online retailers from which I've bought stuff. The task of managing the address list and high-volume mailings is frequently handed off to a third-party firm that specializes in such mailings. The brand name of the content originator is important, so not only does the message include proud and prominent display of the retailer's name, but message headers accurately reflect the source. While the actual outgoing mail server may be from the firm doing the bulk mailing, the From: and Reply-To: fields identify the name of the retailer. For instance, the email flyers I get from computer retailer MacZone have the following From: header line (substituting "example" for the actual domain name to protect the innocent mailing firm):

```
From: "Mac Zone" <maczone_5120@zones.reply.example.com>
```

In my email program, the name in quotes is the one that appears in the list of mail in my inbox, even though the replies (for the purpose of tracking message bounces and list maintenance) go to the actual mailing company. Links in the message point to the readily identifiable URL of the retailer—the same domain at which I entered a business relationship in the first place.

Retailers and bulk mailers that operate genuine confirmed opt-in operations have a big problem. They get plenty of individuals who sign up for their mailings, but who forget that they did, even after receiving a confirmation of the registration requiring a reply before the actual mailings begin. Imagine this scenario if you publish a confirmed opt-in newsletter (as reported by such an individual on a public bulletin board):

1. A user registers to receive the newsletter by filling out a form on the newsletter Web site.

2. The registration is held in a temporary holding pen (which expires in 48 hours) on the newsletter's server.

3. The newsletter computer sends a confirmation message, which includes a coded link that must be clicked on (or copied to the recipient's Web browser) to confirm the registration.

4. The new registrant clicks on the link to confirm registration, signifying that it's okay to send the newsletters.

5. The newsletter computer moves the address from the holding pen to its mailing database.

6. To welcome the new registrant, the newsletter computer sends the current issue, which always contains an unsubscribe link at the bottom.

7. The recipient, for whatever reason, treats the arriving newsletter as spam, and reports it as such to the newsletter's ISP or antispam organizations.

I have great sympathy for bulk emailers that do the right thing and then get falsely accused of spamming. People forget where and when they signed up for things. They have bad days. They have arguments with their bosses and spouses to put them in sour moods. They are in a hurry to get to an important business email message when something that can wait takes up download time and space. But c'mon people! Take responsibility for your actions. If you sign up and confirm to receive mailings from a company, you must be willing to accept messages from that company. If you're forgetful, then keep a log of where you have signed up. Keep copies of the confirmation messages in a folder on your email program. You don't have to jump up and down with glee each time a new offer or issue arrives, but for Pete's sake, don't report it as spam. If you subscribed and now don't want it anymore, then unsubscribe like a sensible human being.

Here's another situation to watch for. A new employee of a large corporation runs the risk of being assigned a mailbox name that had been used many months earlier by a former employee. If the previous owner of that name signed up for stuff, and didn't unsubscribe when he or she left, then it's possible that some lists may still contain the address, and the new employee will view the unwanted stuff as spam. Ideally, the corporate server would have been rejecting mail for that address while it was inactive, and senders would remove the bounced address from their databases. Now back to the real world.

In other cases, a mailing may have the "odor" of spam because it contains wording that automated spam filters link to "spamminess." If the filter is using automated reporting, the message might be reported to the mailer's ISP as being spam, even though the recipient signed up for the mail and failed to add the sender to a personal "whitelist" of approved senders. Sometimes spam reporting, especially automated spam reporting, can wreak havoc with innocent bystanders. Their ISPs, usually out of fear of being labeled spam-friendly, react to spam reports too swiftly and harshly without looking into the actual situation. It takes days for an innocent mailer to recover from one of these collateral damage attacks, and in the meantime, his or her Web site may be forced offline, or other outgoing (nonautomated) email gets blocked by some recipients' mail server spam filters.

The root cause of these kinds of problems is the volume of spam that has made mail server administrators and antispam advocates hypersensitive to activity that has even the appearance of spamminess. Here we have yet another cost that spammers force others to pay.

So much for genuinely good bulk emailers. They're a genuinely rare breed and are not to be labeled spammers.

You can also find borderline cases where a sender with his or her own address list database is in a quandary about what's "safe" to do. A savvy and well-connected businessman I've known for many years (I shield his name) revealed during an early 2004 conference speech that he had collected well over 100,000 email addresses during a long career in his industry. He was faced with an opportunity to exchange lists with another professional organization. These weren't a couple of sleazy spammers conspiring with each other. Rather, these were two established businesspeople with respectable brand names offering high-end business services, and who believed that their lists complemented each other. Should he, or shouldn't he?

I believe he was approaching the problem from a somewhat myopic marketing view, looking only from the inside out. He failed to take into account the "contract" that each list owner has with list members. Complicating the matter is that he had gathered his list over a long period of time, from sources that included business cards handed to him and conference attendee lists. What are those peoples' expectations with respect to receiving bulk mailings years later? My friend fears that if he attempts to requalify his list by asking everyone to go through a modern confirmed opt-in process that he'd lose a large percentage of names. Would that weaken his reach or offering?

My own sense is that, due to increased personal, technological, and legal sensitivity to spam, he would be better off with a smaller, confirmed opt-in list. His privacy policy should include parameters about what kinds of third-party mailings, if any, registrants might receive. He should limit his list exchanges to organizations that have compatible published privacy policies so that those recipients would not treat his mailings as unsolicited spam.

This route, in my opinion, would be the best way to protect the value of his own brand from being labeled spam-friendly, while targeting a much more receptive audience.

Now we come to the arguments offered by dyed-in-the-wool spammers. They are convinced that their activity is legally, if not morally, protected.

The first words out of a spammer's mouth in defense of his action is a call for the protection of rights to commercial free speech. This concept—or at least the name of the concept—appears to have a grander footing in the United States than in most other countries. Ever since the Declaration of Independence indelibly stamped a set of inalienable rights on the psyche of Americans, the notion of such rights has bloomed well beyond the intent of the authors of the Declaration. Without checking the validity of their statements, Americans (and not a few other Westerners) start spouting about their rights whenever they don't get what they want when they want it.

"Commercial free speech" is a relative newcomer in pseudoconstitutional jargon (the framers never carved out special speech rights for commerce). The idea became part of the American legal lexicon in cases surfacing in the 1970s. The expression tends to flow from the mouths of advertisers that find that some law or regulation is aimed at preventing an advertisement from reaching an audience, whether the audience wants it or not. In recent years, American advertisers claimed an infringement on their commercial free-speech rights when they were blocked from sending unsolicited fax messages and were forced to observe a federally mandated "Do Not Call" list for telephone solicitations.

The U.S. Supreme Court has established some guidelines as to what is and is not protected speech in the commercial realm.[1] One of the most important criteria entails whether the content is misleading or unlawful (in the words of the court). Such advertising messages (regardless of medium) are deemed not protected. Of course, in the spam world, the definition of "misleading" has plenty of conflicting interpretations. Some would say that a message's subject line that does not both identify the message as being an advertisement and reveal the true subject of the ad is misleading; to counter that claim, an advertiser would say that a "creative" subject line can be used to entice recipients to read a legitimate message. A more stringent interpreter would say that any message that employs techniques designed to bypass text-based spam filters is misleading, even if all other parts of the message are true and lawful.

---

[1] Named after the plaintiff in the case, *Hudson Gas & Elec. Corp. v. Pub. Serv. Comm'n,* 447 U.S. 557, 561 (1980), the so-called Hudson Test provides a kind of formula for determining whether a communication is protected as commercial speech.

A more difficult problem, however, is determining on the face of it whether a spam message that looks legitimate isn't really a front for a scam designed to separate you from your money, with no product or service sent to you in return. Plenty of slick-looking spam messages, using polished and professional art, contain links that lead unsuspecting users to offshore Web sites that will gladly take your credit card information, even though they have no intention of sending you the prescription drugs, enlargement products, or credit repair kit you ordered. The recipient bears the burden of proof to spot a misleading or unlawful ad, but the finding comes so long after the message arrived that it makes no difference that such a message was not protected commercial free speech.

In the annals of public forum and newsgroup postings by spammers and antispammers, a spammer, proclaiming the free speech right, typed the phrase as "free speach," misspelling "speech." Antispammers picked up on the error (not just an isolated typo, by the way) with elaboration, and began referring to this defense of spamming as the "frea speach" defense.

All of these commercial free speech discussions are, naturally, confined to the jurisdiction of one country at a time. Can a restriction against a misleading and unlawful spam message originating from a different country have any teeth? Likely not.

But let's take an ideal situation: An American advertiser sends millions of unsolicited messages to other Americans with a clearly marked Subject: line and a message that offers a lawful product that, if ordered, is actually delivered to the buyer. This is the scenario envisioned by most American high-volume mailers. Regardless of how they obtained the target email addresses, the millions of messages are, in their eyes, protected as commercial free speech.

Spammers refuse to acknowledge, however, that nothing about free speech requires that anyone listen to the message. Antispam advocates are not against automated mailings, even those of commercial nature, provided the recipient has explicitly requested mailings from the sender. In the antispam view, a recipient who has not given such permission ahead of time is not required to receive any missive—and certainly not when the recipient has to pay for receiving the message.

Bulk emailers are especially irritated by ISPs and private incoming email server administrators who apply spam-blocking techniques prior to the messages ever reaching intended recipients. The senders believe that the recipient should be the final judge about what to receive, not some faceless robot on the server. For instance, what if a user wants to receive unsolicited special offers from known spammers in the hopes of finding some great deal on a thingamajig? If that user's ISP automatically blocks mail that contains a link to a well-known spamvertiser, then the user will never see the message. "Is that fair?" the mailer wants to know.

When I apply my own logic to the scenario and the question, I have to say that such arbitrary blocks are not fair. Yet those blocks would not be in place unless the lack of spam filters caused too many problems for those who don't want to receive it—and those who don't want it are the majority of the addressees at that server's domain. Maintaining a viable spam-blocking system on an email server is a lot of work, and a never-ending battle at that. If the volume had not become so large so fast, and if the receipt of spam by addressees had not become such a thorn in their sides (costly download time, wasted productivity, overloaded inboxes on weekends and vacations, and so on), spam blocking would not be as popular as it has become. For the majority of Internet users who rely on email, spam has become a significant enough resource drain to warrant drastic measures.

Unsuccessful challenges against anti-fax provisions of the U.S. Telephone Consumer Protection Act have reinforced the illegality of shifting the cost of commercial speech onto the recipient. Because the costs of receiving and handling spam—starting with the incoming ISP's need to handle vast quantities of unsolicited mail and ending with the recipient having to spend time to read and/or delete the messages—are borne entirely by the recipient chain, the issue of "rights" has nothing to do with the free speech of the sender. Rather, the primary issue is the "right" of the recipient (and agents) to avoid expense of time, resources, and money caused by unsolicited messages. In other words, the recipient's right to be free of externally imposed expense should trump the right of an advertiser forcing a recipient to spend to hear the sender's free speech.

A few U.S. federal court rulings against American spammer Cyber Promotions, Inc. in 1996 and 1997 covered a lot of legal territory with respect to the right of email recipients to keep spammers out of their systems. In one ruling (covering cross complaints between AOL and Cyber Promotions, Inc.), a U.S. district court explicitly stated that the First Amendment does not give the right to send unsolicited email to a private (i.e., nongovernmental) party.[2] In another case involving Cyber Promotions *(CompuServe v. Cyber Promotions)*, a different U.S. district court ruled that forced receipt of unwanted email is both a form of trespass that causes the mail system to be impaired and causes harm to individuals associated with the system.[3] The aggravation of mail system providers and the

---

[2] The suit was initially brought by Cyber Promotions because it objected to AOL's blanket blockading of all bulk email originating from Cyber Promotions. The court said Cyber Promotions had no free-speech right to force the removal of the blockade.

end users who must exert time and money to fight the inflow is harm enough.

My definition of spam doesn't necessarily require that it be of a commercial nature. Thus, to my mind, there is no distinction between "free speech" and "commercial free speech" when it comes to spam. In fact, the commercial-ness is in the content, and my issue with spam is not the content, but whether I have granted explicit consent to receive a message. A spammer can say anything he wants (within other limits imposed by various jurisdictions with respect to fraud, pornography, hate, and other areas), but there is no right to force me to hear it, see it, or expend any of my resources to receive it.

Akin to the free-speech argument is one that says bulk emailers have the right to earn a living, and that technologies or legislation that prevent their messages from getting through infringes on that right. There's that "right" buzzword again.

The belief is that because the Internet allows anyone to send an email to anyone else at little or no cost to the sender, everyone is entitled to do so, regardless of the possible consequences. In response to criticism of the U.S. spam law signed in December 2003, Robert Wientzen, then head of the Direct Marketing Association, intimated that small businesses wouldn't be able to prospect for new customers if it weren't for the Internet and email. In his words: "That's the price we pay for American spirit."[4]

I assume he was talking about an entrepreneurial spirit that pervades America (and other countries, too). But I didn't know that being an entrepreneur gives one carte blanche to use and abuse the resources of others at will. That seems more like a spirit ascribed to America by its enemies: imperialistic, greedy, and self-centered. And it's not as if unsolicited bulk email is the only way to reach potential customers. Sure, it's comparatively inexpensive because a great portion of the cost is borne by others; but if building a new business were easy and cheap, then everyone would be doing it and there would be no failures. Get real!

While I'm on the subject of the Direct Marketing Association, the organization publishes a document titled "E-mail Delivery Best Practices for Marketers and List Owners." This document is essentially a road map to producing bulk email that is legal in the eyes of the U.S. spam law, as well as suggestions how to squeak by spam filtering. The first section of this

---

[3] The formal legal term for this kind of trespass is "trespass of chattel," which is legalese for "messing with my stuff."

[4] From a Ziff-Davis Net articles at zdnet.com.com/2100-1104_2-5127621.html.

document discusses the idea of permission, since the DMA says that permission-based email is not spam. If you don't look at the details, the idea of permission-based email sounds like a rational way to handle bulk emailing: sending only to those recipients who have given permission to the sender. But the devil (if not *the* Devil) is in the details of how the DMA defines "permission" and "consent."

Warning: Readers with weak dispositions, unmedicated high blood pressure, and hats that need holding onto in wind gusts should take ample precautions before proceeding.

To the DMA, consent comes in two basic flavors: *affirmative consent* and plain ol' *consent*. Affirmative consent, itself, comes in three types. The first is called *double opt-in,* which, as its name implies, requires that the recipient must first contact the sender and ask to be added to the mailing list. This is followed by the sender emailing a confirmation message that contains a coded link or URL that lets the recipient confirm that he or she wants to receive the mailing. If the confirmation does not get back to the sender, then the address does not get added to the list. That's fine, and is, indeed, the way I define "consent," because no one can sign up on my behalf and get away with it.

The second kind of DMA affirmative consent is called *confirmed opt-in.* This means that the recipient contacts the sender and asks to be added to the mailing list. The sender emails a confirmation of the registration, but by then the address has already been added to the database. Unless the recipient explicitly unsubscribes, the messages will come. This approach, of course, is easily abused by jokesters and evildoers. (Incidentally, this is how one Danny Gonzales [if that is his real name] first started screwing with my domain name. He registered with one of the school reunion Web sites. I received this kind of confirmation note, but to unsubscribe, I needed to know the password that he had used to set up the account in the first place. Since I couldn't possibly know that password, I could not unsubscribe from the list. Although a complaint to the Web site got the account removed, it was too late: that email address had already been added to the spamming world's databases. Now, a few years later, spam intended for that address continues to be aimed at my domain.)

The third kind of DMA affirmative consent is called, simply, *opt-in.* This is nothing more than a sender offering a form and a checkbox on a Web page, where anyone can enter any email address they like. The sender does not send out any confirmation. Upon submission, the address is added to the database.

In the not-affirmative-consent-but-consent-nonetheless category is what the DMA calls *opt-out.* This means that the only action a recipient can take is opting out of an emailing list. If you do nothing, you are consenting to receive email. I suppose that the manner in which the sender obtained your email address in the first place is not relevant to the DMA.

The U.S. law, as evidenced by these DMA "best practices," will certainly lead to plenty of whining from bulk emailers that obey the "rules" but can't get their messages past spam filters at larger ISPs. Too bad. If you limit your notion of consent to what the DMA calls double opt-in, then your delivery rates will improve by leaps and bounds.

Next comes the spammer's well-worn argument that a recipient who does not want to receive a message can "just hit Delete." Antispammers have picked up on this phrase, calling it the JHD defense.

In their efforts to address the spam issue, some lawmakers have bought into this notion. You can see this when the laws they write require all commercial messages to be labeled in such a way that the Subject: line accurately describes the nature of the message. Some go as far as requiring a kind of flag, such as the sequence [ADV], to alert a recipient that a commercial advertisement lies within. The purpose of this flag and accurate labeling is to assist the recipient in just hitting Delete.

As we all know, however, a significant percentage of spam messages have deceptive or ambiguous subject lines—deliberately so in the hopes that we'll open the message. Spammers who employ a combination of deceptive subject lines and Web beacons are hoping to take advantage (I mean that in the worst way) of unsuspecting users who stay with default settings of the most popular email software programs, where simply clicking on an item listed in the inbox causes the message to appear in the Preview Pane. By the time you "just hit Delete," it's too late. You've already contributed to the spamonomy by validating your address.

To spammers, hitting Delete on each unwanted message takes only a second or two. No big deal, they say. But thanks to so many deliberately deceptive subject lines (which continue at a rapid pace, despite legislation forbidding it in many jurisdictions), it takes more than a couple of seconds to delete the average spam message.

What really bugs me about the JHD defense is that it fails to address the problem of spam reaching my inbox in the first place—occupying space on the mail server and adding to the amount of data (and in some cases expensive telephone connect time) downloaded to my computer. Their "solution" does not solve the cost-shifting problem with spam. By the time you've hit Delete, all of the costs associated with receiving spam have accrued to parties on the receiving end.

It doesn't surprise me that bulk email senders, as individuals, appear to have a high tolerance of spam that they receive. I heard one bulk emailer state that because he uses email to market his company's services, he would rather accept spam in his inbox as a price of doing business than suffer the consequences of the opposite extreme: the banning of commercial email. Other senders may look upon spam they receive as market research to keep an eye on what other spammers are doing. To these individuals, the cost of sifting and deleting doesn't enter into their calculations.

Just hit Delete? How about "Just don't spam!"

Another line of defense that spammers use is that most messages provide a way to unsubscribe from future mailings. A significant chunk of those "opt-out links" lead to bogus Web sites or inoperative email addresses. The spammers think that by providing an opt-out provision they're exhibiting good email marketing practices. Feh! When the link does take you to a real Web page, lots of things can happen, but it is unlikely that you'll be completely removed from the list or be free of future mailings from the same basic source. The opt-out link may be coded with your email address or some other identifying number that can be linked to your address by the spammer. If you click to opt out, you are verifying that your address is an active one. Even if the spammer honors your request, he has gathered a valuable piece of information that can be resold to other mailers, or be used in other campaigns by the same sender.

Watch carefully when encountering the wording of some of these opt-out disclaimers. Some of the slicker email marketing firms concoct names for what appear to be separate entities—names like EmailDeals, TodayzBargainz, and the like. These are not the names of the companies doing the mailings, but rather façades with cutesy names. An opt-out link from one of these "outfits" suggests that you can opt out of future mailings from this entity. But the marketing firm behind the operations will use your opt-out address for mailings from its other entities.

Opt-out links that are not coded with your address and that lead to real Web pages should be equally, if not more, suspect. Such pages provide a form into which you are to type your email address. A goodly number of these are genuine email address vacuum cleaners. The address you enter won't be compared against any database from which the original mailing came. But your verification of a fresh address is valuable to the page's owner. Suspicious antispammers commonly enter unique, trackable email addresses into these forms, only to have new spam arrive at those addresses soon thereafter.

Yet another opt-out scam is the so-called global or universal opt-out database. Some of these offers are advertised (via spam, no less) as a paid service. The theory is that honest mailers always cull global list registrants from their lists prior to each email barrage. This scenario makes so many false assumptions that it's laughable, yet the claims they make are readily believed by the spammed individual who doesn't fully understand how the spam world operates. Here are just a few of the problems with this whole idea:

- Just because an opt-out database exists doesn't mean that mailers use it.

- The most egregious and voluminous spam comes from senders who have no interest in cleaning up their lists.

- Any database of opt-out addresses is a pure gold mine of valid addresses.

- Isn't demanding payment to stop doing something harmful the same as extortion?

Don't fall for this nonsense. If a spam message points to such an opt-out mechanism, ignore it. In fact, ignore opt-out mechanisms for all email offers that come your way, except for those which you have subscribed to or registered with in the past.

To end this chapter on a bizarre note, allow me to address an assertion I noticed on a Web page dedicated to blasting antispam forces: You lease your email address (and domain if you registered one), therefore you cannot prevent others from sending email to it. I don't think you'll find words such as "lease" or "lessor" in the contracts for registering a domain name or getting an email address assigned to you by your ISP, but I suppose I can understand that registering a domain name is not ownership in the true sense that you take it to the grave with you. Thus, the annual registration fee could be construed as a lease payment. If you don't pay up, then the domain name goes back into the pool to be offered to anyone else. But I still fail to understand why "renting" my domain name or email address gives others the right to send me email that I don't want to receive.

I've tried to find parallels in other things that we are likely to lease, but I've come up empty so far. Let's see, if I lease an apartment from a landlord, there are certain limits about what I can do to the apartment, and the landlord can demand to be allowed in to check the place. But the lease doesn't force me to let a stranger come in, park his or her butt on my sofa, and blast loud music when I'm trying to sleep. If I lease an automobile, I don't own it. But I am responsible for its upkeep. And if a stranger walks by in a parking lot and slaps an unwanted bumper sticker on the car, I'm the one who has to deal with its removal, just as if I owned the car.

Sorry, I'm just not grokking how a lease grants permission to be spammed.

Elsewhere in this book, I talk about the sanctity of one's email address. If I make it sound as though a human "owns" his or her email address, that's the sense I indeed wish to convey. We're responsible for it. If a spammer forges tons of email with my address in the From: field, I'm the one who gets all the complaints, even though the header information shows the message originated from a mail server in Azerbaijan. An email address has become a part of one's online identity. I suppose in the anti-antispammer's mind, the state leases a driver's license number to me, and the U.S. government leases a passport number to me. If I don't renew those documents, I no longer "own" the numbers; but in the meantime, they are private, personal, and valuable bits of information whose usage should be under my control.

The descriptions of spammers' arguments in this chapter are composites gleaned from published documents (including some legal proceedings), published interviews with spammers, and discussions on numerous online forums. Except for a couple of specific instances as noted earlier, I don't have any sympathy for spammers' arguments. I treasure my "right" to determine who can or cannot put their bits into my email inbox. A spammer doesn't care one whit about how much of my space and time he robs from me.

I don't think either of us will ever change the other's mind.

CHAPTER 9

How Spam Differs from Junk Mail

One of the spammer's arguments in favor of their type of advertising is that spam is no different from the bulk mail that arrives, sometimes voluminously, in your postal mail box. Spammers using this defense cite statistics about how many trees gave their lives to produce the paper on which the flyers and catalogs were printed; or the hundreds of thousands of dump trucks full of junk mail that head to the land fill each year.[1] Then they cite how environmentally friendly email is, regardless of quantity, frequency, or aggravation.

Certainly not all consumers are fond of advertising mail. It didn't get its "junk" moniker because folks love the stuff unconditionally. In Australia, you can even put a sign on your postal mailbox to reject delivery of junk mail.[2] On the other hand, there is a good chance that you are receiving this material in the mail because somewhere along the line you purchased from a catalog or a store that sends out mailings, subscribed to a magazine, attended a seminar, or in some other venue filled out a form that included your name and address. That makes your mailing address a valuable commodity, not only to the company that sold you some goods, but to other companies that rent the seller's mailing list for complementary or related merchandise. Unless you specifically opt out of receiving future mailings from the original company, you'll stay in the database of mailings for a year or more, receiving additional mailings and catalogs from time to time.

---

[1] They forget to mention how much of that gets recycled, but I split hairs.

[2] Unlike the United States, Australia allows advertisers to deliver flyers and catalogs to postal mailboxes without going through the post office. This has led to abuse, overstuffed mailboxes, and a litter problem. Advertisers who do this "letterboxing" by and large respect the wishes of the "No Junk Mail" stickers.

If some of this terminology—address, opt-out, list rental—sounds spammish, you're right, to the extent that many companies and organizations with long traditions in direct mail have tried to adapt their industry to the email delivery mechanism. In truth, the "snail mail" order world is far more sophisticated in linking your address to more detailed demographic information that becomes part of the value of your address when other mailers rent lists. Using computerized techniques called *data enhancement* or *data appending,* mail order companies associate your name and address with information such as the types of products you buy, the size of your order, and how often you buy. If you knew the ways your name and address were being compared and blended into myriad demographic segments and census data, you'd probably freak out.

Just as there are stupid spammers, not all conventional mail order companies are on the ball. If they (or the service bureaus that run the mailing list computers) don't do a good job in a process called *merge-purge* (merging multiple lists and purging the duplicates), you may receive three copies of a catalog in one day mailed to slightly different variations of your name and address. Sometimes your name gets into a demographic category that makes no apparent sense to what you think your mail order buying habits are.[3]

Despite numerous similarities on the surface, substantial differences separate the typical spam message in your computer inbox from the direct mail record club, credit card application, magazine subscription, and gadget catalog offer arriving in your postal mailbox. Here are the high points.

Goal of a Mailing

Direct Mail: The cost of acquiring a new customer is so high that a mailing to a list of prospects is aimed at not only converting a prospect into a paying customer, but, ideally, building a relationship with the customer so that he or she will continue to buy from the mailer in the future. It's not uncommon for a direct mail company to expect to lose money on the first order in the hope of keeping that customer long enough to get another, more profitable order going in a subsequent mailing.

Spam: If the advertiser really does deliver a product or service described in the email message, the primary goal of the high-volume spammers is to make one sale. The cost of goods is so small that there is sufficient profit (even after paying the spammer and/or affiliate) in each sale to make a prof-

---

[3] And yet, when a single, heterosexual male finds a Victoria's Secret catalog in his mailbox, suddenly it's not all junk mail.

it. The chance that a customer will place another order for a product of questionable efficacy is pretty low. In the case of quasi-legal or poor-quality products, the chance that the company will still be in the same place or offer the same product line when it would be time to reorder is doubtful. But there is also a higher probability that the order will not be fulfilled at all. The big exceptions to this "one sale" phenomenon are the prescription drug outfits, which expect you to order extremely profitable refills.

Mailing Cost

Direct Mail: Although paper does "grow on trees," that doesn't make it cheap. Nor is the cost of designing and printing mailing pieces. A multi-million copy print run of a 32-page four-color catalog and bulk postage costs around $0.30 per copy. For mailings in the millions, we're talking real money. And the United States Postal Service doesn't take credit cards for this kind of postage purchase. Cash up front!

Spam: Despite the urban myths that sending email is completely free, high-volume spammer operations do spend some money—some more than others—on their computers and high-speed data lines. They may even hire one or more programmers to work their magic to help them get around various blockades presented by their service providers and the spam detection programs running on their targets' servers and PCs. But the cost of "designing" the mailing piece and mailing it is negligible. When you account for the millions and millions of messages they distribute per day, the cost per message is next to nothing. One Russian bulk mail software provider sells its top-tier anonymous mailing service for one one-thousandth of a penny if you commit to a quantity of 300 million. Yes, $3,000 buys you 300 million outgoing messages, which you must use within 90 days (over 3 million per day).

Prospect Address Cost

Direct Mail: Prospecting for new customers means renting lists from other sources. Magazine subscribers with your ideal customer demographics, and mail order customers from complementary businesses are prime targets, but they're not cheap. Each address, alone, costs in the range of $0.08 to $0.30. Additional charges to a service bureau that performs a merge-purge on the combined lists (to eliminate duplicates) adds to the total.

Spam: Spammy spammers have their own lists that they continuously harvest from the Web and trade among themselves. Newbie spammers and affiliates buy their lists of tens of millions of addresses on CD-ROMs for tiny fractions of a penny each (freshness not guaranteed). A few advertisers actually spend $0.30 or more per address from highly targeted lists of magazine subscribers and other sources that rent their customer lists using the direct mail model. Rather than place these highly valuable lists into the advertisers' hands, the list owners tend to require that the actual mailing process flow through their own trusted service bureaus. Moreover, most of these lists are confirmed opt-in lists that have permission to send third-party offers—not really spam. The high costs of these lists keep spamming riffraff away.

Identity

Direct Mail: A large part of what a mail order company attempts to accomplish is building brand recognition in the recipients' mind. With rare exception, the envelope or cover identifies either the product or company, which the recipient can use to determine if it's worth opening the piece. A practice I don't see much anymore is an envelope that has all kinds of "come on" tidbits about what's inside the envelope, without identifying the sender or product by name. At most there might be a return address on the back flap, but not the company's name. Even if the envelope is mysterious, the identity of the sender is quite clear once you get inside. After all, the company is selling both a product and an ongoing relationship, so it's proud of a brand or corporate name.

Spam: Except for the hapless newbie spammer who buys into an email marketing outfit's lure of riches (and then promptly runs afoul of spam fighters), a significant percentage of bulk automated email uses deceptive or explicitly forged information about the sender in the From: portion of the mail message. All too often, the return address is either a false account or from an account that was fraudulently obtained for just enough time to get a batch of spam out onto the Net. In fact, in a high percentage of cases, the Web site to which the message links does not belong to the spam sender. The sender would rather remain completely anonymous and untraceable through the use of open mail relays and zombie servers that have been installed on thousands of PCs around the world through email-borne worms. Another annoying ploy used a lot by companies that promote email marketing services is to identify themselves by one of dozens of identities. The message will announce you're receiving this offer from so-and-so (there's commonly the word "offer," "deal," or some word ending in "z"), which is a made-up name for the current promotional blast. Whatever they call it, it's not a brand name with which they expect to build long-term customer relationships.

Mail Targets

Direct Mail: Because each piece of mail that enters the physical postal system costs its sender cold hard cash, the sender has a genuine incentive to limit mailing only to those who have a high likelihood of being interested in the product or service. Companies that rent out their customer mailing lists jealously guard those lists to prevent direct competitors from mailing offers for similar products to those same customers. If you subscribe to *Time* magazine, you can be sure the publisher won't rent your name to *Newsweek;* but because *Time's* parent company also publishes other magazines, you may receive periodic offers to subscribe to *People* or *Sports Illustrated.* After that you may also receive offers from book clubs that have rented your name from *Time,* with the expectation that you are an active reader. The science of finding rentable lists of addresses whose profiles closely match the products or services of an upcoming mailing translates into big money because incorrect assumptions cause costly wasted mailings. About the only mailers that use blanket mailings (e.g., to every address on the block or postal code) tend to be local businesses that appeal to a wide audience (e.g., grocery and drug stores).

Spam: Despite the claims of some email marketers that promise "targeted lists," the overriding evidence is that most spammers have one goal: to send their messages to as many live addresses as can be reached in as short a time period as possible. In light of the spam blocking occurring on the popular Internet portals (AOL, MSN, Earthlink, and others, which report blocking billions of messages per day), it is even more important for high-volume spammers to turn it up. The hope is to reach as many inboxes and eyeballs as possible. Unlike a piece of mail that must be printed and stamped, an email message can easily afford to be delivered to any living soul, regardless of interest in the product or service. Such small returns are needed to break even, the waste makes no difference to the senders.

"Do Not Send" Request Handling

Direct Mail: It comes down to money again. A direct mailer doesn't want to send you a catalog if you don't want it. By and large, direct mail senders gladly remove you from their lists upon request because it frees up that mail piece to perhaps go to a more receptive prospect. They also have a reputation they'd like to protect. If you don't like getting a catalog from a hobby crafts mail order company, that company doesn't want you talking trash about the company to your neighbors, family, and friends. Most catalog companies provide a place on their order forms where you can indicate your preference for receiving future catalogs. Calling their toll-free order number can also get you off the list. Unfortunately, glitches in the merge-purge operation can still mean mailing pieces find their way to you, if, for example, your name arrives in a different form from a rented list. But the sender has a sufficient financial incentive to remove you from the list whenever possible.

Spam: Since most spammers care little about their recipients, by and large they do not honor requests to be removed from their lists—removed in the way you'd like. Oh, plenty of lip service is paid in the spam messages about how you can be removed by clicking here or responding there. But, typically, the request to be removed is instead turned into a verification of your email address, only to be more widely distributed among other spammers. Equally common is the bogus address or link to which you are to direct your removal request. When the message's From: or Reply To: address is forged (or is from a stolen temporary account), replying to the message won't get you anywhere. A high percentage of the messages put gibberish into the template where they're supposed to enter a removal address. And any offer on the Web (including the one from the Direct Marketing Association) to register your address for widespread removal is either worthless or a sham. While DMA members may honor your removal request, only a tiny percentage of spam you receive originates from DMA members (whose definition of "spam" is at odds with that of most recipients'). When a spam message provides a link for you to enter your address into a "global removal" database, LOOK OUT!

Perceived Trust in the Sender

Direct Mail: Despite warnings not to believe everything we read, the quality of a slick catalog or other mailing piece makes us want to believe that the sending company is what it says it is and that the company will honor orders you phone or mail in. While there have certainly been occasions when such a slick piece is mailed by a huckster (not unheard of in the financial services world), we tend to trust that someone who has gone to the trouble to design, print, and mail a catalog (most of these costs must be borne up front) is a legitimate businessperson or operation.

Spam: In the spam-fighting community, Rule number one is, "Spammers lie." They tell you that the message you just received isn't spam; they tell you that you've opted in to a list or partner's list when you haven't; they lie about their identities; they lie about the subjects of their messages; they lie about removing you from their lists; some lie that you'll receive the product or service advertised in the message or target Web site. A lot of spammers will tell you they have to lie in order to get around the blockades that stand in the way between them and their targets. Even if you buy that argument (I don't), it means that you cannot place inherent trust in any spam message that arrives. Worse yet, it induces doubt about the trust you place in any immediately unidentifiable mail message arriving in your inbox. It is easy to become suspicious of truly confirmed opt-in mail that you have elected to receive. The lies have damaged the medium.

Who Pays for the Message

Direct Mail: A direct mail piece consists of some printed material and perhaps an envelope (if the piece isn't a self-mailer). As a physical mail piece, the message costs money to design and print. Then there is the cost of mailing the item to you. These costs are inescapable, and must be paid by the individual or organization sending the pieces. At the receiving end, your cost is comparatively tiny. Your cost starts the moment the piece arrives in your mailbox. If the volume of mail increases, many recipients can't do much about increasing the size of their boxes because the boxes are built into existing pods or racks beyond the control or design of the individual recipient. Of course, if your mailbox is on a post at the curb or attached to a wall near your front door, you have the option of buying and installing a larger box to accommodate the larger flow. It is pretty rare, however, for someone to buy a bigger mailbox to ease the crunch from direct mail advertising. Other recipient costs are difficult to calculate, even in the aggregate. True, there is the extra time needed to flip through the items, and then the extra load in the recycling bin to consider. Despite these recipient costs, the sender has expended many more times in real cash to get the piece into the mail system in the first place. The cost of sending physical direct mail acts as a limiting filter to the amount of such mail being inserted into the postal system.

Spam: The expense proportions between sender and recipient invert for email. The sender's cost in accumulating the necessary computers, Internet access, email address lists, and bulk mailing software is almost infinitesimally small per piece.[4] It is the tiny cost per piece that spammers use as their arguments for having such little impact on recipients. After all, a single

---

4 A product seller without his or her own address database will have to pay for addresses, ranging from fractions of a penny to quite a few cents per address. But the disguised senders have their own lists, so there is no incremental cost per address for those spammers.

email message takes up an infinitesimally small amount of space in the Internet infrastructure, your mail server's hard drive, your connectivity time, and your personal computer's disk space. The problem, however, is that the infrastructure and recipients are flooded with so many unsolicited messages that the aggregate volume causes significant disruptions and burdens on the systems. That's not even addressing the unfortunately extremely popular spammer ploy of forwarding their mail through computers they don't own (by way of open mail relays and zombie servers running on worm-infected PCs), which puts additional burdens on those systems as their service is being hijacked without their permission. It is these downstream costs—and the incalculable but tangible annoyance factors—that place the burden on the recipient. It is akin to receiving all direct mail with postage due that you must pay even if you immediately discard the mailing piece; or a collect call from a telemarketer for which you must accept the charges even if you hang up on the caller. A sender's cost that approaches zero encourages senders to insert as many messages as possible into the Internet mail system as frequently as possible.

In view of these comparisons, I fail to see much similarity between advertisements that arrive via postal and electronic mail. The combined cost to me for a month's worth of unsolicited postal mail is tiny compared to the disruption caused by a month's supply of unsolicited email. They're both fruit, but they're apples and oranges.

CHAPTER 10

The Antispammer's View of the World

Spammers and antispammers of the world have one thing in common: No single stereotype defines all members of their respective groups. Yes, even antispammers come in all shapes and sizes, and they react to spam and spammers in different ways. In this chapter you'll begin to understand how antispammers think, and learn how the actions of some not only harm innocent bystanders, but, in the worst cases, go too far to pursue individual spammers.

At the root of virtually every antispammer is a personal quest to rid one's email inbox, if not the entire Internet, of spam. Obviously, someone who doesn't realize that he or she is being spammed won't have the incentive to stop it. But what happens to many email users is that some straw breaks the camel's back. Something like the inbox on the server overflowing over a weekend and rejecting important email because the box is too full; or accidentally deleting an important legitimate message while cleaning out the garbage from the PC's email program; or spending many dollars to retrieve email through a hotel phone system only to discover that most of it is unsolicited and therefore wasteful of time and money.

Many have risen to the call over the years. The World Wide Web is littered with sites that were begun as personal crusades by individuals who were fed "up to here" with spam. Most of those sites haven't been updated in months or years, as the sites' authors became frustrated and disenchanted. In fact, the more they railed, the more spam increased—if not to them personally, then certainly to the rest of email users. Google still lists a lot of these sites, but their owners have gone on to fight other battles, defeated by the ceaseless economic incentive that keeps spammers in business.

In addition to individuals fighting spam, plenty of email server administrators working for companies and other organizations have been forced to take up the cause—if they want to keep their jobs by cutting out the spam that eats into worker productivity. An email administrator who understands the ins and outs of how email works, knows how email servers work, and can use custom programming to keep the bulk of spam at bay becomes a sophisticated ally in the battles against spam. It's not by accident that these folks are avid participants in several volunteer antispam efforts in place around the Internet and the world.

Several formal associations of spam fighters have formed, and a few are still going strong. The three most visible are:

Coalition Against Unsolicited Commercial Email (CAUCE) is a volunteer organization working primarily as an educational resource for anyone interested in fighting spam, especially legislators. It accepts no dues or donations, yet publishes a lot of up-to-date antispam information on its Web site (www.cauce.org) for free access. Although CAUCE works primarily in the United States, sister organizations are on the job in other parts of the world.

SpamCop (www.spamcop.net) examines spam messages and sends formal complaints to the sources of the spam, as well as to the ISPs and upstream providers for the mail senders. It obtains messages from its own spam traps, as well as from subscribers to its free and paid services. Any member can forward spam to SpamCop, which then uses computers to extract the necessary reporting information (hiding your own address from the headers, if you prefer). SpamCop also provides a blacklist database of IP addresses it deems to be spam sources, which mail servers can use to block or filter incoming spam.

The Spamhaus Project, a volunteer organization (currently headquartered in London—www.spamhaus.org), maintains two free services. One, called the Spamhaus Block List (SBL), is a database of IP addresses reported and verified as being sources of spam mailings. Mail system administrators can use this blocklist to help them identify spam arriving at their servers and (typically) block reception of such mail. The other service, Register of Known Spam Operations (ROKSO), publishes results of research performed on what Spamhaus identifies as 200 spam operations ("gangs" in its terminology) supposedly responsible for 90 percent of the spam arriving in U.S. inboxes.

Active participants in these (and other) antispam organizations treat spammers as The Enemy. Antispammers express their views and relate their experiences on public forums. You can access these newsgroups either with a newsreader (commonly found as part of a modern email program on PCs and Macs) or through Google Groups (groups.google.com). The most active discussion groups are news.admin.net-abuse.email and news.admin.net-abuse.policy. Antispammers are quick to post the most recent crop of spam messages in their entirety in the news.admin.net-abuse.sightings group, so you can quickly compare one you received against others just like it. SpamCop also has a series of discussion groups that are run as both mailing lists and newsgroups (info at news.spamcop.net/mailman/listinfo). While most traffic on SpamCop lists deal with support issues surrounding the SpamCop service, you'll also see plenty of general spam discussions. Another active group, the Spam Prevention Discussion List, communicates via a free mailing list. To obtain subscription information and access to the archive, visit www.lsoft.com, and search for SPAM-L.

One point you'll soon learn by lurking in any of these groups is that the antispam community has developed a colorful vocabulary consisting of shortcuts to generally accepted antispam principles. The following is a brief lexicon that explains the terms you'll encounter most often.

Rule #1, Rule #2, Rule #3. A list of three rules has evolved over time. The most commonly reported list is as follows:

1. Spammers lie.

2. If you think a spammer is telling the truth, see Rule #1.

3. Spammers are stupid.

You may see occasional references to Rule #0 (Spam is theft) and others. Among the lies you tend to encounter in spam messages are:

- Forged header information

- False or misleading Subject: line

- False From: line

- Untrue statement about your having requested the information

- Nonworking unsubscribed links

- Advertising copy stating that an illegal product or service is legal

Evidence of spammer stupidity usually comes in the form of mistakes caused by inadequate quality control of the automated processes that spammers use. Chapter 14 illustrates the point with numerous examples. But recent technical advances in redirecting spam origination points to overseas ISPs and zombie PCs indicate intelligence levels not attributable to anyone stupid. Therefore, while a lot of lesser spammers display stupidity, don't underestimate the upper echelon (where Rule #1 reigns supreme).

LART. Used as both a noun and a verb, LART is an acronym for Luser Attitude Readjustment Tool. "Luser" has numerous explanations for its origin (some dating back to text terminal days at MIT), but it generally describes a human computer user (not necessarily a clueless "loser"). A LART is an emailed, written, or telephoned report of spam abuse to the ISP or other provider in the chain between originator and receiving mail server. The desired destination of a LART is an abuse desk at an Internet provider that can investigate and act on the report promptly. The desired outcome is to get the spammer to stop spamming altogether, if not by changing his ways, then by getting tossed from his ISP. You can also use the term as a verb, as in "I LARTed the spammer's upstream provider."

Listwashing. The act of a spammer removing the email address of a constant LARTer from the database so that the LARTer will no longer receive messages and complain to the spammer's ISP. Some recipients are satisfied to be listwashed (thus reducing their individual spam load), while other antispammers dislike listwashing because it can reduce the number of complaints that might ultimately lead to the spammer being disconnected from his current ISP.

Mainsleaze. Usually a provider of Internet connectivity or related services that tolerates or actively seeks the business of spammer operations. Also used to refer to the predominant spam gangs, such as those listed in Spamhaus' ROKSO list.

Cartooney. A lawyer—real or imaginary—who threatens (or threatens to threaten) an antispammer with lawsuits. A cartoon-attorney. Such threats tend to be all bluster with no legal footing behind them, and are intended to intimidate an antispammer. The most extreme recent case of cartooney activity was a libel suit filed by a nonprofit organization named eMarketersAmerica.org against blocklist compilers Spamhaus and Spam Prevention Early Warning System (spews.org) in April 2003. The plaintiff claimed to represent numerous unnamed email marketers and ISPs in Florida (home of numerous ROKSO "honorees" and where the suit was filed). The organization was founded four weeks before the suit was filed, and its domain name registrant is the same lawyer who brought the suit— and who happened to be the personal attorney for a well-known Boca Raton spammer. The court refused to issue the requested injunction against the blocklists' publication. Then Spamhaus hired its own attorney, who planned to fight the suit in court, which would have forced the plaintiffs to reveal details about the relationships and operations of eMarketersAmerica.org's members. By September 2003, eMarketersAmerica.org pulled a

"Nevermind!" on the court. In October, the court dismissed the case "with prejudice" because the plaintiff failed to participate in its own case. By December 2003, the eMarketersAmerica.org Web site had disappeared from the Internet. Unfortunately, the cartooney won a small victory because even though the suit was dismissed, the Florida court wouldn't award legal costs to the defendants.[1]

Joe-Job. A tactic of a spammer who is really irritated by a particular anti-spam advocate or organization. The trick is to make a spam barrage appear to originate from the mail server of the target or list the target's Web site as a spamvertiser in the hopes that thousands of bounce messages and complaints will land at the target's feet. In the attack that spawned the name (an attack on the joes.com domain), the messages intentionally broke every rule of bulk email etiquette to cause the most damage to the reputation of the victim. While some spam recipients occasionally feel as though they're being joe-jobbed because they receive a few dozen bounces, such incidents are most likely just random accidents of zombie PC's spam servers. Real joe-job attacks flood the victim with thousands of messages. Other joe-job tactics include a spammer issuing a spam run advertising child pornography with links to the victim's Web site or email address.

Hat. Used with a color adjective to describe the attitude of an ISP or other service related to spam propagation and prevention. A white-hat provider is a good guy, who acts promptly and decisively on verified spam reports (i.e., suspends or cancels the spammer's account). A black-hat ignores abuse complaints or even promotes spamming activity. When a provider acts unpredictably when addressing abuse complaints, it may be labeled a gray-hat.

Lumber Cartel (LC). A wholly fictional and mythic organization of companies dedicated to the publishing and mailing of paper catalogs and other physical advertising mail. An invention (in 1997 or before) of a poster to a spam-related newsgroup who claimed that this organization was funding antispam activities as a way to keep advertising in print rather than via email. The joke has been around so long that most LC parody Web sites no longer exist. Even so, antispammers sometimes include "tinlc" ("there is no Lumber Cartel") in newsgroup messages as a self-deprecating reference when they succeed in getting a spammer booted from an ISP.

---

[1] You can read the original complaint and Spamhaus' responses at www.spamhaus.org/legal/answer-03-80295.html.

Chickenboner. Derived from the original 1997 phrase "beer cans and chicken bones," claimed by newsgroup poster Ron Ritzman. It was intended to promote a stereotype of the lone (and Rule #3 stupid) spammer in a mobile home surrounded by take-out chicken boxes. While leaders of notorious spam gangs tend to be more upscale in their lifestyles, it is believed that many of them rely on numerous "chickenboners" to perform affiliate mailings on behalf of the gangs.

Frea Speach. An antispammer's way of referring to the commercial free speech argument of spammers. It derives from a misspelling in a spammer's forum posting, claiming "free speach." Antispammers picked up on the spelling error, and propagated it to both words to reinforce the Rule #3 stereotype.

Spam Trap. A common technique by spam-gathering organizations, whereby specially coded email addresses are embedded in the HTML code of the organization's Web pages so that email harvesting programs will add the addresses to the spammer's databases. Any email message sent to that address is immediately labeled spam because no individual had ever used that address to register with, or subscribe to, any Web site, mailing list, or other service. When a sender to the address claims to send only to addresses that have opted into a list, the spam trap owner knows the sender is lying (see Rule #1).

Clueless. Used to describe anyone who doesn't understand the ins and outs of the email system, server administration, or personal email management. The more vocal and critical posters to antispam newsgroups are quick to label an inexperienced user or administrator as clueless, rather than help the individual increase his or her knowledge and skills. Anyone who posts to one of these groups and reveals naiveté in his or her server administration and security mechanisms risks being labeled as clueless.

A goodly amount of spam filtering at ISPs and among incoming email server administrators utilizes the services of one or more BLs—blocklists, blacklists, or blackhole lists, depending on whom you ask. These lists contain IP addresses (not domain names) associated with the origination of spam messages or sites that promote and support spamming activity (e.g., Web sites that sell email address harvesting software). The purpose of a BL is to help incoming email servers compare the IP address of an incoming message against the list. If the IP address of the server attempting to send a message matches a number on the list, then the incoming server can choose how best to ignore or divert the message, depending on how the administrator manages spam.

That's the theory, anyway.

In practice, applying BLs to incoming spam can be tricky business, for several reasons. First, there are many BLs from which to choose, and each one uses different criteria for determining who gets on the list and how (if ever) an entry leaves the list. For instance, SpamCop assembles its list from the highly automated system that analyzes thousands of spam message reported to it every day (including messages that arrive at its own spam traps). The system keeps track of the frequency, recency, and basic content details of each message. When an IP address is reported enough times within a 48-hour period (regardless of content), the address is added to the list. If activity stops, the listing may be removed automatically within another 48 hours. In contrast, the Spamhaus Block List (SBL) gets its candidates from other sources, and assigns a weighting system that determines how long an address stays on the list.

Of course, the holy grail would be a perfectly accurate and up-to-date blocklist, but none exists. Instead, spam fighters can choose from more than two-dozen distinct BLs on the Internet, plus many others dedicated to listing IP blocks from individual countries. Lists come and go, and some lists contain so many IP addresses that they recommend blocking more mail than they allow in.

Nevertheless, BLs play an important role in spam filtering—if they are applied sensibly. For example, a filter might use several blocklists and see on how many lists an incoming message's IP address appears. If the IP is listed on a majority of them (and some BLs may be given more weight than others because of their accuracy track records), then the message is blocked entirely or is shunted to a suspected spam holding area. Some of the major mail server spam-blocking software products on the commercial market utilize a blend of BLs as part of their filtering technologies.

Occasionally, however, an email administrator may rely on too few BLs, or, in more radical cases, only one. Herein lies a potential problem that exhibits itself from time to time. Take, for example, an ISP or mail server administrator that treats the SpamCop BL as gospel—a tactic that SpamCop, itself, recommends against, but can't control others from using that way. If the SpamCop analysis software makes a mistake, if the SpamCop user's mail server is misconfigured, or if the spammer has found a new way to spoof Received: headers, SpamCop can accidentally list the spam reporter's IP address or another forged IP address listed in the header. The SpamCop reporting system tries to minimize these possibilities by showing a list of IP address owners associated with each spam message. The reporter can then uncheck the ISPs that shouldn't receive a LART. However, if the user slips up, and the list includes his own ISP, that user could end up on the receiving end of a nastygram from his ISP because he reported himself as a spammer.

These accidents happen. Authorized SpamCop "deputies" monitor the SpamCop mailing lists and try to remedy legitimate complaints quickly. But trying to convince others on those mailing lists that an IP address on the BL is not used for spamming leads to fireworks.

Vocal antispam activists have zero tolerance for anything—and I mean *anything*—that emits even the faintest aroma of spam or spam activity. Thanks to antispammers' firm belief in Rule #1, the more one protests his innocence (per Rule #2), the more the antispammers believe the protester is a spammer trying to "work" the system to get an IP address off the BL while still spamming.

Sparks fly when a bulk emailer (including a legitimate one) that isn't active in the antispam community tries to communicate with the antispam community in public forums. If the bulk emailer uses the preferred terminology promoted by organizations such as the Direct Marketing Association, the emailer may use the expression "double opt-in" to describe the way he handles subscriptions—believing that he is doing the right thing by recipients. But the more virulent antispammer sees that term as a red flag signaling spammer-speak. The antispammer's preferred description is "confirmed opt-in." Yet if the mailer followed the DMA's definitions, a "confirmed opt-in" subscription system is not as rigorous as what the antispammer calls by the same name. The parties are speaking entirely different languages, and don't understand the fine points of each other's tongue.

Cooler heads usually prevail in these discussion threads, but not always. In truth, spammers have tried to con their way off blocklists by way of discussion groups (the preferred communication medium for some BL removal requests). Just as so many spam message authors have lied their way via disclaimers and bogus unsubscribe links only to make knowledgeable recipients wary of all claims, so, too, have the discussion "trolls" poisoned the minds of many group participants. The first thought is to suspect a newcomer of being a troll, who is either trying to con the system or mess with the tempers of the veteran participants. Thus, if you passionately profess your innocence using the "wrong" terminology, and especially if you make any kind of cartooney threat, you'll be doomed. Look up the word "invective" in the dictionary, then harden yourself to receive plenty of it.

Blocklists have one more potential problem that occasionally hurts unsuspecting individuals and companies by causing their mail to be blocked at some recipients' servers. A BL's owner has the option of listing not only individual IP addresses, but entire blocks of contiguous address numbers. Justification for such extensive blockage is sometimes quite valid, particularly when a black-hat ISP invites spamming activity (or explicitly fails to act on spam abuse complaints). If spam analysis finds mail coming from two or more IP addresses in a 256-address block managed by the same ISP, many antispammers believe that it is a valid practice to put the entire block on the BL as a preemptive strike against mail that is, or will soon be, originating from IPs managed by the same provider.

A lot of this kind of IP block filtering goes on in mail servers around the Internet. It can cause all kinds of headaches for the technically unaware. I visualize an unsuspecting Web neophyte (someone that veteran antispammers would call "clueless") finding a banner ad on a Web site for inexpensive Web and email hosting—say, something a father needs to set up a site for his sixth grader's soccer league. It would never occur to that budding Web site author to investigate the IP range of the ISP to see if any of its addresses were listed on BLs. Heck, he doesn't even know what an IP address or BL is. But the Web space is cheap, and off he goes to create the Web site (probably with the help of his sixth grader acting as server administrator). Part of the site includes a place to sign up for newsletter mailings. Several of the parents sign up with their work email addresses.

Unbeknownst to the soccer team site, its ISP also hosts a few sites that have been reported as spamming or sell spam-related products. Moreover, the ISP does not react quickly enough (or at all) to prevent the spew or close the offensive Web sites when reports arrive at its abuse desk. As a way to punish the ISP, the BL provider lists an entire contiguous block of IP addresses managed by the ISP.

This activity really happens. In early 2004, customers using wireless network (Wi-Fi) connections at public places served by carrier T-Mobile found their messages blocked by some incoming mail servers. Because T-Mobile Wi-Fi connections were reported as the source of a spam mailing, all adjacent T-Mobile Wi-Fi IP address groups were added to one or more blocklists.

The blocklist provider doesn't care much about legitimate mailers that are also assigned an IP address in that block. In fact, the BL provider (cheered on by lots of antispammers) hopes that enough innocent people will be affected so that they pressure the offending ISP to either change its ways or lose customers.

When newbies learn about this BL stuff, their heads spin because they don't understand much about how email works, and they become very upset at being punished for doing nothing wrong. If they're guilty of anything, it's associating with an organization (the ISP) whose other customers in the same IP block are genuine Bad Guys—information that the innocent had no notion of investigating beforehand. They fail to understand why they should go through the hassle and expense of finding another ISP whose IP addresses are not blocked en masse. Even if the addresses aren't blocked today, they could be tomorrow.

This scenario doesn't occur often, but it has happened in the past and will happen in the future. On the one hand, I'm uncomfortable with this approach because it smacks of the same kind of stereotyping that has led to tons of human misery ("That fellow with a 'Q' in his name stole from me; therefore all people with 'Q' in their names are thieves and should have their thumbs cut off"). On the other hand, in pure self-defense within my own spam filters, I find myself converting a few individual spam addresses within a block into the entire block when I see multiple related addresses arriving in recent spam (usually from distant countries). I'm not doing this to punish the ISP, but to keep more spam sources from that same provider out of my inbox next week. If that ISP were really intent on eliminating spammers from its customer base, it wouldn't be shifting the same spammer to other IP addresses within its block or allowing new spammers to occupy available slots.

Blocklist supporters make an important distinction that is lost on BL victims. Because reports of being blocked usually name the specific BL containing the offending IP address, a sender who is blocked believes that the compiler of the BL is physically blocking the mail. I understand how this feeling can arise. If you get a report that your IP address is on a BL, and you visit the BL's Web site to find out more about the reports that led to the listing, you indeed get the feeling that the list creator is the only one responsible for rejecting your mail. But bear in mind that there is no single authoritative BL, and the choice to use one or several BLs (and relative weights assigned to each) belongs to the incoming email server administrator or the developer of server-based spam-fighting tools.

To challenge the BL system, many listees have sued BL compilers over the years. One of the major lawsuit lightning rods in the late 1990s and early 2000s was a service called Mail Abuse Prevention System, L.L.C. (MAPS). Typical charges in these cases included defamation, interference with business, and unfair practices. The suits usually began with a request for a restraining order against MAPS for including IP addresses (or blocks of IP addresses) on its list. Some jurisdictions granted the orders; others did not. Over time, BL compilers have adapted their listing criteria to rely on more objective observations of actual spam. If the eMarketersAmerica.org fiasco against Spamhaus and SPEWS is any indication, BL compilers are being more careful to keep restraining orders at bay.

One of the arguments that bulk emailers use against BLs is that any email system that filters email based on a BL listing also blocks mail from those sources even when the recipient was foolish enough (okay, that's my wording) to sign up for mailings that also go out to harvested addresses. In other words, the power to censor mail is put in the hands of the incoming email system, rather than the recipient's. In many cases, the recipient doesn't even know that such email is being blocked because the server operator does not say which, if any, BLs are used for spam filtering. If the ISP does not let account holders supply individual lists of permitted senders (called *whitelists),* then the censorship is complete.

I hate to admit it, but there is logic to that argument. Yet ISPs and mail server administrators are under the gun from users to filter spam, in some cases to prevent as much of it as possible from even entering the receiving mail system (something that BLs can assist in doing). To keep spammers' messages out their systems, the email operators don't want to give away which methods they use for filtering, out of fear that such information will help spammers find ways around the filters.

History shows that, too often, systems developed in a spirit of trust and mutual respect become targets of abuse by those whose aim is to exploit the freedoms offered by those systems. When exploiters demonstrate that they can cause harm to participants of those systems, everyone loses some of those freedoms, to protect the majority against the minority of exploiters. For decades, any airline boarding-pass holder could waltz through the terminal at will ten minutes before departure. But then hijackers and terrorists exploited the security-free system and brought weapons and bombs aboard to commandeer and blow up planes. As a result, all airline passengers, including the unarmed, law-abiding ones, had to subject themselves and possessions to being searched, scanned, and probed before getting near a commercial aircraft. With each new breach of the airline passenger security system, the clamps on our liberties squeeze tighter. We're already taking off our shoes. If some jerko terrorist invents an undetectable underwear bomb, airport security inspections could get really ugly.

Airport screening stinks. Spam filtering stinks. But if we don't yield some of our freedoms to these intrusions, the terrorists and spammers will make air travel and email, respectively, unusable by all.

One thing is for sure: blocklists have had a negative impact on spammers in recent years. A lot of spam gets filtered or blocked daily, meaning that response rates per million must be declining. Aside from the occasional press interview by master spammers that indicate the trouble caused by BLs, more objective evidence comes from Internet traffic winding its way across the Internet.

In 2003, variations of the Mimail worm (Mimail-E, -H, and -L) were coded to cause massive "packet attacks" on a few of the more active BL communities, including spamhaus.org, spamcop.net, and spews.org. This kind of attack, called a Distributed Denial of Service (DDoS) attack causes the target servers to receive so many requests at one time (150,000 or more per second) routed through a large number of relays that the servers become overloaded and cannot serve genuine requests. That same year, separate from the Mimail worm, several BL-related sites suffered DDoS attacks, causing some to close down permanently. Others found sufficient resources to beef up their systems with distributed servers sharing the load around the world, making it easier to keep the service available even when under attack.

Spammers are also modifying the ways they forge message headers to try to trip up some automated BL systems. For example, the SpamCop system analyzes the sequence of Received: header lines in a suspected spam message to determine where the forged portion begins, thus signifying the presumed origination point of the message. As described in Chapter 11, "Header Trick #4," some spammers assemble a credible, but completely false, Received: header chain to trick SpamCop into bypassing the real insertion point (usually a zombie PC).

This type of forgery takes extra processing on the spammer's part—processing that eats into the number of messages that can be delivered each hour. They wouldn't bother, however, unless they believed the tactic improved delivery rates by tricking BL-based spam filters and protected their hidden zombie servers from discovery.

Speaking of underhanded tricks, a small number of the most virulent antispammers take the fight to extremes that make a lot of other antispammers queasy. Pushed too far by a spam flood from one source whose identity becomes known to spam fighters, these spammer haters (notice the distinction between spam haters and spammer haters) resort to spammer-like and hacker tactics to take revenge on their enemies. In August 2003, the *New Zealand Herald* told the story of 100-million-messages-a-day spammer from New Zealand named Shane Atkinson and his brush with antispammers. It's not uncommon for antispammers to research known spammers to obtain as much personal information as possible, and then make that information known publicly. In Atkinson's case, antispammers published his home address and telephone number. At that point, he started receiving nasty phone calls, and his email address had been subscribed to what he describes as "tons of email lists," including a gay dating service. He went public to explain that he feared for his own safety and that of his family, and was getting out of the spam business.

Publishing the whereabouts of known spammers is nothing new. In fact, you can find a fair amount of address and phone information about some of the most notorious spammers at the spamhaus.org Web site's ROKSO list. (You also find records of past serial criminal activity on many of them, but that's a separate story.) A small minority of spam victims have no reservation about turning what they consider to be email harassment on its ear, and harass the spammers. DDoS attacks on spamvertised Web sites and related support industry servers are not uncommon, but there are so many such places that an attack can have only little effect on a spammer who runs sites on dozens or hundreds of domains and servers around the world. DDoS attacks are also illegal in many jurisdictions.

I suppose the revenge seekers get some momentary personal joy from carrying out their attacks and pranks, but I don't see how that helps the antispam cause. Just because spammers forge their way into email boxes, criminally hijack computers, and eagerly attack or joe-job antispammers, why should an antispammer stoop to the same level? Such activity is just as repugnant as the original offenses. Yes, it's frustrating when spammers host their Web sites at foreign ISPs that don't respond to complaints. But wouldn't the antispam energy be better directed at helping eliminate the spammer's economic incentive? Why not educate everybody in your family and all of your friends and their families about the spamonomy and how to appear invisible to spammers? Teaching your father-in-law about the dangers of 419 scams and cheap "medz" will do more good than igniting a paper bag full of dog poop on a spammer's doorstep.

Antispamming attitudes vary among recipients, but anyone who recognizes an incoming message as spam will find that they have the most in common with one of three groups:

- Computer geeks

- Legal geeks

- Lay consumers

Each group sees spam differently, although all would agree that they don't want to receive it anymore. What separates them are their approaches to dealing with the problem.

Computer geeks look not so much at the message that the spammer is trying to convey, but rather at the traces left by the spammer to help identify the origin of the message, as well as patterns in the message to assist in filtering future messages that use the same tactics. It is rare that an antispammer who enjoys the technical aspects of the chase actually sees the message as the spammer would like everyone to see it. Messages that arrive with HTML coding to display Web-pagelike content get examined at the source code level—all those angle brackets and gibberish that load images and change font colors in the message. Message headers contain valuable information that help knowledgeable antispammers find out where the computer that sent the message is located (at least in which country), and whether the message originated in a mail server or a likely hijacked PC. They don't know whose home or office it's in, but they'll know the cable or DSL provider that supplies the connection (which, in turn, should be able to track down the infected computer from its customer base if it has the desire and manpower).

It's the geeks who are ultimately responsible for the technical solutions that assist all spam fighters with blocking and filtering spam, whether that occurs on the mail server or on the PC. Because spammers use a variety of techniques to attempt to bypass existing restrictions, the computer-literate antispammer is more likely to be active in spam reporting (through organizations such as SpamCop). If they "roll their own" antispam solutions, they monitor the source code of incoming messages carefully, particularly those that get past their own filters to counteract the tricks that spammers use to get around known filtering and blocking technologies.

The second group, legally trained spam recipients, look less at the source code and more at the parallels that may exist between the spam epidemic and existing case law. They also try to find ways of crafting new laws that will both act to quell public complaints and stand up to a court test if challenged by a spammer. An antispammer lawyer trots out venerable precedents, such as trespass of chattels, theft of service, and fraud to bolster claims against a spammer.

Lawyers and prosecutors don't have to rely strictly on antispam laws to pursue some offenders. Spam that tries to get recipients to buy some penny stock may run afoul of stock trading laws (under the auspices of the Securities and Exchange Commission in the United States). Spam that sells prescription medications with "no doctor's prescription necessary" may be pursued by an agency responsible for medications (the Food and Drug Administration in the United States).

Legislators typically walk a fine line between the interests of various constituencies. On the one hand, consumers complain vigorously about spam and want the government to put a stop to it (as if that were possible); on the other hand, business groups won't stand for laws that impede their free hand at hawking their wares. Unfortunately, with few exceptions, the business interests have won major battles for the hearts and minds of legislators. So far.

By "lay consumer," the third category, I mean the nontechnical email user who has no particular training in computer programming or law—two areas that are used by others to attempt to fight off spam. I'm talking about the everyday user who must communicate at work by email or the student who exchanges messages with friends and family. Some consumers have a more difficult time than others when it comes to ignoring the content of spam messages, especially when they first begin receiving them. They may get tricked by the misleading subject lines into opening messages. Or they can't figure out why they receive offers for bizarre products. If they open a message that has graphically pornographic content, they are revolted by it, and hope the same thing doesn't get to the kids.

This consumer class receives the most spam, but generally is the least vocal about it. They may submit an occasional complaint to their ISPs, employers, a government agency, or congressperson, but they wouldn't have the faintest idea about how to track down a spammer themselves. They may believe that the From: address visible to everyone is the actual address of the sender, because neither they nor their friends put anything but the truth in the From: and Subject: lines of their own messages. When a marketer explains that the recipient supposedly registered to get these messages at its site or a partner's site, these consumers may simply shrug and accept that as being true. After all, they also get catalogs in the mail from new companies they haven't bought from in the past—it must be the same with email ads. And the lay consumer certainly doesn't know how much trouble the spammer went through to get the message past filters and find a place for the Web site that takes orders for whatever is on offer.

For the corporate email user, it's impossible to know from the From: and Subject: lines that the message from an unknown name with the subject "Meeting changed" isn't coming from a new employee in a different department. Double-click that message, and BAM: a graphic that would make most adults blush.

A lay consumer is also the most at risk when it comes to media coverage of spam and antispam efforts. When the U.S. CANSPAM act was signed into law in December 2003, the television news had all kinds of teases and 20-second reports about how the law would "get the spam out of your email." The media frequently misunderstood the law's language about investigations into a possible "Do Not Spam" list, and made it sound as though the list was going into effect immediately—a knee-jerk reaction to the popularity of the U.S. "Do Not Call" list aimed at reducing telemarketing calls. How confused are the consumers now that the law hasn't slowed spam one bit?

As I'll discuss in Chapter 17, of the three antispam groups, the one that is capable of responding the fastest, acting with impunity, and having the most damaging effect on spammers is the lay consumer. The consumer holds the bulk of the spamonomy in his and her hands. If the geeks and lawyers help reduce the amount of spam that reaches the lay consumer as a start, the consumer can finish the job—but only if sufficiently aware of the tricks being perpetrated with every message that gets through.

CHAPTER 11

Spammer Tricks Part One: Headers

This chapter and the next are designed to expose the tricks that spammers employ (or try to employ) to get their messages past spam filters or blocks into your inbox, and, if they're really good with their tricks, in front of your eyes. The stuff explained in these chapters will sometimes get a little technical, but you must understand that spammers are hoping that unsuspecting consumers won't be motivated or technologically aware of these things. They're playing you for a sucker, plain and simple. Once you understand these tricks, you'll learn what to look for in a benign way that makes you appear nonexistent to spammers.

In all of the examples shown in these chapters, I have disguised email addresses, IP addresses, or any other identifying mark that would provide antispammers with a way to carry out revenge against the perpetrators. I use \x\ to signify a string of characters, such as an identifiable address or domain name. This intentional obfuscation is called *munging* (the first "g" is soft, and thus rhymes with "sponging" or "lunging"), and is a common technique that spam reporters use with the copies of spam they submit to antispam archives and reporting systems.

The following compendium was culled from a large sampling of real spam messages that I captured at my mail server. Where possible, I try to ascribe an intention to the deception. It's not easy to guess the specific motivation for the usage of a particular trick, because not all spammers have equal skill nor understanding of how antispam techniques work. While Rule #1 (Spammers lie) prevails throughout, Rule #3 (Spammers are stupid) frequently shows evidence of proof. I've reserved an entire chapter later for Rule #3 samples.

121

Header Trick #1: *Using an open proxy or zombie PC on a cable/DSL network.*

Example:

```
Received: from mdi-ger.de (adsl-67-125-157-
\x\.dsl.irvnca.pacbell.net [67.125.157.\x\]) by
\x\ (8.12.10) id hB4MYkm5011107 for <\x\>; Thu,
4 Dec 2003 15:34:48 -0700 (MST)
```

Intended Victim(s): Spam source investigators, virus-infected computer owners

Description: The most prolific spammers spend substantial effort disguising their actual entry points to the Internet. The increased popularity of IP-based blocklists as spam-fighting tools means that maintaining even several outgoing mail servers is a losing proposition. The one part of a message header that cannot be easily forged is the IP address of the mail server from which the message was sent on its final leg of the journey to the recipient's incoming mail server. A properly configured incoming email server logs the IP address of the server sending the message and records that number in the topmost Received: header. The IP address usually appears inside square brackets. In the example above, the IP address of the last outgoing mail server to touch the message is shown as:

```
[67.125.157.\x\]
```

The incoming server may also be configured to perform a *reverse DNS lookup* of the IP address and record the way the server associated with the IP address identifies itself in publicly accessible records (this all happens in less than a blink of an eye while the incoming email server is carrying on its little introductory exchange with the sending server). For our example, the IP address resolves to the following URL:

```
adsl-67-125-157-\x\.dsl.irvnca.pacbell.net
```

Although the company is now known as SBC Internet Services (if I read my telephone company Ouija board correctly), the owner of this IP address is listed as Pacbell.net, a provider of DSL connections to a large swath of the United States. From the looks of this particular IP address and reverse identity, the block of IP addresses from which this one comes is from a DSL network in or near Irvine, California, and the particular computer is very likely owned by a customer with a hijacked computer.

Notice the domain name as it appears at the start of the Received header: mdi-ger.de, a domain registered in Germany (and not connected to the Internet as I write this). That this domain does not match the reverse DNS lookup data for the sending machine's IP address is highly suspicious. A mismatch does not automatically prove a forgery, however. When email servers change configuration, get sold to other companies, or get shifted to another division of a company, not all of their inner server settings are immediately updated. In fact, at the time the example message came through, SBC had not yet assigned new SBC-specific domains to the servers that identified themselves as being Pacbell (although it took the company less time to change the signs on the San Francisco Giants' baseball park from PacBell to SBC than it's taking to change all of its server identities).

Open proxy servers and zombie computers (both PCs and servers) typically act as their own SMTP servers, appearing to the recipient's server as if the mail originated just one hop away. This is excellent for the spammer because there is no apparent breadcrumb trail leading back to the actual origination point. At the real origination point, a computer locates the IP addresses of available servers and infected computers (through automated probing of numerical IP addresses, or buying IP numbers from services that do the probing for them). Then, with the knowledge of how to communicate with these proxies, the real originating computer sends instructions containing the target email addresses and the message content (more about this in a moment). Routines in the zombie PC's program assemble the messages (sometimes filling in blanks with random words or concocting From: field data out of pieces of addresses sitting in the queue or perhaps even pulled from the PC owner's address book). Finally, the SMTP engine starts spewing out reams of spam. The IP address of that SMTP server is the IP address of the zombie PC connected to the Internet via a DSL or cable modem (occasionally also a dial-up network connection).

The account owner of that particular IP address at the time of the spam spew is not guilty of spamming, per se, but is unknowingly abetting spammers by failing to patch and disinfect his or her computers or turn off default settings of any mail servers that may be connected to the network. Most of the IP addresses dished out to cable and DSL customers are dynamic. Each time the modem resets (or the ISP decides to reset the modem remotely), the computer gets a new IP address for the next spam spew. This makes it very difficult and problematic to assemble lists of zombie computer IP addresses for use as spam blocklisting. If the IP address of today's zombie Dell PC were listed in a blocklist, a squeaky-clean Macintosh using that same IP address next week would have its email blocked at incoming email servers that observe such a BL. The more strident antispammer would say, "Great! Block all the addresses in that IP group to send a message to the ISP." Some blocklists do just that.

Any bulk email message from an unknown sender whose source appears to be a broadband provider is most commonly employing a zombie PC or hijacked proxy server. Here is a list of the common broadband domains that have machines being abused in this manner (with notes in parentheses):

adelphia.net	(Pennsylvania-based regional cable broadband provider)
ameritech.net	(U.S. regional dial-up and DSL provider, owned by SBC)
apol.com.tw	(Taiwanese ISP, Asia Pacific On-line Services, Inc.)
attbi.com	(Formerly AT&T Broadband, now owned by Comcast)
charter.com	(U.S. regional cable broadband provider)
comcast.net	(Huge U.S. regional cable broadband provider)
cox-internet.com	(U.S. regional cable broadband provider)
hinet.net	(Taiwanese ISP, owned by Chunghwa Telecom)
nf.net	(Newfoundland ISP, owned by Rogers Cable)
pacbell.net	(Former Pacific Bell DSL provider, now owned by SBC)
rogers.com	(Ontario, Canada-based broadband provider)
rr.com	(Virginia-based broadband provider (Road Runner), owned by Time Warner)
swbell.net	(Former Southwestern Bell DSL provider, now called SBC)
telesp.net.br	(Brazilian ISP—Telefónica)
telus.net	(Regional Canadian dial-up and DSL provider)
veloxzone.com.br	(Brazilian ISP—Telemar Norte Leste)
videotron.ca	(Quebec-based cable broadband provider)
wanadoo.fr	(French DSL provider run by France Telecom)

Of this illustrious group, comcast.net has the worst reputation when it comes to responding to complaints from antispam activists. I know for a fact that spam I received in early 2004 from hijacked computers connected to the Internet via comcast.net outweighed all other similar providers.[1]

By the way, PCs aren't the only systems that get hijacked in this way. Any computer connected to the Internet is vulnerable, even when the machine's owner is a savvy server administrator. David Barroso Berrueta from Palencia, Spain, discovered that someone had exploited a security hole in a popular server-based photo album program he had installed on his server. The program is called Gallery, and he, like many other thousands, ran it to provide an easy user interface for displaying and navigating through a

---

[1] Comcast announced in June 2004 that it had begun tightening its grip on excessive outflow from customer computers suspected of acting as zombies. Let's hope it is successful and that other providers follow suit.

photo collection. While performing some routine analysis of his Web site, he saw an unusual amount of outgoing traffic that he couldn't easily explain. After much monitoring and research (explained in very technical detail at www.securityfocus.com/guest/24043), he discovered that his server had been hijacked by a hacker whose goal was to send out batches of spam (under 6,000 at a time) while disguising the actual origination point. The programs that the hacker (or, more likely, a computer program run by a hacker) installed on David's server were frighteningly clever in the way they received instructions from the "mother ship," hid their own tracks after running each batch (executing 100 or more spam flows at the same time), and reporting results back home. In his tracking and research, David found controlling signals coming from multiple sources in numerous countries, very likely other hijacked computers acting as relays to reach his machine.

Although the producer of the Gallery software program has issued an update that fixes the hole exploited in this report, there is no guarantee that all installations of the software have been patched by users. But there's a darned good chance that the originator of this scheme will remain hidden because the multiple levels of indirection through multiple foreign countries will thwart all but the most deep-pocketed prosecutor who could assemble the correct charges against the hacker.

Header Trick #2: *Making you believe you have an account at some organization*

Example:

```
Subject:   Your Monthly Account Statement -
           November
```

Intended Victim(s): Gullible recipients

Description: There are lots of variations on this scam, but somewhere in the message is a lie about you being a member of some club or buyer's group. The subject line shown in the example is taken from a message sent by an outfit that claims to let members accumulate "points" when they buy certain products through its Web site—like a frequent flyer program for people who buy gift books or pet food.

These outfits and their programs may be legit, but if they turn blind email addresses into "members" without their permission, they shouldn't be entitled to anybody's business. They use the subject line to get unsuspecting suckers to open the message and read their offers. If you don't recognize the sender's identity in the list of unopened mail, or if the subject line doesn't give the name of the company, don't touch it.

Header Trick #3: *Forging the From: field with a bogus free Internet email service account or address assembled from pieces of other spam targets*

Example:

```
From:  "Shelby Ferguson" <Case50@mn.rr.com>

From:  "Krystal Payne" <sscn600j@yahoo.com>
```

Intended Victim(s): Incoming email servers, amateur spam fighters, single users

Description: The big mistake that nontechnical recipients of spam make is assuming that the From: field of an email message accurately represents the sender's email address. Nothing could be further from the truth. As described in Chapter 4, the email system does not use the From: field for any part of the message's journey from sender to recipient. Nor does the recipient's email server perform any kind of validation or authentication of the From: field information.[2] The original SMTP mail specification was deliberately designed to accept the From: field at face value—back when the comparatively tiny population of the ARPANET behaved themselves, for the most part.

So when you receive a spam message, open it, and get outraged that you were conned into viewing the spew, your first inclination is to look at the From: field to see who sent you the garbage. The field can contain a couple variations in format for an address. One is a simple email address, like the following:

```
From:  freedomiseasy@excite.com
```

When the data consists of only an email address, that address appears in your email inbox listing as the From: field of the message.

But if the address if formatted by enclosing the address in angle brackets and preceding that with any characters (usually in quotes), the header field looks like this:

```
From:  "Lisa Trueheart" <freedomiseasy@excite.com>
```

When the brackets are present, email program inbox listings display only the part before the bracketed address. The text preceding the brackets can be anything, and is not necessarily related to the address. That's why some of the spam items in your inbox listing have other phrases in the From: listing, as another opportunity to sway you into opening the message.

The point is that spammers can put anything they want in the From: field of the headers that their servers send out. Spammers who try to hide their

---

[2] This practice may change in the near future, as discussed in Chapter 15.

identities use a variety of techniques to fill this From: field with information that has all of the appearance of being in good form, but in truth is bogus. Most commonly, they use email address domains from one of the free email services on the Internet. Popular ones include:

hotmail.com

yahoo.com

netscape.net

centrum.cz

email.com

freenet.co.uk

excite.com

The user names for these addresses are usually phony, comprised of random characters or some phrase intended to convey part of the sales pitch of the message. Occasionally you'll encounter a laughably odd combination, as one I received with a message whose body was entirely in Russian:

```
From: "Fumigate H. Devolving" <\x\@nicholastse.net>
```

When addresses include plain-language names, the majority of them have female first names. This is an old trick to prey on what was once the predominance of males being computer users. The assumption was also that male computer users would likely be nerds and geeks who have never once in their lives ever uttered more than a few clumsy syllables to women with names like Ashley, Kristen, and Lara. Ooooh, to have received a message from "Jessica"—I've gotta open it, in case it's a secret admirer from the twelfth floor. In the last year or so, however, the spammers must have finally realized that women do as much emailing as men, so the phony From: fields include an increasing percentage of men's or ambiguous names ("It's Pat!"). It's also easier to program for random name assembly across genders. A real win-win for the spammer.

I think it's safe to say that anyone who is building a legitimate Internet-based business will not only have registered a domain, but will want to use it for correspondence and to advertise the domain name as a brand name. A mass-produced mailing campaign with a free email account address in the From: field is a clear tip-off that the sender is concealing his identity, and should therefore be avoided.

Spammers, however, don't only use bogus free email accounts. They also use other peoples' genuine email addresses in the From: fields of their messages. They get the addresses the same way they get the recipient addresses, and randomly pull one to plant in the From: field of one or a batch of messages. A related technique is to assemble the three pieces of a From: field's data (plain-language name, user ID, and domain name) from three samples of addresses in the database. Really. I'm not making this stuff up (like the spammers are). I have received advisories that messages showing my domain as the From: field had invalid recipients' addresses. Attached to the advisories were copies of the original messages, which clearly show a plain-language name I've never heard of, a completely unrelated user ID that is none of the ones I use or could have been harvested anywhere, and my domain (I occasionally set up my mail system to receive all messages to any user ID as a way to sample incoming spam).

If you ever receive these kinds of "bounce" messages from AOL or other services, the reason is that the magic combination of your user ID and your domain got planted into the From: field of a batch of spam sent to addresses that are no longer valid. When you receive these notices, you'll be perplexed and mad ("How dare anyone use my address without my permission!"), but there isn't anything you can do about it. Don't bother writing back to the service that bounced your message in an effort to clear your good name: The entire bounce process is automated, and the bouncing system isn't keeping track of your address as a troublemaker.

But the spammer has accomplished a couple of major feats at the expense of others. First, he has concealed one part of his identity. Second, he has provided a place far from his inbox for invalid address bounce messages to go. Since the worst spammers have no interest in cleaning their lists, they don't want to know about bounces, only about how many messages they've sent.

Header Trick #4: Forging a credible Received: header chain

Example:

```
Received: from \x\.whtmrs01.md.comcast.net
(\x\.whtmrs01.md.comcast.net [68.33.60.\x\]) by
\x\ (8.12.10) id hB4N0VmG016280 for <\x\>; Thu,
4 Dec 2003 16:00:32 -0700 (MST)
```

```
Received: from [41.159.201.105] by
\x\.whtmrs01.md.comcast.net SMTP id
4R79KcBuv3GbbN; Fri, 05 Dec 2003 02:02:57 +0300
```

Intended Victim(s): SpamCop and other automated header analysis systems

Description: This trick has been used much more frequently since the rampant distribution of spam-centered Trojan horse programs. Under control of the "mother ship," these worm-infected zombie PCs become slaves, as their hidden SMTP servers relay thousands of messages while connected to their broadband providers. When spam from a zombie computer is reported to a service such as SpamCop, the header might have just the topmost Received: header line, like the one shown in the example. When the SpamCop parser sees no earlier Received: line in the header, it recognizes the source of the message and sends its spam report to that provider.

The spammers needed one more Received: to try to fool the SpamCop parser into seeing the zombie PC's IP address as being an innocent or legitimate relay in the transmission of the message. In communicating with the zombie PC (to issue its commands to send out the messages), the controlling computer obtains the IP identity of the PC (probably using the same routines that incoming email programs do to fill out their portion of the topmost Received: header line). This allows the PC's hidden SMTP server to write that identity as the source of the topmost Received: line and compose a phony second (earlier) Received: line, showing that the message came from some IP address to the SMTP server that is now sending the message to the recipient.

To a quick human or computer analysis of the two Received: lines, the sequence appears completely normal. If the message is construed as spam for other reasons, then the injection point of the spam "must be" the IP address at the beginning of the lower Received: header line. Note that this IP address is enclosed in square brackets, generally the sign that the address is one that the receiving server has verified. But this is where things get, um, interesting.

The "mother ship" supplied this IP address for use in this phony-baloney position of the header. Importantly, a search for the IP address in a database called whois reports that the number is within a block of IP numbers assigned to somebody. The problem, however, is that this particular IP address is in one of the many address blocks held in reserve by the Internet Assigned Numbers Authority (IANA), the organization that allocates IP address blocks to Internet providers. The IANA has huge numbers of blocks held in reserve, and random addresses from these blocks are commonly used as the phony source of these kinds of spam. I've seen similar insertions of IP addresses for various government agencies. I don't know if SpamCop or other spam analysis programs send LARTs to the government agencies, but if they do, I'm sure the agencies are not amused when accused of sending spam. Maybe that's another goal of the spammers who use this trick.

Header Trick #5: *Inserting random characters and spaces in the Subject: line*

Example:

```
Subject:  Join the Revolution!   wpamrmcswvrfqbl
```

Intended Victim(s): Content-based spam filter software

Description: Early server-based spam-fighting software operated primarily on text or pattern matching. For example, the software would have a list of subject lines or subject line phrases that had been recently reported by other users of the spam-filtering software. Upon arrival at the incoming server, a message first passed through the filter program, which applied lists of "rules" against the text of the message. The servers are fast enough to apply hundreds of rules in the blink of an eye, so the process didn't appreciably slow down the delivery of mail that survived the complete test.

Somewhere along the line, a spammer figured that adding some gibberish or random characters to the Subject: line would trick the filtering software because the line would no longer match the string of characters in the rule. This tactic is extremely primitive because the spam filtering is more interested in finding a match of the readable words anywhere in the Subject line, regardless of surrounding junk. Even so, a number of spammers (or perhaps just the cheap spamming software programs they bought from other spammers) continue to use this worthless technique.

To me, the presence of gibberish in the Subject: line, which is visible in the inbox list of messages, is a clear sign of spam, and makes it all the easier to delete without opening. Perhaps to make the gibberish characters less visible, some messages insert dozens of blank spaces between the readable subject portion and the garbage—in the hope that the inbox list column isn't wide enough to let the garbage characters appear. Of course, viewing the source code of the header or entire message reveals the gibberish, confirming your suspicion that it's spam.

You'll also find random characters appended to message bodies. The goal is the same, but the aim is also to trick more sophisticated content analysis, which can generate a numerical value—called a *hash*—that characterizes the content of the message. Adding random characters and words in each email is called *hash busting,* described more fully in Chapter 15.

Header Trick #6: *Forging the Message-ID: header field*

Example:

```
Message-ID:
<21d201c3bb3c$c69657fb$416d76f9@rte.ie>
```

Intended Victim(s): Spam analyzers (human and computerized)

Description: One of the lines suggested by the RFC 2822 message format standard is labeled Message-ID. Many email servers insert this header line if they find it missing, usually identifying the server's domain (after the @ symbol) and an identifying number that theoretically can be associated with a mail log entry maintained by that server. Not all mail servers add this line, so its absence does not mean that the message is automatically spam. But neither does the line's presence mean that the message isn't using forged headers.

The text from the example above comes from a spam message whose topmost Received: header line starts out as follows:

```
Received: from rte.ie
(PE245040.user.veloxzone.com.br
[200.164.245.\x\])...
```

The final incoming email server records the IP address of the sender (shown in square brackets), and performs a reverse DNS lookup to discover the sender is a customer of veloxzone.com.br (Brazil), most likely a zombie PC or customer's mail server that has been hijacked as an open proxy. The `rte.ie` identifier at the start of the line was forged by the true originator of the message, who also supplied the Message-ID line as part of the message content to be issued in the spew, purporting to come from the same domain (the Irish Public Service Broadcasting Organization).

I suppose that the spammer is trying to make somebody believe that the presence of the Message-ID line makes the message look real, as if it had originated at rte.ie. But the IP address recorded by the receiving server proves that to be false.

Header Trick #7: *Inserting a To: or CC: address that is not yours*

Example:

```
To: dannyer@ms52.hinet.net
```

Intended Victim(s): Nontechnical recipients

Description: Newcomers to the receiving end of spam probably wonder how a message with someone else's address in the To: or CC: fields in the header could have made it to their inboxes. Recall from Chapter 4 that a spammer (or his proxy SMTP server) can fill out the message's envelope (invisible to humans) with the actual delivery address, and it does not have to match anything else in the header. The message from which the example above was taken was actually addressed to a user at the dannyg.com domain. The incoming mail server directs the message to the inbox of the envelope addressee, even if the To: field is missing.

It looks like magic, but it's not. The process is basically the same that makes blind carbon copies (BCCs) work as they do to deliver the same message to a list of addresses that none of the recipients see in their own copies.

Header Trick #8: *Using a Subject: line that is complete gibberish or random words*

Example:

```
Subject: evfporate permeaje nr f
```

Intended Victim(s): Spam filters and maybe puzzle fanatics
Description: When a Subject: line isn't in a foreign language yet still looks like it was typed by a chimpanzee on crack, it's hard to know for sure what the motivation was. The above example came from a message that was pushing some cheap stock (I was being given a chance to get the "INSIDE SCOOP" on a stock that was "about to blow up").

While it's unlikely that a spam filter that looks for keywords in the Subject: line would reject a message with gibberish there, the message (to my mind, anyway) becomes much easier to spot as garbage without even having to open it. If this message had reached my email program, it would have been listed with that subject with a (bogus) sender "Tabatha Harmon." Why would Tabatha be sending me a message with a garbage subject line? To peak my curiosity perhaps? Or is she a narcoleptic insider who happened to drop off for a moment while filling out the Subject: line of this hot tip she wanted to mail to me?

More recently Subject: lines have been arriving with a blast of random real words, sometimes assembled in amusing or poetic combinations. Here are some examples:

```
Subject:  simon inconsistent skyscrape talismanic
          vandal lyman whom palmetto an

Subject:  Nothing to say but amazing sciatica

Subject:  Need health insurance 2002? no cost
          coverage quotes...cauliflower

Subject:  blackmail away krypton pneumonia
```

```
Subject:   bombast junk r

Subject:   Turn-key business dud
```

The words are an attempt to trick more sophisticated statistical content filters (Chapter 15) to help get the messages into your inbox. Don't be lured by such messages from senders you don't recognize. You'll be gravely disappointed to read the run-of-the mill medz or body part spam offer inside.

Header Trick #9: *Using a provocative (and, generally, spammy) Subject: line with an unknown From: line*

Example:

```
Subject:   hello

Subject:   Someone wants to Date You

Subject:   The safest way to invest your money

Subject:   don't be by yourself, I'm here

Subject:   try and beat this

Subject:   Danny, What is Your Status

Subject:   I saw your profile

Subject:   Are you doing ok?

Subject:   hi

Subject:   I saw you in church Friend

Subject:   Re: Hot stuff!

Subject:   randy looked at this

Subject:   Re: Payment  Past  Due, acct wv
           bpzotsrwjojrlsvms

Subject:   Please Respond!

Subject:   Did you sent me this message?

Subject:   YOUR PAYPAL.COM ACCOUNT EXPIRES

Subject:   Re: Do you remember me

Subject:   Howdy partner!

Subject:   Open only if you wish to read a
           personal prediction about yourself
```

```
Subject:   please scan for errors by 12/01/03

Subject:   Danny, URGENT- Your Account will be
           DELETED !

Subject:   Someone is looking into your background
           at our website
```

Intended Victim(s): Unsuspecting, curious, lonely recipients

Description: The spammer has multiple hurdles to leap from the moment an outgoing spam batch begins to the time the payoff (whatever form it might take) is complete. Even assuming that everything is all clear at the far ends of the journey—sending the spew and hosting the spamvertised destination—a spammer must:

A. Get the message into your inbox (past any spam filtering).

B. Get you to open the message (past any human suspicion).

C. Get you to click, reply, or call in response to the offer.

In the "old days," an email marketer spent most of the time on C, carefully crafting the message to produce the highest click-through or order rate possible. The marketer would test various approaches, keeping track of which variations received the best response, then tweak the next batch to use more of the features that seemed to get more targets to act.

These days, C is still important, but steps A and B present the biggest challenges. Spam filtering at some high-volume ISPs kills a ton of spam before it even reaches the recipients. Filters running on other ISP systems, corporate email servers, and personal email programs prejudge suspicious email, and segregate it into a "possible spam" category, making the recipient highly wary of those messages (I hope!). For those messages that do make it past the filters, the spammer doesn't know how sensitive a particular recipient's "spam radar" might be, so he needs to do his best to convince or, more likely, con the recipient into opening the message. Once the message is open, then the hard work that went into honing the message (for step C) takes over.

Various antispam laws, including the new CAN-SPAM law in the United States, call for commercial messages to avoid deceptive Subject: lines. But such deception continues because it had been successful in the past and enforcement is lax.

How you react to a message from an unknown sender depends on too many social factors to categorize with any meaning. By and large, however, the less experience you have with mail, the less suspicious you are of such messages. In one's early Internet days, receiving *any* mail is a thrill, especially if it comes from some mysterious person who appears to want to communicate with you. If you don't rely on email for important business or personal communications, then spam may be the only email you receive, and you may feel obligated to read it to justify your email presence.

That's what the spammer is really counting on.

Until you build a level of cynicism about the Internet, and spammers' tricks in particular, you may be caught up in the desire to be polite to your correspondents, including those you don't recognize by name. You may not yet understand that your email address is just one of millions in a spammer's database, and no genuine personal connection is in the offing. All the sender wants is to know that your address is "alive," some personal identification data from you, your money, or any combination of the three. You're a wounded zebra about to be smothered by hungry lions. You're potentially somebody's dinner.

Rule #1 (Spammers Lie) earns its position for a reason. The more provocative the Subject: line, the thicker your defenses must become.

Header Trick #10: *Merging identifiable personal information into the Subject: line*

Example:

```
Subject:  Danny  Goodman your acct for \x\ AVE
          is Ready
```

Intended Victim(s): Unsuspecting recipients

Description: Paranoiacs of the world, unite! Several companies in the direct marketing industry have built their businesses around a technique called *overlay* or *enhancement*. Their job is to find all known data about an individual or address and collate it for use by direct marketers. While no human is necessarily tracking you as an individual by name, your snail mail address is frequently targeted because of some past behavior that has been tracked (mail order purchases, real estate transactions, legal actions, credit activity, government license registrations, and the like).

This gets creepiest if you own real estate and owe money on a mortgage. Between public real estate transaction documents and your credit record, it's not uncommon for a postal mail solicitation to arrive from a financial institution (not your own) with information about your approximate outstanding mortgage balance. They're soliciting you to refinance with them. They not only know the approximate balance, but the address of the property. When you get an e-mail with this information "baked" inside it, your skin might crawl because somewhere, somebody has made the connection between your email address and this other personal data.

The Subject: line shown in the example included the street address of property I once owned. Naturally, the spammer used the other tactic of making it sound as though he and I have an ongoing relationship, since my "account" is now "ready" (for what?). Checking the source code view of the message, I saw that the message was an offer to refinance the property at that address (repeated in the message). The spamvertised link (which included a supplementary name/value data pair with my email address) was to a fairly new domain registered to an organization on the spamhaus.org ROKSO list—another one of the slimy lead-generating companies that feed replies to mortgage brokers for hefty referral fees. The address in the From: field was another domain registered to the same gang (all operating out of the same post office box in Arizona). Despite the fact that the message included my name and a property address, it was not a personal message—just another from a spew barrage utilizing automated mail-merging techniques as old as the hills. What was newish, though, was the linkup between physical and email worlds.

Be prepared to have your regular life and email life become associated with each other. It means that messages (using mail merging) will appear to be more personal, when, in fact, they're no more personal than the thousands of other messages that include your email address as the destination.

I've shown only the most common header tricks here. Others abound, but their impact is on a more technical level. Header tricks are all about deception, whether the victim is a human deceived by a phony Subject: line or a header analysis program that follows blind alleys down forged Received: lines sequences. In the next chapter, we jump into the message body, where even defter sleight of hand tries to make fools of us all.

CHAPTER 12

Spammer Tricks Part Two: Messages

In this chapter, I continue the parade of spammer tricks, here focusing on the message body. Most of the body tricks are designed to bypass computerized routines that perform spam filtering and reporting, while others are explicitly meant to trick the recipient in a variety of ways. If you simply view or preview messages employing most of these tricks, you won't notice the tricks because they're buried within the HTML coding. In fact, most of these tricks rely on recipients using email programs that render HTML just like a Web page. The "biggies," such as Microsoft Outlook (all flavors), AOL, MSN, and the Web-based email services like Hotmail, all do this.

To uncover whether a suspected spam message is trying to pull the wool over your or your mail software's eyes, you'll need to look at the source code view of the message. Despite the complexity of reaching the source view in some email programs, it is something I strongly recommend that everyone do for every suspicious message.[1] Viewing a message's source code (without first viewing or previewing the message) is the safest way to scan a message to find out if it's something you want to read "for real."

The problem with viewing the source code is that a lot of times it looks like pure gibberish to the nontechnical user. In many cases, you are, in fact, seeing gibberish, as various tricks confirm. But even a legitimate message that has HTML coding in it (as all messages from AOL and MSN, for example, do) can look pretty scary with all those angle brackets and strange words surrounding the message content. That said, the more you see this stuff, the more comfortable you'll be with it, even if you don't understand all of the codes and

---

[1] I supply instructions for Outlook users in Chapter 17.

numbers in the message. As it turns out, it's relatively rare to receive a legitimate HTML-only email message from a friend that has loads of HTML coding in it. One of the giveaways of a spammer is overuse of HTML to create colorful headlines and formatting designed to make the message look more like a Web page than a mail message—where even more content tricks are possible.

Message Trick #1: Inserting Junk HTML tags

Example:

```
ge<kkpgorhcdbqqnzc>t y<kzjkqmtbcol>our mon
<kzhbsrzdqnmeibb>ey bac<kcbumuybchihjc>k!
```

Intended Victim(s): Content-based spam filters; newbie source code viewers

Description: HTML tags are codes inside angle brackets. Tags are used to mark up text to provide context for parts of a document. Web browsers (or programs that act like Web browsers) interpret the tags as guides to laying out the page content. For instance, a paragraph in a typical HTML document begins with a tag denoting the start of a paragraph (<p>) and ends with the same tag name preceded by a slash (</p>). Therefore, a simple paragraph in HTML looks like this:

```
<p>This is an HTML paragraph.</p>
```

A Web browser (or email program that renders HTML) has a built-in style that it applies to any text surrounded by paragraph tags, including separating the current paragraph from its surrounding paragraphs.

As a way to prevent old browsers from becoming obsolete with the addition of new tags to the HTML language, browsers ignore any tags that they don't know about. But only the tags are ignored; the content between the unknown tags still appears on the page. This is exactly what this "junk tags" trick is designed to do: break up the visible content with tags that aren't part of any HTML version known to mankind.

Content-based spam filters commonly list patterns of text that appear in spam. For example, if a filter looked for the phrase "your money back" as an indicator of spam, then it could reject, delete, or label as "suspected spam" any message in which that string of characters appears. By inserting garbage HTML tags within the phrase, the spammer hopes that a content-based filter will not see the phrase. The extra tags present no problem for the recipient understanding the message, however, because the human viewer of a recipient's email program sees only that phrase, and none of the garbage tags.

Notice in the example that the junk tags being used are not the same, and that other than the first character ("k" throughout the entire message), the length and makeup appear to be random. This, again, is an effort to prevent content filters from noticing any telltale patterns. Blocking spam if it contains the string <k would not be a good idea because there is one valid (although rarely used) HTML tag that begins with k (<kbd>). Besides, the next spam run could use different first letters for its junk tags.

Junk tags don't have to be long strings. Here is one excerpt that uses short tags to break up the otherwise telltale mortgage offer:

```
<ZM>If <X>y<KDD>o<KY>u
are payi<QDYJ>n<KZT>g
<KMVY>more th<YMAA>an   3.6<XSP>%
<Y>on <XI>you<KFA>r
m<QG>ort<CJHV>g<QR>age,
<CDT>we <KY>c<ZP>a<X>n   save
<KU>yo<Z>u money!<br>
```

Because HTML renderers (unless instructed otherwise) ignore massive amounts of spaces, tab characters (accountable for the big gap in the second line above), and carriage returns in the source code, the recipient of the above segment sees one regular line of text reading: "If you are paying more than 3.6% on your mortgage, we can save you money!"

Fortunately for spam fighters, however, some parts of an HTML message cannot be obfuscated by junk tags, particularly the URL associated with the "click here" action button or image in the message. The URL may link to a spamvertising Web site that is easily matched from a list of such reported sites. Also, more intelligent content examination of messages that employ this trick will spot other patterns, such as the profusion of tags compared to the amount of unbroken text outside of the tags.

Message Trick #2: Auto-login "click here" links

Example:

```
<A href="http://xewdoycoieuuyc@www.\x\.biz">Click
here</A>
```

Intended Victim(s): Content filters, spam-reporting parsers, wannabe anti-spam experts

Description: A valid link that you are supposed to click in a spam message to reach the spamvertised Web site must contain a URL assigned to the href attribute of the <a> tag. Unless the HTML for the message contains another tag earlier in the message (the `<basehref>` tag) that specifies a default URL path for all links in the message, the URL shown in the `<a>` tag will begin with `http://` followed by the rest of the Web address of the spamvertiser's Web site.

Not known to everyone, however, is that this kind of address can include a prefix that the server can treat as a login user ID. More generically, this part of a URL is called *userinfo* because it typically holds a user ID for an account name. The userinfo prefix goes between the `http://` and an @ symbol, in front of the actual Web address. A Web site's server can easily be programmed to receive and record the userinfo portion of any page or image access. If the spammer has programmed the spam run to merge a coded version of your email address, email address database record, or some other identifier associated with your address into the message at this point, the Web site server can record the activity, thus validating your email address as live and fresh if you click the link.

But a Web site server can also be programmed to ignore the information to the left of the @ symbol (and the symbol itself). Therefore, a spammer may include random characters in this prefix location to try to trick content filters that look for instances of URLs in previous spam attempts. This is rather a waste of time in my opinion, because a knowledgeable spam filter creator will be more interested in the part of the URL that cannot change—the domain name after the @ symbol—and simply look for matches to the basic Web site address. Maybe spammers think antispammers will waste time by trying to figure out what the prefix means, thus diverting their attention away from the more easily filterable components of the message.

Slightly more sophisticated uses of this technique try to trick nontechnical users who may peruse the source code of a message to see if the URL is something they recognize. The prefix portion of the URL may contain what appears to be a URL of a site they do business with. Numerous identity-theft phisher messages use this technique so a nosy user would see, say, `citibank.com` at the beginning of a link's source code and believe that the link really goes to a Citibank Web site. But now you know to look further along the URL for the @ sign, and then start noting the real destination. For example, the following link (from a spam wanting me to "verify my account information") navigates to a site in Russia (at the da.ru Web hosting site):

```
<a href="http://www.citibank.com:
ac-fPdYOwoq3F@\x\.dA.RU">
```

Whenever you see a long, convoluted URL, look for an @ symbol, and ignore everything that comes before it.

Message Trick #3: *Claiming you to be a member of an organization with which you have never registered*

Example:

```
You received this email because you're a member
of \x\.
```

Intended Victim(s): Forgetful, lonely, and/or gullible recipients
Description: This may be the most common lie in spam messages bodies. The variations on this Big Lie are endless. For example:

```
You received this message because you registered
at one of the sites in the \x\ Email Network or
opted in through one of our partners.
```

```
You received this message because you are regis-
tered with \x\,  with the email address:
\x\@dannyg.com.
```

```
This is a professional communication for indi-
viduals affiliated with the insurance industry,
who opted-in to receive the email advertisements
we send on behalf of our advertisers, and our-
selves.
```

```
If you believe this e-mail has reached you in
error or if you no longer wish to receive our
Select Correspondence, follow the link below to
unsubscribe.
```

Even if the spammer believes he is telling the truth, he is using unacceptable definitions of "opt-in," wherein the existence of a harvestable email address on the Internet means that the addressee has opted in to receive mail from anyone as often as the sender wants to send it. The spammer may have also been fooled by an email address supplier that lied about the names being opt-in.

In the earlier days of spam, these bogus assertions stating I had requested to receive the mailings used to get my dander up. I took it as an insult to my intelligence, especially since a lot of the messages were sent to addresses harvested from my Web site. When they used the "partner" garbage, I would see red. Eventually I came to realize that the more forcefully a message professed that I had joined, registered, signed up, opted in, or otherwise requested to be sent mail, the less I should believe it. This gets difficult sometimes because the sites that you really do sign up for—and they're the good ones, right?—may state the same thing in their regular mails to you, while providing you a way to unsubscribe from future mailings. It means that you do need to be aware or keep records of those places where you sign up for mailings, and sign up only after checking out the sender to determine whether promises about guarding your privacy are trustworthy.

Message Trick #4: *Making phony claims about knowing your computer problems*

Example:

```
Subject: Warning: Your PC may be infected

[snip]

Have you noticed your computer is running slower
than ever?

The reason for that may have to do with online
advertisers adding SpyWare or AdWare to your
computer without your knowledge. "Spyware" is a
common term for files that are installed on your
system without your knowledge that allow compa-
nies to monitor your Internet activity. "AdWare"
is software that will show you popup ads over
and over. What they don't tell you, however, is
how these files can be extremely dangerous to
your PC and could cause major problems with your
PC.

\X\ removes Spyware and Adware that threaten your
privacy. If you have downloaded music or videos
from the internet, there is a 98.7% chance your
computer is infected with Spyware or Adware.

We are offering every computer owner, including
yourself, the opportunity to scan your computer
to see how many "SpyWare" infections your PC has
free of charge.

To scan your computer for free, click here:

http://www.\x\.com/redirect.php?rid=93551b5b51,=0
2bj5yZ55mbhRGQnlnbuFGZ

Our goal is to put an end to shady online adver-
tising so that Internet users can enjoy the
World Wide Web without having their privacy
intruded upon.
```

Intended Victim(s): Nontechnical computer users

Description: With so many PCs compromised with adware and spyware installed by machine owners who downloaded a variety of free software, it's likely that a spam message targeting owners of sluggish machines would find plenty of recipients eager to learn more.[2] The subject of this kind of message makes it sound as though someone has been monitoring your computer's activity. If you have spyware installed on your machine, someone may, indeed, be monitoring your machine, but that's not why this spam arrived. Such messages go to all kinds of users, including Mac users who aren't affected by PC adware or spyware.

It's true that adware and spyware can sap a PC's processing power and invade your privacy. That garbage infected your computer because you (or someone with access to your machine) welcomed geeks bearing gifts (Chapter 13). Even worse, however, are spam offers that promise to help you uncover and remove offending software. I'd be more wary of these offers than the stuff that may already be on a PC. These guys are counting on you believing that they are concerned with your best interests, and that you'll gladly follow their lead to install and run whatever program they recommend to get rid of other programs.

WATCH OUT!

The offer in the example is a free scan. Because I had not heard of the product name (disguised above), there's no way I'd install it to perform the scan. I would wager that the "scanner" you have to install becomes its own piece of spyware. In the meantime, there are genuinely free programs that do the job and have been checked thoroughly by independent labs to make sure they do not put their own adware or spyware onto your machine in the process.

And note the gall of this advertiser to deride shady online advertising—in *his* spam. Not the best example of online chutzpah, but getting close.

Message Trick #5: Distorting drug names

Example:

```
Subject: How To have real v~a~l~i~u~m, x_a_n_a_x
& v_i_c_o_d_i_n  Today
```

Intended Victim(s): Spam-filtering software

Description: Lots of content-based spam filters are on the lookout for the well-advertised drug names, such as Viagra, Valium, and many more. Online

---

[2] Chapter 13 covers this subject in depth.

drugstores are among the most successful spam-fueled businesses, particularly those "pharmacies" that sell from outside the United States and/or break U.S. law by supplying drugs without a prescription from the buyer's regular doctor.

Demand for lower prices on medications, and the ability to bypass the controls that a drug abuser's physician would place on quantities, will probably keep this segment of the spam world in business unless the drug companies (no particular friends of mine, unless they can step in to eventually get the drug spammers out of our inboxes) and governments step up their efforts to close the loopholes that allow spammers to solicit for business. Of course, if you buy prescription meds from a spammer, you also run the risk of getting counterfeit drugs that are either not the same quality as the real thing or may be downright lethal.

Because drug spam is so prevalent, you see hundreds of variations on the brand-name spelling to prevent the messages from being filtered by ISPs. Techniques include similar-appearing character substitution, intentionally close misspellings (so you know what is meant), and interposing symbols between the characters (as shown in the example). Here is a list of variations for Viagra that arrived in one day's spam:

```
V.i.a.g.r.a
Vi-a-gra
V'l'a'g'r'a
V|agra
vi@gra
V|i|a|g|r|a
Vi@ gra
Via.gra
VIA-GRA
V*I*A*G*R*A
Via-gr-a
V-i-@-g-r-a
V1@GRA
V.I.A.G.R.A
V1AGR@
vi-agra
V'l'a'g'r'a
```

Then there is the technique discussed in Message Trick #1 of inserting garbage tags in an HTML message body to foil the content filters:

```
Vi<!--iTVTg -->agr<!--PipHJ -->a
```

Some medz spammers aren't necessarily too bright. I've seen messages where they mention Viagra numerous times, mostly with corrupted versions to fool the filters, but then they include a couple mentions with it spelled the correct way. Rule #3, I guess.

Message Trick #6: *Distorting other common spam filter words and phrases*

Example:

```
rem©ve
```

Intended Victim(s): Content-based spam filters

Description: One class of content-based spam filter programs not only looks for the presence of certain words and phrases common to spam, but they also assign weighted values to their presence. For example, one filter rule could search a message for a pattern of text that starts with the word "remove," followed anywhere later in the message by the word "click." If the message body contains the phrase "To remove yourself from future mailings, click here," then the rule assigns a point value to this particular message. Matches for additional phrase, word, or character patterns accumulate additional points. After all of the pattern rules are applied to the message, the filter sees if the total point value is above or below the threshold set by the administrator. If the number is over the line, the filter flings the message into a holding bin on the server or deletes it outright (depending on how the administrator has configured the filter).

Content filters pass each incoming message through scores of rules in numerous categories (e.g., disclaimers, make-money-fast, diploma mills, and so on) to determine how it should handle the message. Volunteer supporters of publicly available filter utilities, such as Procmail, keep the rule sets up to date based on recently received spam trends. Spammers try to stay one step ahead of the filter folks by creating new variations on words they use all the time. For some spammers, it has become a kind of game to see how far they can bend the spelling of words and still get the meaning of their messages across to recipients. Recent research reports that the human mind can easily decipher a wide range of intentional errors in spelling. Some recipients may even treat these kinds of messages as a test or puzzle to see if they can understand the "hidden" meaning—like the kids do with their Instant Messages and cell phone short messages. Ah, exactly what the spammer hopes will lure victims to opening and reading their messages.

Message Trick #7: *Using base64 encoding for the message body*

Example:

```
TG9vayBhdCB0aGlzIGRlYWw8aHRtbD48dGFibGUgYm9yZGVyP
SIxIiBjZWxscGFkZGluZz0iMCIgY2VsbHNwYWNpbmc9IjAiIH
N0eWxlPSJib3JkZXItY29sbGFwc2U6IGNvbGxhcHNlIi
```

Intended Victim(s): Content-based spam filters; casual source code viewers

Description: One of the standards on the Internet is a way to convert characters and symbols to a very restricted set of characters. The resulting set has only the letters A through Z (in uppercase and lowercase), the numerals 0 through 9, and the plus (+) and equal sign (=) symbols. Given the 26 letters of the alphabet (for a total of 52 by treating uppercase and lowercase separately), the numerals, and two symbols, you have a total of 64 possible characters. These characters are easily accommodated even by "ancient" computer systems, making them the lowest common denominator among all computer systems. Just as our regular decimal numbering system is called *base10* (with numerals 0 through 9), this 64-character system is called *base64*.

Through the "magic" of math-based conversions, a string of characters containing other symbols, such as the HTML tag angle brackets, quote symbols, and even some accented characters, can be translated into the 64-character set. The nature of the process causes the same original word or phrase to be encoded into a different base64 result if the surrounding text differs from a previous message. Putting the base64-encoded sequence through a reverse conversion process spits out the original characters in all their glory.

Web browsers (and browser rendering engines in HTML-equipped email programs) know how to convert base64 text into its original form. After the spammers compose their email "page," they pass the HTML source code through a base64 encoder program to get the version they'll insert into the message body. Their goal is to trick content-based spam filters that won't necessarily know the base64 encoding for key words they normally look for.

This hasn't stopped content filters, however, because sophisticated filters can also decode base64 text when they see it and run the decoded version through their lookup tables and rule sets. Decoding base64 text is not a particularly intensive computational process, so the added step doesn't bog down the spam filters.

A base64 encoded message does, however, stop the casual source code viewer in his or her tracks. But even then, there are plenty of pages on the Web where anyone can copy the base64 source code into one field, click a button, and see the results in another field (Appendix B). If nothing else, the decoded version lets you see the real source code of the message in a completely safe environment. You can see the URL of the spamvertised Web sites, as well as their dorky disclaimers.

Message Trick #8: *Padding messages with blocks of hidden real words or names and literary selections*

Example:

```
<CENTER><FONT face=Arial color=#616161
size=+1>All Pop</stoichiometry saga immigrate
matrimony thayer carbide cord bloodbath>ular
Me</aiken fontainebleau uninominal
sanitate=20>dications Prescribed &amp; Deli</ogle
sunder czerniak agglutinin delicatessen>vered
Ov</wiretap dreary logician dearie remunerate
midweek incise>ernight!</FONT></CENTER>
```

Intended Victim(s): Bayesian and other statistical content filters

Description: One of the most useful spam-filtering technologies is a modern application of a theorem proven by the eighteenth-century British mathematician, Reverend Thomas Bayes (1702–1761). IANAMM (I am not a math major), so Bayes' formulas might as well be Egyptian hieroglyphics to me. But I marvel at the ingenuity of applying the Bayesian notions of probability to the content of email messages.

Bayesian filtering works best on an individual level because it gets smarter over time when an individual "teaches" the filter about his or her incoming email habits. A Bayesian filter begins life in some ways like a plain-old content filter, with a library of text strings that are known to be employed in spam. For each message that gets through the filter, you tell the filter whether it is a real message or spam. For a legitimate message, the system analyzes the content and adapts its filtering to recognize words and phrases that are most likely to be from mail you want to receive. Over time (and not too long, as it turns out), the filter becomes very proficient at recognizing real messages, while dumping the rest into a holding pen for inspection later for potential false positives. Even if a valid message contains a word or phrase that is commonly associated with spam, the message would have either enough other traits to be treated as legitimate or spam, depending on the predominance of those traits. The more you train the system, the smarter it becomes.

Spammers are fully aware of Bayesian filtering, and dislike it a great deal. The biggest problem that it presents to spammers is that the spammer cannot pretest the filter against a message (or at least not easily). When it comes to other pattern-based filters (particularly server-based filtering), spammers can easily get accounts at the big services and send proposed messages to their own accounts, tweaking the content until the messages get past the filters. Then, spameroo! But because the best Bayesian filtering operates on the individual level, at best, spammers can try to test prospective messages against their own trained systems, which won't have anything like the knowledge of a paleontologist's Bayesian filter.

Thus, spammers try to trick Bayesian filters by loading their email offers with words and names that have nothing to do with the spam offer. In the example above, the words seem to have been selected by their infrequency in typical email English language, presumably to make the Bayesian filter treat the words as coming in a legitimate email. Other attempts at this technique bury large passages from public domain literature above and below the spam offer, hoping that these passages will weigh heavily in favor of allowing the message to pass unscathed through Bayesian filters. Viewing the source code of such messages, you get some Shakespeare or Lucy Maud Montgomery with your male member enlargement patch offer. Zounds and egad!

A developer of a Bayesian filter add-on program called POPFile wrote an analysis about how a spammer could potentially learn about an individual's Bayesian filter characteristics. For the snooping to be effective, the spammer would have to get through a particular Bayesian filter one time, and code the page with one or more Web bugs that report back to the source about the specific recipient and the content of the message that made it through. Theoretically, this is possible, but the amount of processing time and database storage needed to put such an operation into place is antithetical to the massive-volume, automated mentality of the big spammers. And, if you are a good email recipient, you would never even view or preview a message you didn't immediately recognize without first checking the message source code for Web bugs. Right?

Text-burial techniques vary. In the example above, the words are included inside junk HTML tags (Message Trick #1). Unlike most real HTML tags that adhere to the industry standards, a start junk tag does not require a balancing end junk tag. The author of the example above chose to use all end tag formats.

Another text burial technique is to assign the page's background color (usually the default white) to the text. This way, upon closer analysis of the document, the padded text appears to be part of the document body. But white text on a white background is invisible when viewing or previewing the message in your email reader. I've seen what I can only deduce to be desperation on the part of numerous spammers using this trick. When the spam offer occupies fewer than 10 percent of the message body (in bytes), and the laundry list of random words and names fills the other 90 percent, it's clear that this type of filtering must be effective where it's deployed.

Message Trick #9: *Invisibly tracking your viewing or previewing of a message, and verifying your email address as being active*

Examples:

```
<img
src=http://\x\.com:8080/clickopen?msgid=3395019&e
mail=6v500vhf70h" width="1" height="1">

<img
src="http://hnml.track.\x\.com/_o.jpegg?cid=78480
01&ln=1&kin=105933515&email=DANNYG@DANNYG.COM"
height="1" width="1">
```

Intended Victim(s): All unsuspecting recipients, especially those with Preview panes visible in their email programs

Description: The trick of embedding an invisible image into an HTML-based email for tracking purposes is one of the dirtiest tricks in the spammer's repertoire. While it's true that some legitimate confirmed opt-in email outfits do this with newsletters and offers that I have genuinely subscribed to receive, I'm okay with that because I know that I have voluntarily registered my email address with these folks. But I absolutely do not want to verify to a spammer that the address on any message that manages to get into my inbox is a working address. To do so lets spammers put my address into collections of fresh addresses that they can resell to others for additional spam. The tactic affects all computer types with HTML-capable email viewers, including those running on Macintosh and Linux operating systems. All you have to do is preview a message containing one of these Web bugs or beacons, and you've given yourself up to the spamonomy, putting money into other peoples' pockets without your permission or knowledge. It's despicable.

Here's how it works: An email message that comes with HTML-coded content is treated like a Web page in most modern email programs. In fact, on most PCs, the "engine" that displays such email is the same one that the Web browser uses. An HTML-capable email program allows HTML messages to display a variety of fonts, variable font sizes, font and background colors, tables, and images downloaded from a Web server. Thus, the images are not delivered with the email message until you view or preview the message, at which time a code in the HTML instructs your email "browser" to fetch the image from a Web server. The address of the image (its URL) appears in the HTML as part of an < img> tag, more precisely, the URL assigned to the src attribute of the < img> tag.

The key to the tracking scam is the additional information at the end of the URL—the part after the question mark. You'll find a question mark in a URL whenever the address contains some extra information that is "submitted" to the server at the address to the left of the question mark.[3] When the submission arrives at the server, a program inspects the data to the right of the question mark and acts on that information, in whatever way the program author wishes to handle it. In most cases, the data is in the form of what is known as a name/value pair—really, nothing more than a label and some data associated with it. In the first example above, there are two name/value pairs: msgid and email. My guess is that the number assigned to msgid identifies the precise email message content, while the number assigned to email identifies the listing of my email address in the spammer's database. If I view or preview this message in an HTML email window, then the spammer's program logs which message made it through spam filtering for my address and confirms that my address is alive and well. In the meantime, the spammer's program sends back to my email window just enough data to simulate an image to satisfy the < img> tag. Beacons are also the technique behind proof-of-readership email delivery services.

Notice another point about this tag: The dimensions of the "image" are set to one pixel high and one pixel wide—a speck at best if it were a black dot on a white background. If the image were completely transparent (a common feature of images used as spacers in displaying tricky tables in HTML), you would not see it at all, nor would you notice the one pixel of space it occupies on the email page. Most image-based Web beacons occur at the bottom of the message, where even the speck won't interfere with anything.

Not all unwanted sales pitch spam messages contain beacons, but many do. The only way to know that the message contains a beacon is to view the message source code. You may see just codes, like the one shown above, or more explicit listings of your email address either in plain view or encoded in some fashion. In Chapter 17, you'll learn how to prevent yourself from getting scammed by the Web beacon.

---

[3] This question mark business isn't an industry Web standard, but it has become a universally accepted practice.

Message Trick #10: *Sending a bogus confirmed opt-in request*

Example:

```
Thank You for requesting \x\ Daily Garfield
Cartoon, through our friends at the \x\ network.
Your subscription is not yet confirmed, and if
this email has reached you by mistake you need
do nothing—you will receive no further emails
from \x\.
```

Intended Victim(s): Gullible and forgetful recipients

Description: If I didn't receive so many of these from a variety of senders, I'd almost believe they were sent as a result of someone (not me) physically typing my address into some registration form to try to get me to sign up for some mailing.[4] But I'm convinced that these are simply disguises for regular ol' spam using purchased or harvested lists. Passing an otherwise proper confirmed opt-in verification is just another spammer lie. Whenever a "confirmation" includes an aggressive sales pitch, I am immediately suspicious.

Links associated with these "requests" contain the kind of codes I'd expect from a genuine confirmed opt-in service. And, by and large, the same requests don't keep popping up—at least not frequently enough for me to notice them.

It may also be that the senders who keep sales spiels out of their confirmation messages are trying to do the right thing with questionable lists that they acquired in good faith from list vendors that lied about their opt-in-ness. If that's the case, then I laud the senders for taking some steps to cleanse the list, but I'd rather they more fully vet their list suppliers before risking their reputations with these bogus sign-up verifications. After all, if the list suppliers use harvested or purchased addresses, there is a good chance my address will be on a future list. A second request like this will mark the sender as a spammer through and through.

A rise in confirmation messages after the U.S. CAN-SPAM law took effect makes me wonder, though, how serious these requests are. Here's one I received that speaks volumes:

---

4 While scanning one day's spam, I noticed three different confirmations arriving at my server within nine seconds. The sign-ups were for a gambling newsletter, the cartoon shown in the Message Trick #10 example (associated with some kind of cooking recipes), and a sweepstakes game. All of the headers were very different (one was forged), and the confirmation URLs were hosted on three different ISPs. I don't think there was any connection among the three "offers."

```
Hello Danny...

It appears you have requested information from
one of our subscribers. In order to receive this
information, we require your confirmation that
you actually wanted it.

Here is a brief description of the information
you requested:

If you requested this information, please click
the link below:

http://www.\x\.com/confirmit.htm?tag=187EE699-
3A17-4DF7-9993-811607875AFE

If you did not request this information, please
just ignore this confirmation request and you
won't receive any further information
```

The place where the information I "requested" would appear is blank. Yes, it's true, I requested nothing from you. Why are you bothering me with this phony confirmation? All I can hope is that this spammer will, indeed, drop my address from his database because I will not respond. Well, I can dream, can't I?

Message Trick #11: *Using numeric IP addresses (not plain-language domain names) in clickable links and image retrievals*

Example:

```
<a href="http://64.125.86.\x\/p.html">Watch the
hot blonde Paris H!LTON ...</a>
```

Intended Victim(s): Nontechnical recipients

Description: Web addresses aren't always the plain-language URLs you see at most Web sites. In fact, as described in Chapter 4, every time you click a link or choose a bookmark in your browser with a plain-language URL in it, your browser looks up the numeric IP address corresponding to that name in one of thousands of Domain Name Service (DNS) machines around the world. This lookup is necessary because computers communicate with each other on the Internet only via their numeric IP addresses.

As a result, it's no big deal for a link in a Web page or email message to use a numeric IP address; it's just not particularly user-friendly. Respectable e-commerce sites spend tons of money promoting their domain brand names to get them ingrained in the minds of the public. In most browsers, and lots of Web-enabled email programs, when you roll the mouse atop a clickable link, the URL associated with that link appears in the status bar of the program window to let the user know ahead of time where the link will be going if clicked.

Using IP addresses as link addresses is meant to disguise the domain of the destination. It may be a case that a legitimate site has been hacked, and the IP address contains a reference to a directory that the hacker has installed on the machine without the owner's knowledge. The domain name of the site might give away the deception. Many of the eBay phishing scams have links to sites whose domains are clearly located in South Korea. If the link in the mail has only an IP address, a curious roll of the mouse pointer atop the link doesn't tip off the user that the destination is Korea, rather than eBay's real site. Links to pornographic sites also commonly use numeric IP addresses, although I'm not sure why, unless the initial link destination is hijacked and redirects the user to the real porn site.

Message Trick #12: *Sending an HTML message consisting of nothing but a link and an image*

Example:

```
<html><body>

<center><a
href=3D"http://Dannyg.\x\.com/host/default.asp?ID
=mik"><img src="http://mj.\x\.com/pics/gvl.gif"
height="270" width="405"></a></center>

</html></body>
```

Intended Victim(s): Content-based filters

Description: The thought behind this approach is that the less information supplied directly in the message, the less likely that content-based filters will reject the message. Unless the Subject: line of the message accurately reflects the subject of the advertisement, neither a computerized filter nor a snoopy source code recipient will know what the ad is for. But when you view or preview the message with its image, you get the full spiel in all of its polished graphic-ness. You'll probably see an area of the image that says "Click Here," or the like. But by surrounding the image with the <a> tag, the spammer has made the entire image clickable: no matter where you click on the image, you'll go to the same place.[5] I get the impression that

---

[5] The same technique appears very frequently in banner ads, where you are presented with what look like several buttons for different options, but the entire image is just one linked hotspot. The advertiser just wants the click-through.

there are tons of image libraries for every prescription medicine on the market, which many of the pill pushing spammers call upon. It's rare that the domains of the image and the link that leads you to the order form are the same or are even hosted on the same continent.

The bad news for spammers, however, is that some content-based filters are getting smart enough to flag messages that provide nothing or little more than <a> and <img> tags. I also find a lot of spam now combining this technique with boatloads of attempted statistical filter busters described in Message Trick #8.

Message Trick #13: Labeling the message as a reply in the Subject: line

Example:

```
Subject: RE: At last, smart filtering technology
that works
```

Intended Victim(s): Forgetful recipients

Description: When you scan a list of messages awaiting in your email program's inbox, you may be drawn to those that begin with the RE: prefix. Most email programs insert this prefix into any message that the sender initiates in reply to something you sent to the sender. When spammers produce a new message with the RE: prefix, they are trying to trick you into opening the message under the assumption you want to read a reply to a message thread you are already engaged in. Some email users generate a great deal of mail in a day, hence they may not remember the subject of every message they sent. But by and large, you would recognize a subject that was of enough interest to you that you initiated a message to begin with. Anything else you should treat as potential spam.

Naturally, spammers obey Rule #1 to varying degrees, so the subject after the bogus RE: prefix may be designed to resemble a non-specific subject that you might have written or previously replied to:

```
RE: Important
Re: Your winning ebay auction
Re: Word file
Re: hi
re; Your Order
RE: Status of your account
```

Spammers also exploit the nasty habit email users have for forwarding all kinds of tripe to their friends, family, and colleagues. Email programs usually plug the FW: prefix in front of the original Subject: line when forwarding a message. Spammers would love it if those who actually received their messages also forwarded them on to their best friends. But since the spammers can't count on recipients doing that, they start the whole process by labeling the original spam message with the FW: prefix, under the assumption that someone receiving a forwarded message is more likely to open it so as not to offend the "considerate" person who forwarded the message in the first place. In a large corporation, the fact that the name in the From: field is strange may not be out of the ordinary.

This RE: and FW: technique is popular enough among the most deceptive spammers that you should be immediately suspicious of any message bearing these prefixes when you don't recognize the sender's identity. Nine times out of ten, such messages will be spam or viruses trying to get past content filters and unobservant recipients.

Message Trick #14: *Inserting white garbage text into the message*
Example:

```
<font size="+5" face="Arial, Helvetica, sans-
serif"> <strong><a
href="http://www.\x\.com"><EM>Cli</EM><FONT
color=#ffffff size=2>d</FONT><EM>ck</EM><FONT
color=#ffffff size=2>d</FONT><EM>here</EM><FONT
color=#ffffff size=2>d</FONT><EM>to</EM><FONT
color=#ffffff size=2>d</FONT><EM>ord</EM><FONT
color=#ffffff size=2>d</FONT><EM>er</EM><FONT
color=#ffffff size=2>d</FONT><EM>n</EM><FONT
color=#ffffff
size=2>d</FONT><EM>ow!</EM></a></strong></font>
```

Intended Victim(s): Content-based spam filters
Description: If spammers want to include their offer in text, they must get you to act in some fashion—clicking someplace to visit the spamvertised Web site, usually. The most effective verbiage reads something like: "Click here to order now!" Naturally, any content-based spam filter worth its salt will be on the lookout for things like "click here" and "order now" as telltale signs of spam. If the filter is intelligent enough to bypass all HTML tags that could get in the way of the strings (including junk tags), then the remaining message would still be visible to the filter, and the message would be escorted to the Suspected Spam folder. That means that the spammer needs to go one step further and insert some extra junk into the text, but do it in such a way that the recipient doesn't see it. Time for some HTML tricks.

When you surround HTML text with a link (`<a>`) tag, the text not only becomes clickable, but the default style applied to the text includes an underline and a blue color (or purple if the link had been recently visited by the browser). An underlined blue text link is very common on Web pages, and most Web users know what it means. But if you insert some extra text that has the same color as the background, that text won't be visible to the user and a content filter would be fooled by it. One (old-fashioned but still useful) way to specify a color for a piece of text in HTML is to surround the text with a `<font>` tag and assign a color in a format that specifies the color in what is called a hexadecimal triplet (values for red, green, and blue components of a color using base16 numbering, well known to programmers). The hexadecimal color for white is #ffffff (essentially, full blasts of red, green, and blue to form white). Of course, the extra text will take up some space, so it's best to make the extra text small enough not to hurt the readability. The following illustration shows what the recipient sees from the HTML example shown above:

Cli ck here to ord er n ow!

What the user doesn't see are the intervening small "d" characters in white inserted between some spam-alert keywords.

If instead of the white color specified in the message HTML the color were black, the instruction would look like the following:

Cli_dck_d here_d to_d ord_der_d n_dow!

Therefore, a smart content-based filter that looked past the HTML tags would see the text "Clidckd hered tod ordderd ndow!" and perhaps be fooled. Only if the spammer utilized the same letter and letter positions on lots of spam would the filter ever associate this string of text with spam.

So-called white garbage text is nothing new, nor is it used only in the way shown here. Large chunks of random words, random characters, or paragraph-long excerpts from public domain literary works find their way into messages intended to fool Bayesian filters (a tactic called "hash busting"). Because there aren't too many ways in HTML to specify white text, the spam filter folks quickly updated their capabilities to look for `<font>` tags whose `color` attribute values were equal to the limited ways "white" could be referenced (`color="white"`, `color=white`, `color="#ffffff"`, and `color=#ffffff`). Spammers discovered this, and altered their tactics to use other colors that were nearly white, or at least white enough to be unseen by typical recipients. Here's an example from the wild with a near-white color that can't be seen:

```
<font color=#fefefe>toyr akywhdzy k gnsqopbqrx
ckykebxwgigozs j.</font>
```

The hope was that there would be too many combinations for the filter makers to block.

And thus the whack-a-mole game continues: spammers keep popping up their heads, and filter writers keep bopping them with mallets.

Message Trick #15: *Using a misleading message body to trick you into clicking through to the spamvertised Web site.*

Example:

```
Received: from isp.co.nz ([65.167.41.\x\]) by
dannyg.com (8.12.10) id i0E1ULpa098187 for
<\x\@dannyg.com>; Tue, 13 Jan 2004 18:30:26 -0700
(MST)
Message-ID:
<85c701c3dac4$902aa2e9$1eada812@isp.co.nz>
From: "Jesse Baker" <bakerfg@ghl.de>
To: \x\@dannyg.com
Subject: hello
Date: Wed, 14 Jan 2004 13:32:26 -0400
MIME-Version: 1.0
Content-Type: text/plain
Content-Transfer-Encoding: 8bit
X-UIDL: J]n!!9~a"!:+=!!QGk!!

Hey!
Oh my god it's been am so long since we talked
last!

I have been wondering s how you have been doing?

We never get a chance to see each other anymore.
qvf

I sent you something last time and was wondering
if you got it?

If not i included it below so let me know if you
like it
http://www.\x\.com/?rid=1002

Get back to me as soon as you can, alright?

Thanks

Your love!
jkzajbck
```

Intended Victim(s): Unsuspecting lonely hearts
Description: This is the kind of message content deception scam that drives me to distraction. One day I received two of these messages in the space of 15 minutes. The two messages had different From: names, different spamvertised Web site domains, different zombie PC origination points (Comcast and Sprint networks), and different forged points of origin (New Zealand and Germany). A few random pieces of the messages (an errant character in the "I have been..." sentence, the three characters after the "We never" paragraph, and random characters in the last line) differed between each message. Everything else about the two messages was identical, including the formatting and line breaks.

What is the subject of this offer? It's impossible to tell from the content. It purports to be a personal message from a long-lost, um, apparently very close friend. The first names of the two forged From: fields are Jesse and Haley, names that could be male or female. Because I'm a male recipient, I guess I'm supposed to believe they're female admirers; a female recipient could easily interpret the message and names just the opposite.

So, again, what's the offer? Despite the different domain names in the two messages' links, they both ultimately lead to the same spamvertised Web site hosted in Romania (both domains claim to be registered from Belize). The product or service? Prescription meds.

Now I feel betrayed by my two lovers. They simply wanted me to order meds from Romania. I suppose it didn't help their credibility that two of my (unknown) girlfriends sent me the same message only 15 minutes apart (Rule #3 in action). I'll never love again. Boo hoo.

Message Trick #16: Displaying a phony link URL

Example:

```
<a href="http://www.visa.com:UserSession=2f6q9uuu
88312264trzzz55884495&usersoption=SecurityUpdate&
StateLevel=GetFrom@66.235.192.\x\/visa.htm">
http://www.visa.com</a>
```

Intended Victim(s): Recipients who don't view the message source code
Description: This trick is less meaningful in spam (it's used there, too), but really comes in handy for the scammers who send the identity theft phishing messages. The main goal of these messages is to make you believe that they come from a Web site or financial institution where you have an account. The message proclaims that you must click a link to visit the company's Web site to verify your account information. Typical phishing tricks

include blending logo images retrieved from the real institution into the email message.

To make their ploy even more believable, they place what appears to be a URL in the message as the text to click to reach the supposed verification Web site. The trouble is, the text that looks like a URL is just text, and has nothing to do with the destination of the link; the true destination is the URL that is assigned to the href attribute of the <a> tag surrounding the visible text. The fact that the visible URL is blue and underlined is merely the way that Web browser engines (by default) display any text that goes between the HTML <a> and </a> tags. Most of the time you'll see something like "Click here" in that spot, but in this case, the scammer tries to trick even the HTML-aware recipient into thinking that the link is to the underlined URL.

In this example, too, the scammer tries to head off the more knowledgeable user by employing another URL disguise technique that is useful in email programs that show a link's URL in the window's status bar. Notice that the long URL value assigned to the href attribute of the <a> tag starts with the visa.com domain, followed immediately by what look like name/value pairs of extra data submitted with the URL. In a real URL, a question mark separates the link address from the name/value pairs; in this phony-baloney URL, the scammer uses a colon. The length of the meaningless name/value pairs is intended to be wide enough to keep the real part of the URL (after the @ symbol) out of view in the status bar. That's right, the real URL of the link is a numeric IP address—to a Web site run by a lowlife who had an account at a Santa Monica, California, Internet service provider.

Message Trick #17: Providing a bogus unsubscribe URL

Example:

```
<a href="http://www.moveaheassdsdf233.com/Dbt/
re.php">nomail</a>
```

Intended Victim(s): Anyone who doesn't know not to try unsubscribing from the worst of the spammers

Description: Some antispam laws around the world require that commercial messages contain a link or other free way to unsubscribe from the list. When unsuspecting recipients get messages they don't want, their first instinct may be to unsubscribe from the mailing if such a link presents itself. As described elsewhere throughout this book, this is usually a bad idea. When the message (as revealed through its source code view) utilizes additional spam tricks, it's even more reason to avoid the unsubscribe link.

The above example shows a link (<a>) tag that turns the word "nomail" into clickable text, with the URL appearing in the status bar of some email readers. Notice that the right end of the URL points to a server program called re.php—a program that will remove me from the list. The problem, however, is that the domain provided in the URL does not exist. If you click on the link, your Web browser comes to the front and tries to load the URL. You'll get an error message that the site doesn't exist. To an experienced old guy (yeah, that's me), the presence of letter sequences "asd" and "sdf" are usually clues to someone typing garbage letters (look at an English computer keyboard to understand). Other tip-offs that an unsubscribe link in a message won't work include IP addresses for active spamvertised links, lots of garbage character hash-buster text in the body, and Received: headers indicating transmission through a zombie PC or proxy server.

Providing a phony link does not satisfy any of the legal requirements for unsubscribe links. The laws read that the links must work. This one does not. Nor do the ones whose links consist of email addresses. Of course, I'd never unsubscribe from a mailing I didn't subscribe to. The spamonomy won't stop unless we make the spammers believe nobody's home.

Message Trick #18: *Encoding URLs with HTML numeric character references*

Example (partially edited to disguise actual URL):

```
<a href="http://pecos@&#119;&#119;&#119;&#46; \x\
&#112;&#105;&#108;&#108;&#115;&#46;&#99;&#111;&#1
09;&#47;&#105;&#110;&#100;&#101;&#120;&#46;&#112;
&#104;&#112;&#63;&#112;&#105;&#100;&#61;&#101;&#1
18;&#97;&#112;&#104;&#55;&#55;&#57;&#48;"><B>V1AG
RA Just $1.80</B></font></a>
```

Intended Victim(s): Automated spam analyzers and amateur spam investigators

Description: This one gets a little nerdy, so fasten your seatbelt.

To accommodate a variety of written languages in HTML rendering engines, the HTML standards body adopted a system that allows any character (including those of non-Roman languages, such as Chinese, Arabic, and Russian) to be conveyed in a document. It is up to the Web browser (and its operating system) to provide the necessary support to display the character in the desired font, but the key point is that the character value is preserved in the document during transmission to the user's machine.

The technique is called a *character reference,* meaning a standard way to reference any given character among all known written languages. Through work of other standards bodies, unique numeric values have been assigned to each character of all languages (yes, it's a lot of characters!). In HTML, a character can be referenced by its number in the format:

```
&#n;
```

where "n" is the number (however small or big it may be). If you had the Appendix B lookup table for the characters in the Latin character set used in most URLs, for instance, you find that the number for the lowercase letter "w" is 119. To represent that letter in an HTML page with its character reference, you could write:

```
&#119;
```

The sequence "www." would then be:

```
&#119;&#119;&#119;&#46;
```

where 46 is the number for the period (dot) character.

In everyday use, numeric entities are rarely used for Latin characters because it's obviously more convenient to use and edit with the real characters; moreover, regular characters need fewer bytes to convey a given character than its corresponding character reference: "w" is 1 byte; "w" is 6 bytes.

When an HTML-capable mail viewer encounters numeric character references like these, the rendering engine acts just like a Web browser: It converts the references to their characters, ready for us to read. Link URLs in this form are clickable, as in a browser window, but you won't be able to decipher the URL without clicking on the link to visit the site—forcing a click-through for which the spammer may get paid a few cents. You can, however, preview the URL without visiting the site with the help of a converter (Appendix B).

So why does a spammer go to all the trouble of encoding URLs this way? Obfuscation, my friend. In truth, it doesn't slow down the experienced spam tracker, so the spamvertised site will eventually be reported—perhaps not with the same volume as if the URL were in the clear, but enough to get the site in trouble with an ISP that acts against spammers using its service to host spam destinations. In fact, the domain to which the unedited URL in the above example pointed was no longer accessible a month after the spam arrived. The domain registration is still valid, so it could pop up again at some other host, which is why I don't want to advertise the complete domain.

Message Trick #19: *Attaching an executable file*

Example:

```
------------CF4999440015005
Content-Type: application/x-zip-compressed;
name="photos.zip"
Content-Transfer-Encoding: base64

Content-Disposition: attachment; filename=
"photos.zip"

UEsDBAoAAAAAMgAhS+R0AohIDIAACAyAAAOAAAAcGhvdG9zL
mpwZy5leGVNWpAAAwAAAAQAAAD//wAAuAAAAAAAABAAAAAAA
AAAAAAAAAAAAAAAAAAAAAAAAAAAAAAAAAAAAAAAAAAACAAAAADh+
6DgC0Cc0huAFMzSFUaGlzIHByb2dyYW0gY2Fubm90IGJlIHJl
biBpbiBET1MgbW9kZS4NDQokAAAAAAAA
...
```

Intended Victim(s): Recipients lacking up-to-the-minute antivirus protection

Description: Viruses, worms, and Trojan horse infections arrive mostly via email attachments. The attachments come in many file formats, including the most popular Windows-specific types:

.bat	Executable Windows and DOS batch file
.exe	Executable application file
.pif	Program information files, which are capable of executing embedded program code
.scr	Screensaver files, which are capable of executing embedded program code
.zip	Compressed ZIP files, which, when unzipped automatically, run their expanded programs

Such files are usually accompanied by a message that tries its level best to trick you into opening the attached file: promises of sexually explicit photos; "cool" screensavers; even security patches that purport to come directly from Microsoft itself (they don't, but the From: fields of the messages try to trick you into believing otherwise). The subject of the message containing the above example was:

```
Subject: Re[2]: our private photos
```

It's trying to make believe this message and attachment have been passed around the "in crowd."

Resisting the temptation to open these files is incredibly difficult, especially for young and computer-newbie recipients who have never experienced the "thrill" of having their computer infected by whatever payload arrives in the attachment. Because some of these payloads propagate themselves via email to addresses in the infected machine's address book, you may receive one of these enticements from the computer of someone you know. The From: address may be your best girlfriend, but she didn't send you the file. If you're not expecting the file from her, check with her first to make sure she actually sent it, and that she knows what it is and where it came from. Don't let yourself be conned by the clever, familiar, or threatening wording in the message. It may be the virus writer's words leading you and your computer astray.

Message Trick #20: *Shaming users of safe email programs into using HTML-enabled mail viewers*

Example:

```
This message contains an HTML formatted message
but your email client does not support the dis-
play of HTML. Please view this message in a dif-
ferent mail client or forward this email to a
web-based mail system.
```

Intended Victim(s): Users of older email programs

Description: Some messages include both plain and HTML segments so that recipients with both types of email programs will get the "benefit" of the sales spiel. For example, if you create an email message in the heavily HTML-reliant AOL or MSN mail programs, you actually send both an HTML formatted version and a version that has the tags stripped from the message so that others with non-HTML Web programs can easily read your message. But because a lot of spam designers believe that their HTML layouts are so effective at snagging customers, they don't want anyone to see their message unless they get the full Technicolor (and trick-enhanced) effect. To draw recipients to the HTML version, they place something like the message shown above in the example in the plain-text part of the message.

Frankly, if you have an email program that doesn't render HTML, you're giving yourself a big break. You won't see some of the spam, nor will you accidentally transmit Web beacon data back to the server or accidentally click through a link to put money into the spammer's pocket.

Alas, the world is heading toward HTML email programs as the default setting, so the vast majority of users with those settings in their Outlook email program see HTML-rendered content. Poop!

Message Trick #21: *Embedding a self-loading computer infection into an HTML frame (`<iframe>`) in the message.*

Example:
```
<HTML><HEAD></HEAD><BODY>
<iframe src=cid:Y3150b6Xn73C5d height=0 width=0>
</iframe>
<FONT></FONT></BODY></HTML>

--X5Gcez2KnM0ycO
Content-Type: audio/x-midi;
     name=Sids.pif
Content-Transfer-Encoding: base64
Content-ID: <Y3150b6Xn73C5d>

TVqQAAMAAAAEAAAA//8AALgAAAAAAAAQAAAAAAAAAAAAAAAA
AAAAAAAAAAAAAAAAAAAAAAAAAAAAAAAA2AAAAA4fug4AtAnNIb
gBTM0hVGhpcyBwcm9ncmFtIGNhbm5vdCBiZSBydW4gaW4gRE9
TIG1vZGUuDQ0KJAAAAAAAAAAYmX3gXPgTs1z4E7Nc+BOzJ+Qf
s1j4E7Pf5B2zT/gTs7Tn
...
```

Intended Victim(s): Recipients with unpatched Windows 95, 98, 98SE, and ME systems

Description: This is a nasty one that takes advantage of a security flaw in the browser engine that comes with Internet Explorer (IE) 5 and 5.5 (and can persist through an upgrade to IE 6 if you perform only a minimal install of the upgrade). Microsoft issued a patch for this hole in 2001, but as we all know, not everyone installs security patches in a timely fashion (or ever).

In the code above, the HTML portion of the email message body has little more than an `<iframe>` tag set. An iframe acts like its own window embedded within an HTML page. In this case, the size of the iframe window is zero, meaning you aren't supposed to see any remnants of it. What's so evil about this exploit is that it does its dirty work when you simply view or preview the message—no double-clicking or opening attachments necessary. More important, the URL of the data that loads into this window is a special URL that points to a batch of content that arrives with the message. The `<iframe>` attribute that says `src=cid:Y3150b6Xn73C5d` references the ID of the content segment that comes after the HTML portion.[6]

While the label of this base64-encoded stuff claims it is a type of sound file (in the popular MIDI format), the name of this embedded attachment is a file name ending in .pif, an executable format. In an unpatched system, the

---

[6] See Message Trick #23 for more about Content-Type declarations.

browser engine has complete faith in the content-type label, and believes the content is one of the safe types. In truth, the data is potentially deadly, and will start executing as soon as all of the base64 data loads into the iframe (nearly instantaneously).

This exploit still survives in spam, as this example from December 2003 demonstrates, but it is becoming less frequent as more users upgrade to Windows XP and patch their older systems. Still, plenty of machines connected to the Internet remain vulnerable to this exploit, especially in places where keeping systems up to date may be a low priority, such as homes and schools, where users typically aren't careful about avoiding spam or any suspicious message. The subject of this message was `Hello, darling`, a difficult tease to resist if you aren't acquainted with the evil ways of hackers, scammers, and spammers.

Message Trick #22: *Capturing and reporting system information via JavaScript*

Example:

```
<!-- www2.\x\.com/ web tools statistics hit
counter code -->
<script language="javascript">
```

{some JavaScript code here collects system/browser data and writes it to the end of an <img> URL like a web bug}

```
</script>
```

Intended Victim(s): Recipients with JavaScript enabled for email
Description: I've spent the last eight years of my professional life immersed in JavaScript, so I'm well aware of its strengths and weaknesses. The trick I'm reporting here is nothing more "sinister" than can occur in any Web page you visit, and it reveals no genuinely personal information stored on your computer. But I believe you should be aware that information about your browser and computing system can be passed to a Web server when this trick is being used and you have not turned off JavaScript for email browsing.

Any Web page viewed in a browser with JavaScript turned on (which it is in most browsers, by default) can obtain information about your browser version, operating system type, monitor size, system language, system clock time zone setting, and some other less valuable pieces of environmental information. Information about your browser version and operating system type is sent to a Web browser for each page and image request anyway, even with JavaScript turned off—information passed along as data called the

USERAGENT. Additional items, such as system language, monitor size, and time zone setting are not part of the USERAGENT string, but over the years have been deemed innocuous enough to be accessible to JavaScript in regular Web pages. Scripts can make practical use of this information, such as adjusting time-based calculations to work in your time zone, or sizing a window to fill the screen (although I personally hate it when sites start screwing with my browser window sizes and locations).

When the script that comes in the above example runs, it reads the properties of the browser and system, accumulating the pieces of information into a sequence of text. After the data is gathered (it takes a tiny fraction of a second), the text is appended to an image URL, and the script literally writes the `<img>` tag and its data-encrusted URL to the browser page, thus causing the data to be delivered to the server at that URL. A program on the server can capture that data and do with it as it pleases.

The examples I've seen of JavaScript gathering this kind of data in an email are primarily geared toward gathering statistics about the systems used by the mail's viewers. The scripts execute when you simply view or preview the message. Unfortunately, because the scripts arrive by email with your address on it, the address can be associated with the system statistics being gathered. Therefore, your personal identity can be associated with your system and browser information.

Now that the explanation is out of the way, take it from me, Mr. JavaScript: JavaScript has no place in an email message. Look through all of your email program's preferences, and see if you can turn off scripting for email (and for newsgroup reading, if that's an option). Leave client-side scripting to the Web page browser, where it can do a lot of good.

Message Trick #23: Using quoted-printable HTML content-encoding types

Example:

```
<img src=3d"http://images=2epaypal=2ecom/images/
pixel=2egif"=height=3d"29" width=3d"1" border=
3d"0">
```

Intended Victim(s): Casual human spam investigators and some content-based filters or analyzers

Description: This tactic isn't so much a trick as a recognized Internet standard that just looks funky when you view the source code of an HTML-based email message. If I were to go into full details, a pocket protector would soon start growing in your shirt pocket. I'll try to keep it simple.

Due to the historic aim of the Simple Mail Transfer Protocol (SMTP) to reduce complexity, the early standard limited the range of characters that could be guaranteed to survive a journey from sender to recipient. When a more modern email message contains separate portions that are readable in a plain-text mail reader and in an HTML-aware mail reader, these portions have to be compartmentalized and labeled in the message body so that the mail program knows which section it should display. This same kind of compartmentalization is how a file attachment is glued onto a message body— leaving it up to the receiving email program to separate out the attachment that the recipient can use, independent of the message.

To help the receiving email program know what's what, messages usually contain advisories about the kind of content being conveyed and in what form the data is encoded. For a text-only email, you commonly find the following fields in the header:

```
MIME-Version: 1.0
Content-Type: text/plain; charset="US-ASCII"
Content-Transfer-Encoding: 7bit
```

The MIME-Version line needs to be there, but you can ignore it for this discussion.[7] The Content-Type field indicates that the message body is all plain text, using a character set known as US-ASCII, whose characters (letters, numerals, punctuation, and control characters such as Tab and Carriage Return) number no more than 128 (the highest number that can be represented with combinations of seven binary digits—0000000, 0000001, 0000010, etc.). If I'm losing you, don't worry. There is no test later, and I describe this only to set up the next contrasting tidbits.

When the message body is composed only as HTML, the message headers typically read as follows:

```
MIME-Version: 1.0
Content-Type: text/html
Content-Transfer-Encoding: quoted-printable
```

Thus, the entire content consists of text with HTML markup. The text also uses a type of encoding known as "quoted-printable," which means that the original content may contain any kind of known character (such as a Chinese pictograph character), but the data for the character is represented in a special format that allows it to be conveyed using the very limited 7-bit

---

[7] MIME stands for Multipurpose Internet Mail Extensions, a standard that has been at Version 1.0 since 1982 (RFC 822). Although the standard anticipated the possibility of future versions, to date, the version remains unchanged.

range of characters (the US-ASCII character set, which is "printable" on an old-fashioned teletype printer). The conversion operation is rather nerdy, but suffice it to say that the process is made possible because every known language character has a standard number associated with it. To represent the number in a compact (and mathematically convenient) way, the hexadecimal (base16) counting system is used, a system that we humans would be using if we had 16 fingers and 16 toes. Decimal numerals are 0123456789; hexadecimal numerals are 0123456789ABCDEF.[8]

The impact of quoted-printable encoding is minimal on regular running English text, which means we can usually read those words even when viewing the source code. But some encoders prefer to use hexadecimal equivalents for various symbols, line breaks, and even punctuation, including those that would otherwise be part of the US-ASCII character set. To denote a hexadecimal character in this type of encoding, the character is preceded with an equal sign (=). We humans who look at the source code of such encoded messages see all these = signs and weird two-character thingies afterward, like =3D. When a program on the decoding end sees the = symbol, it knows to throw away the visible = sign and treat the next unbroken batch of characters as a hexadecimal number corresponding to some character. For example, upon encountering the sequence =3D, an decoder tosses the = sign (it's just acting as a kind of switch, after all) and does the equivalent of looking up the 3D character in a hexadecimal table to see which character it decodes to. Hexadecimal 3D is a real equal sign (=). Aha! That's why when you see an HTML tag attribute assigned this way:

```
height=3D0
```

the browser treats it like:

```
height=0
```

Similarly, if the sender (or his encoding routine) tries to hide a link URL with this kind of encoding, the source code displays:

```
www=2Edannyg=2Ecom
```

Hexadecimal 2E corresponds to the period character, leading the email program to render:

```
www.dannyg.com
```

---

8   The RFC document that describes this encoding system wants hexadecimal numerals letters (A—F) to be all uppercase. In practice, email programs and browsers interpret lowercase versions without any problem.

Thus the spammer has yet another way to try to obfuscate a spamvertised URL. Occasionally, you also see the spammer go one step further, by breaking up the URL with a carriage return in the middle of it. This also gets a little tricky to explain, but bear with me.

Quoted-printable content is limited to a line length of 76 characters. An encoder (or author) can insert what is called a "soft" line break to act just like a word-wrapping instruction at the end of a line. A trailing = sign at the end of a line (as seen in the source code view of a message) signifies such a soft return. The email program that decodes the text simply removes the soft line breaks when restoring the content for display in the email view or preview window. Thus, a spammer could intentionally break up spammy words or spamvertised Web site URLs with such a soft break (or insert junk tags to get the lines to extend long enough to force the encoder to make the breaks) in the hopes that content analyzers will be thrown off course:

```
Get cheap presc=
criptions at <a href=3D"www=2Eexa=
mple=2Ecom">Medzzzz</a>
```

Software that decodes quoted-printable content restores the above gibberish to normal HTML for interpretation in the email view or preview window:

```
Get cheap prescriptions at <a
href="www.example.com">Medzzzz</a>
```

While the encoding scheme shown here was originally designed for practical reasons, it can be abused to obfuscate telltale signs of spamminess.

Message Trick #24: *Lying about recording your subscription IP address and timestamp*

Examples:

```
You are receiving this message as a subscriber
of the \x\ Network or Partners.

We take Privacy Very seriously, and have IP
address and timestamp on file for every sub-
scriber.

----------------------

DANNY GOODMAN. You requested the information con-
tained in this e-mail when you signed up on
01/27/04 using dannyg@dannyg.com from IP
```

```
202.111.81.133. If you no longer wish to receive
information on unique products and services
through our network, you can opt-out by clicking
on the link below.
```

Intended Victim(s): Nontechnical recipients.

Description: More proof that Rule #1 (Spammers lie) permeates the email marketing business. The first example shown above is from a message sent to an address that could have only been harvested (not from my Web site, by the way). I wonder which IP address the first one has on file. Since I couldn't have personally signed up with that particular address (and certainly didn't go through any confirmed opt-in process with the sender or "partners"), maybe the IP address is that of some slimy email marketer who harvested the address in the first place, and figured that any harvestable address has opted in to the world. My guess, however, is that there is no such record or timestamp on file.

The second example confirms Rule #1. It's pretty bold to actually present an IP address as proof of my registration. Expecting a user to be shocked and awed by the inclusion of a supposed IP address at time of "registration," I guess the sender of the second message didn't expect me to check it. But I did check. I would have had to be physically located in China to sign up to that sender's mailing list. The unsubscribe link referenced in the message leads to a Web site hosted in Hong Kong.

(Note to the two spammers: If either of you think I'm going to inquire or correct you, you've got another thing coming. I'll just keep reporting your spew and sending the messages to Dave Null on the server.[9])

Message Trick #25: *Boosting search engine ratings through URL redirection*

Example:

```
http://rd.yahoo.com/zljqdt8lqmp03ccxxk7031voqziyj
ztx2c06zy50sxum41ps4owko/*http://www.\x\.biz/?a=0
0005&c=17
```

Intended Victim(s): Shoppers using search engines to locate Web sites to buy spamvertised products

Description: Getting a Web site to rank high in a search engine's results is an important marketing tool, and not easy to accomplish. If you hear about a new product by way of a spam Subject: listing but don't want to follow the

---

9 Dave Null is a pseudonym for the Unix trash directory whose path is /dev/null. That's where all my blocked incoming spam goes when I'm not trolling for the latest evidence of Rules #1 and #3.

link to the spamvertised Web site, you might head to a search engine to find relevant sites independent of the spam. But some spammers are coding URLs in their links to navigate to the spamvertised sites via search engines that redirect visitors to the final destination. The rd.yahoo.com redirector appears to be the most popular route.[10] The Yahoo server reads the URL and passes you on to the other site, tracking the URL as you go. It may give Yahoo's search robots reason to visit and crawl through the site and add it to its search listings.

Obviously, search engines frown on these transparent attempts at rigging the system. You should be on the lookout for such links in the source code of suspected spam, and avoid clicking the links at all cost.

Message Trick #26: *Embedding encrypted JavaScript within an HTML document attachment*

Example:

```
Received: from 24.102.229.xx (CPE000ae61dd0a0-
CM014510004036.cpe.net.cable.rogers.com
[24.102.229.xx]) by dannyg.com (8.12.11) id
i2PN2qfn075670 for <dannyg@dannyg.com>; Thu, 25
Mar 2004 16:03:14 -0700 (MST)
Received: from unknown (HELO ADDGCAF)
(192.168.144.86)
   by 24.102.229.xx with SMTP;  25 Mar 2004
14:55:32 -0800
Message-ID: <00f501c412bc$3d9bf880$a38a50d5@ADDG-
CAF>
From: "elli" <recites@mexopals.com>
To: "dannyg@dannyg.com" <dannyg@dannyg.com>
Subject: where you at
Date: Thu, 25 Mar 2004 14:55:17 -0800
MIME-Version: 1.0
Content-Type: multipart/mixed;
      boundary="-----
=_NextPart_000_00F2_01C412C6.4373553B"
X-Priority: 3
X-UIDL: ]lO"!$H#"!b[W"!P&,!!

This is a multi-part message in MIME format.

-------=_NextPart_000_00F2_01C412C6.4373553B
```

---

10 Yahoo has additional redirection servers, including rds.yahoo.com. The "rd" stands for "redirect," so expect those letters somewhere in the subdomain name.

```
Content-Type: multipart/alternative;
    boundary="-----
=_NextPart_001_00F3_01C412C6.4373553B"

-------=_NextPart_001_00F3_01C412C6.4373553B
Content-Type: text/plain;
    charset="utf-8"
Content-Transfer-Encoding: quoted-printable

this is plain text part
-------=_NextPart_001_00F3_01C412C6.4373553B
Content-Type: text/html;
    charset="utf-8"
Content-Transfer-Encoding: quoted-printable

<!DOCTYPE HTML PUBLIC "-//W3C//DTD HTML 4.0
Transitional//EN">
<HTML><HEAD>
<META http-equiv=3DContent-Type
content=3D"text/html; charset =3Dutf-8">
<STYLE></STYLE>
</HEAD>
<BODY><B>This message</B> has a sweet girl wait-
ing for you</BODY>=
</HTML>
-------=_NextPart_001_00F3_01C412C6.4373553B—

-------=_NextPart_000_00F2_01C412C6.4373553B
Content-Type: text/html;
    name="inspirations.html"

Content-Transfer-Encoding: quoted-printable
Content-Disposition: attachment;
    filename="inspirations.html"

<script language=3D"JavaScript">
Tillich =3D new Array(234,
63,48,64,14,205,189,35,163,69,209,
239,134,9,167,5,255,121,121,151,31,
233,220,233,126,94,96,60,13,53,197,
[snip]
112,120,255,111,27,209,123,21,11,199,
49,85,187,170,56,108,153,79,223,78
);
gained =3D new Array(214,
87,68,45,98,243,176,41,174,79,220,
229,186,107,200,97,134,71,116,157,18,
```

```
[snip]
21,42,27,184,145,246,247,100,205,130,
147,208,201,206,239,252,133);
hopelessness =3D 1151;
fission =3D 108;
var plucking =3D "";
for(overtures =3D 0; overtures < hopelessness;
overtures++)
   plucking =3D plucking +
String.fromCharCode(Tillich[overtures]  ^ =
gained[overtures % fission]);
document.write(plucking);
</script>

--------=_NextPart_000_00F2_01C412C6.4373553B--
```

Description: Although this message contains a laundry list of tricks, the one I want to point out is associated with the final portion: an HTML document that shows up in your email reader as an attachment to the message. This trick is difficult to guard against unless you are suspicious enough about the Subject: line to investigate the source code of the message.

The three content segments of this message are: (1) an empty plain-text message; (2) a short HTML message that is intended to lure you to opening the attachment; and (3) the HTML document attachment. Opening the attachment brings your browser to the front and loads the attached file into it.

The document, however, consists of only a JavaScript script that runs when the "page" loads. I've snipped dozens of lines of numbers that are formatted similarly to the surrounding lines.

This script uses a two-level encryption technique that is well-known to experienced JavaScript (and other) coders. Characters for the message content are conveyed as numbers (one character per number), and the script applies a numerical key to pull characters from specific locations within their collection and then decrypt the numbers into their regular characters. With the characters fully decrypted, the script writes the HTML content to the browser window. In this case, the page advertises (in wording unsuitable for children) an adult Web site.

A study of several messages from this spammer indicates that he uses random numbers for his encryption/decryption keys from message to message. He even uses random words for script variable names in an attempt to fool pattern-matching spam filters.

Because the JavaScript associated with this message runs not in the email program, but in the browser, the spammer is more likely to get his page read—as long as recipients open the attached HTML document. Although this particular message doesn't include any nasty HTML or JavaScript tricks in the page it loads into the browser, other such HTML attachments may not be so gentle. You could easily find yourself in popup hell (if you don't have any browser popup blocking) or open to other exploits if you haven't kept your Windows software up to date.

This example should reinforce your aversion to any attachment that arrives with an email message you don't recognize. Even a seemingly benign HTML attachment could be trouble.

Thus ends a survey of tricks within message bodies practiced by spammers, as well as scammers and virus writers. New techniques crop up all the time, as filters and content analyses improve. That spammers resort to many of these tricks provides ample evidence that content filtering and spam reporting (LARTing) do have an impact.

An entirely different set of tricks perpetrated on unsuspecting users don't always arrive via email. The results are potentially far more damaging to your privacy and computer than any spam message. Even worse, you or someone using your computer helped set you up to be robbed, as you'll discover in the next chapter.

Beware Geeks Bearing Gifts

Any marketer on planet Earth will tell you that the word "free" is the most powerful tool in a promoter's vocabulary. What an amazing hold the notion of "gettin' somthin' fer nothin'" has on the human psyche. It's an irresistible attraction.

Precisely what hackers and scammers are counting on.

Thanks to the public's eager adoption of free downloads of music, video, software, screensavers, pornography, and other stuff, millions of PCs around the world are now burdened with add-in programs that run in the background to do things like:

- Change your browser's home page to an advertising site or portal not of your choosing.

- Display pop up windows advertising products that are related to the content on Web pages you visit.

- Replace a Web site's banner ads with ads from other sources.

- Capture every character you type, including Web site addresses, user names, and passwords, and report the content to individuals you don't know.

- Intercept Web searches by taking you to a search engine not of your choosing.

- Turn your PC into a proxy server for mailing spam and/or redirecting spam links to the spamvertised Web sites.

- Install additional software on your machine at the whim of a hacker somewhere else on the Internet.

- Take complete remote control of your PC.

It's not just gullible computer newbies who have their computers overrun by software known as adware, spyware, and malware (as in malicious). The avenues of entry for most of this stuff include the following:

- Installation of free programs (including well-known music-sharing services) and some media players

- Anonymous or forged viral emails containing executable attachments

- Instant messaging (IM) and Internet Relay Chat (IRC)

- "Greeting cards" from anonymous senders and even best friends

- Web pages and emails exploiting numerous unpatched security holes in Microsoft Windows and Internet Explorer for Windows

- Blatant software installations whose long-winded, legalese license agreements tell the user in language as clear as mud that the software does potentially nasty stuff

- An infection spread over a local area network (LAN) initiated from a computer that got infected via email, Web site, IM, or IRC exploit —including the laptop that was connected to a home network last night

Most users whose PCs are infected with spyware (I'll use that term to encompass it all) don't know that somebody else's software is controlling their Web browser or forwarding home banking logins to heaven-knows-where. Inexperienced computer users typically attribute bizarre behavior of their machines to the mysteries of PCs, and shrug their shoulders when the browser starts up today with a different home page hawking cheap vacations or mortgage refinancing. Any home computer used by youngsters is extremely vulnerable because kids tend to put more trust in free software offerings put before them; their friends pass along links to "cool stuff" that is easily downloaded for free, and then infects the new machine.

Despite the risks, there is plenty of good stuff available for free download on the Internet that doesn't carry any of this spyware baggage. Knowing which free software is good and which will open your machine to Bad Guys is very difficult to determine. The Web sites hosting the most vile software could look very slick and professional, while the safest open source package may come from a page that looks like it was thrown together in two minutes.

Recognizable brand names of free downloads don't necessarily offer assurances about receiving spyware. Although their policies change from time to time, well-known music-sharing applications Kazaa and Grokster have checkered histories in this regard. Based on alerts I've seen from a Windows firewall program that tell me when a program on my computer is trying to access the Internet, even the free player for RealAudio unexpectedly, and otherwise silently, reaches out to some place on the Internet each time I start Windows.

A fair amount of spyware gets installed as separate programs coupled with the free download—the classic definition of a Trojan horse program. If you apply antispyware programs to disable the spyware, your free program may not work. In a reverse twist, if you uninstall the free program, the spyware stays on your machine, doing its dirty work just the same.

Then there are the free downloadable solutions to the problems of spam, adware, and spyware. Can you trust these programs to be devoid of other nasties? Some you can, some you can't. I certainly wouldn't trust any pointer to such a "solution" arriving in a spam message. I mean, c'mon! How dare you use spam to flog an antispam solution? What kind of antispammer could you possibly be?

The truly sad part of this spyware business is that the two most threatening aspects of the Internet—information (including identity) theft and proliferation of spamming—are the chief beneficiaries of the truly evil spyware coursing its way around the world. Millions of innocent and naïve PC users' machines have already been compromised. Corporate computing installations are spending fortunes to provide filters that prevent the arrival of potentially damaging email attachments; they also monitor local network activity in search of suspicious traffic bearing the signatures of spyware bit exchanges. But small businesses and home users are at significant risk unless they take special precautions.

Guarding against the installation of spyware on a PC takes time and sometimes money—both of which tend to be in short supply for home and small business PC users—while spyware vultures may be lurking behind every free download you encounter. It's a shame that users have to play system security engineer just to keep their machines free of this garbage; but with new tricks exploiting newly discovered system vulnerabilities all the time, you can't just run on autopilot and expect your system to be safe for time immemorial. It takes a combination of (safe) software installation, frequent software updating, and an amazing amount of self-control by all users of a particular computer to keep a machine spyware-free. To that end, I herewith provide a necessarily long checklist of tasks you must perform to remove whatever junk is currently on your PC and keep further spyware infections from ceding control of your computer to Bad Guys.

Removing Spyware

This may be the most difficult task to accomplish fully because you won't know for certain that every Trojan horse, keylogger, screen capturer, or email address harvester has been eliminated from your system. Users who have experienced malware infections commonly recommend running two programs, which appear to complement each other in catching some items that the other misses. The programs are:

- Ad-aware, by Lavasoft (www.lavasoft.de/software/adaware)

- Spybot-Search & Destroy (www.safer-networking.org)

Both suppliers accept donations to help keep the programs updated with the latest data files. If you run these programs and they clean out junk in your system, aren't the developers deserving of a donation? They may have saved you from a year of clearing up personal identify theft.[1]

Make sure you download updated data files from these vendors at least once a week, and run the programs after receiving each update. Remember that spyware authors are inventing ways to work around these spyware removers. If you don't keep the programs updated and don't run them regularly, you are opening yourself up to infection.

Blocking Spyware

The worst spyware is the stuff that communicates with the outside, particularly to convey your personal data to others or download other applications (like spam proxy servers). No one who connects to the Internet should be without firewall software that monitors all network activity. You can purchase commercial firewall software from reputable vendors like Symantec and McAfee, or you can download a terrific free utility called ZoneAlarm (www.zonelabs.com). The product comes in a simple free version and two more powerful paid versions (ZoneAlarm Plus and ZoneAlarm Pro). Even the free version does a great job of preventing network activity (incoming and outgoing) that you have not authorized. If some new program installed on your PC tries to access the Internet, you receive an alert about which program it is, at which time you can grant or deny access. It's a super tool that should be on every Windows PC.

---

1 It's possible that malware stoppers will also halt a good program that you need. For instance, a friend of mine discovered that Spybot-Search & Destroy wanted to uninstall a commercial software program that establishes secure connections to remote networks. You can easily restore any such accidental removals.

You should also install a quality antivirus package. Look through the computer magazine and help Web sites for the latest reviews and recommendations. Here are sites and publications that I rely on for well-researched information:

- *PC Magazine* (pcmag.com)

- *PC World Magazine* (pcworld.com)

- CNET (cnet.com)

Avoiding Spyware

To avoid getting spyware installed on your machine, you have to use your head and be less eager to install goofy dancing chicken software on your machine just because it's free or your neighbor told you it's "cool." You can expect that any free media-oriented software will come with adware or spyware strings attached. If a product is available as an advertising-supported free download and a paid, advertising-free version, you can be assured that the free version will be installing adware along with the program, and that adware may not go away even if you later uninstall it or upgrade to the paid version.

More established vendors of these items cover their butts by explaining (after a fashion) what rights you give up by downloading and installing their gizmos. You'll likely be confronted with an installation dialog window that asks whether you want to install the stuff; then you'll see another window present what lawyers call the End User License Agreement, or EULA (pronounced YOO-lah) for short. This is where all the fine print is. No matter how much I encourage you to actually read these agreements before clicking the "I Agree" button, I know you won't sit through all the legal mumbo jumbo. Even if you did, you probably wouldn't truly understand how much permission you're about to give away. Wording in a EULA has been known to deprive licensees of seemingly simple rights. For instance, the EULAs for several Microsoft OS service packs and the .NET Framework contain a provision that prevent the agree-er (you) from disclosing the results of benchmark tests on certain components without Microsoft's prior written approval. What, you didn't see that clause?

Since probably you're not going to read (or understand) the EULA, my best advice is to cancel any software installation unless the software meets one or more of the following criteria:

1. The software was created by the maker of the operating system you're using, and you have asked explicitly to have the software downloaded to and installed on your system.

2. The software is a commercial product that you have purchased.

3. The software is a free product that has been vetted by one or more independent sources as being free of spyware and adware.

On the flip side:

1. Never—and I mean *never*—install software or "patches" that arrive as attachments in an email, especially from someone you don't know. Microsoft does not ever send patches via email.

2. Never install a program linked from an email that claims to be from a system administrator, unless you can verify independently that the sender of the message is *your* system administrator or IT department (e.g., in a corporation or on campus).

3. Never install a "media player" to retrieve a greeting card, invitation, or other social come-on that you are supposed to retrieve by way of a link in an email or instant message—including messages from people you know.

I know, I know. I'm sucking all the fun out of your computing. But better that than some stranger sucking all the passwords from your computer and money from your credit lines.

A Safer Bet

The vast majority of the world uses Microsoft Windows and all the other software that comes with it, such as Internet Explorer and Outlook Express for email. That such a high percentage of the universe has that software installed makes it an outstanding target for hackers, scammers, and spammers who know about the security vulnerabilities of those systems. Microsoft is pretty good (not perfect, mind you) about issuing updates and patches to its software to plug the security holes, but not every user performs the updates or does so in a timely manner. It's certainly understandable for home users who access the Internet via comparatively slow dial-up connections. I mean, downloading multimegabytes of patches at 57.6 kbps (if you're lucky) is more than most dial-up users can bear. With so many Windows PCs sitting out there unpatched and using older versions of the OS—lots of home users are still running Windows 95 and 98—hackers, virus writers, and other scum have a nearly endless supply of targets to choose from.

Even brand-new Windows computers are at grave risk because they typically do not include the latest operating system patches. If you buy a new PC, the very first job you should tackle after establishing an Internet connection (and before downloading any email) is to visit the Windows Update Web site. Install all critical updates at once. Do it before a criminal's IP address probe finds your vulnerable, unpatched machine and hijacks it.

A predominance of a single type of system is reminiscent of an agricultural practice (or accidental phenomenon) known as a *monoculture*. One of the criticisms lodged against monocultures in nature is that they make easy targets for bad things that attack them (such as disease-bearing insects). Widespread installation of Windows has certainly drawn its share of pests.

If you want to avoid being one of the targets, become a different species. In the personal computer world, that means using a different operating system, such as MacOS X, Linux, or Unix. Switching operating systems is a tall order, and virtually impossible in any organization that has standardized its applications and internal support structure around Windows. Suggesting a change of OS is not something I do lightly.

At the risk of sounding like a Microsoft basher or a shill for Apple, let me simply state that, from my own experience as a long-time Macintosh user, I feel a hundred times safer in my daily online experience on the Mac than I do when I need to run a Windows machine for some short-term application testing. First of all, any virus-laden email that manages to get through my mail system defenses is going to be a Windows application that simply won't install or run on a Mac. Even if I make a mistake of double-clicking the attachment, nothing bad happens. Similarly, any attacks that try to come my way via Web pages loading ActiveX controls, Instant Messaging, or Internet Relay Chat have no effect on my computer. The same would be true if I were running a Linux PC.

That's not to say that MacOS X (which is based on a version of Unix) and Linux couldn't be the target of the same kind of virus-writing, scam-promoting losers who target Windows today, but as long as these operating systems remain minorities, they won't be attractive targets. In the meantime, I keep my Mac antivirus software and system updated, and I keep a firewall running. I may be smug, but I'm not stupid.

All that said, there is ample evidence that virus and worm writers seek vulnerabilities wherever they exist, trampling on the monoculture theory. In March 2004, a destructive worm known as Witty targeted the comparatively small population (approximately 12,000) of servers and PCs that ran various security products by Internet Security Systems (www.iss.net). As analyzed by Cooperative Association of Internet Data Analysis (CAIDA),[2] this worm exhibited at least three notable characteristics:

---

[2] CAIDA (www.caida.org) is a mostly U.S. government-funded research organization focusing on Internet infrastructure measurement and analysis.

1. It spread extraordinarily quickly among the small population.

2. It eventually crashed infected machines with random hard disk overwrites.

3. It was unleashed only one day after a vulnerability was announced and patched.

It's that third item that should scare the pants off every computer user. If you are not continually vigilant about the availability of security updates for your operating systems and other software, virus writers may get you before you install a patch. With shorter times between vulnerability discovery and virus release, the likelihood of being caught unprotected increases dramatically.

Despite so much of this book being devoted to spam, the real theme is alerting all computer users—especially those without technical expertise—to be aware of bad things that are happening behind their backs, under their noses, and inside their computers. Spammers, scammers, and hackers prey specifically on nontechnical users of this highly complex technology. Unfortunately, technology isn't always quick enough, or sufficiently well designed, to protect you. The Bad Guys are using the human element to exploit you, so you must use that same element to fight back and protect yourself.

CHAPTER 14

Rule #3: Spammers Are Stupid

It should be clear by now that I don't really believe all spammers are stupid. In fact, some are frighteningly intelligent in the way they conceal their identities by relaying commands to hijacked proxy mail servers that have wormed their way into PCs around the world. But these scary spammers comprise a short list—albeit a short list that is long on spam volume. Nevertheless, spam comes from all kinds of folks, including those who don't necessarily understand all of the technology that they use, or those who put too much trust in computers and the spamming software they bought from another spammer (so they could "work from home," "profit from the Internet marketing boom," and "get rich quick"). Randomness, or lack thereof, can also make a spam sender look idiotic.

Yes, plenty of spammers make mistakes that are in plain view of anyone silly enough to pour through reams of spam message source code listings. (That's me over there with my hand raised.)

Because we who don't like spam need a good laugh once in a while (other than the occasional guffaws induced by cartooneys), let me share a few samples from my incoming spam cesspool.

Spammer Stupidity #1: *Forgetting to check if the randomizer is working*

Example:

```
Subject: Re: %RND_UC_CHAR[2-8], a few minutes
```

183

Why It's Stupid: I really laugh every time I find one of the template markers for random words intact in a message. It's so sloppy and careless. It's usually a sign of a clueless newbie spammer who missed a few steps while following instructions in the "make a million from home" spamming kit he bought from some other (smarter) spammer.

In one message I received, the spammer was supposed to fill in some bogus information about the HTML program used to generate the message—as if the message were created as an individual HTML message from the sender. Except he forgot to replace the "random" placeholders:

```
<html><head>
<meta http-equiv="Content-Language" content="en-
us">
<meta name="GENERATOR" content=" %RANDOM_WORD
%RANDOM_CHAR ">
<meta name="ProgId" content=" %RANDOM_WORD %RAN-
DOM_CHAR ">
<meta http-equiv="Content-Type"
content="text/html; charset=windows-1252">
<title> %RANDOM_WORD </title></head><body>
<p align="center"><b>Get a degree from a national
university!</b></p>
```

It's probably a demonstration of how smart you have to be to get one of the phony university degrees he's selling.

Then there is the sloppiness that confirms spam fighters' suspicions about how much of a message header can be forged with meaningless junk (formatted to improve readability):

```
Received: from mail.\x\.com (mail.\x\.com
          [69.150.137.\x\]) by dannyg.com
          (8.12.11) id i4FC15So063216 for <dannyg
          @dannyg.com>; Sat, 15 May 2004 06:01:06
          -0600 (MDT)
Received: from %RNDLCCHAR312%RNDDIGIT13.
          videotron.ca (83.222.25.188) by %RNDLC
          CHAR13%RND DIGIT13-%RNDLCCHAR13%RNDDIG
          IT13.videotron.ca with Microsoft
          SMTPSVC(5.0.2195.6824); Sat, 15 May
          2004 16:54:04 +0400
Received: from Kimberly%RNDLCCHAR13%RNDDIGIT13%
          RNDLCCHAR13%RNDDIGIT13%RNDLCCHAR13%
          RNDDIGIT13%RNDLCCHAR13
          (118.241.222.162) by
          %RNDLCCHAR315%RNDDIGIT13.videotron.ca
```

```
(InterMail vM.5.01.06.05
%RNDDIGIT3-%RNDDIGIT3-%RNDDIGIT3-%RND-
DIGIT3-%RNDDIGIT3-
%RNDDIGIT59) with SMTP id <%RNDDIG-
IT916.%RNDUCCHAR25
%RNDDIGIT23.%RNDLCCHAR57%RNDDIGIT13%RND
DIGIT13.videotron.ca@
curfew%RNDLCCHAR13%RNDDIGIT13%RNDLC-
CHAR13%RNDDIGIT13
%RNDLCCHAR13%RNDDIGIT13%RNDLCCHAR13>
for <dannyg@dannyg.com>;
Sat, 15 May 2004 17:00:04 +0400
Message-ID:
<%RNDDIGIT36%RNDLCCHAR13%RNDDIGIT13%RND
LCCHAR13%RNDDIGIT25$ %RNDDIGIT59$%RNDL-
CCHAR13%RNDDIGIT13%RNDLCCHAR13 %RNDDIG-
IT13@Kimberly%RNDLCCHAR13%RNDDIGIT13%RN
DLCCHAR13 %RNDDIGIT13%RNDLCCHAR13%RND-
DIGIT13%RNDLCCHAR13>
From: "Monroe Hoffman" <YGKGYJ@chello.no>
To: <dannyg@dannyg.com>
Subject: bdaboy you!
Date: Sat, 15 May 2004 10:55:04 -0200
MIME-Version: 1.0
Content-Type: multipart/alternative;
boundary="—2653074283271501372"
X-UIDL: FT3"!00N!!^On"!*0Y!!
```

The topmost Received: header line was written by my email server, but the next two Received: fields are intended to falsely implicate Canadian ISP videotron.ca by assembling a sequence of random uppercase (RNDUCCHAR), lowercase (RNDLCCHAR), and numeric (RNDDIGIT) characters in bogus mail server identities. Even most of the Message-ID: field is random.

In another case, here's the full body of a message from a stupid medz spammer:

```
<html>
<body>
<b>%CUSTOM_RX1</b><br>
%CUSTOM_RX2<br>
%CUSTOM_RX3<br>
%CUSTOM_RX4<br><br><br>
<A HREF="http://iqa.\x\.com/FP">Thanks for
Shopping</A>
<br>
```

Um, I think the sales pitch is missing here, doofus. There's a placeholder for a bold headline and three other statements, all supposed to be filled with some prescription medicine blather. "Thanks for Shopping?" Thanks for being an idiot and wasting the world's Internet bandwidth.

Spammer Stupidity #2: *Using random words in the Subject: line*

Example:

```
Subject:   Re: because i don't lyfhz
Subject:   Re: housed the roman oeaeoqzg jmyasq
           llwo
```

Why It's Stupid: Spammers must believe they're being clever by using random words (often followed up by random garbage) in the Subject: line of messages to trick spam filters. Of course any spam filter that merely filters based on Subject: line content is pretty worthless anyway, but even if the message gets through, what are recipients' reactions to this gibberish? Are they curious enough about it to find out what it's supposed to mean (as if the message body would reveal the meaning)? It would seem to me that anyone who doesn't like spam will delete such messages unopened because both the sender's name/address and the subject are meaningless.

I showed you some ridiculous examples of random word combinations in Chapter 11, Header Trick #8. But this random thing can also get in the way of spam that isn't using random words. One message I received had the following Subject:

```
Subject:   Fwd: Women with cows movs f
```

I thought it was just another one of those gibberish random-word-generated lines. Unfortunately for the spammer, the subject really did relate to the offer (a link to some bestiality pornography site). The subject line was so outrageous at first glance, that it seemed immediately deleteable.

Spammer Stupidity #3: *Wasting time and programming to insert an obviously forged Received: header chain*

Example:

```
Received: from 128.121.100.64 ([219.153.1.174])
by dannyg.com (8.12.10) id hB4N8RmO017855; Thu,
4 Dec 2003 16:08:28 -0700 (MST)
Received: from (HELO om2pd) [77.139.217.54] by
128.121.100.64 with ESMTP id 6F19FBD0A84; Thu,
04 Dec 2003 17:07:13 -0600
```

Why It's Stupid: The message that had these header lines listed six To: addresses (not shown), all for my domain. Most of the addresses were either harvested or corruptions that have been floating around the address collections. This amount of consolidation of addresses to my domain is fairly unusual, but it did let me know that these six addresses are gathered together in at least one collection circulating in the spamonomy.

Perhaps the fact that all of the To: addresses were to my domain influenced the spammer's program to first look up the IP address of my domain, and then insert it into the second Received: header line (the bogus "originating" IP of 77.139.217.54 is one of those IANA reserved blocks), and instructed the outgoing server to identify itself as my IP address (128.121.100.64) when connecting to my email server. But my email server logged the actual IP address of the sending server ([219.153.1.174]), a server in China. Any spam reporting analysis would immediately see the disparity between the *actual* and *reported* IP addresses, and treat the actual address as the insertion point for the spam.

Spammer Stupidity #4: *The "I know nothing" disclaimer defense*

Example:

```
Third-party offers contained in this email are
the sole responsibility of the offer originator.
```

Why It's Stupid: This kind of disclaimer may be more a sign of Rule #1 (Spammers lie) than Rule #3. Anyone reading this disclaimer within the context of the message in which it appeared is left scratching his or her head about who is saying this, and about whom. First, the headers of this disclaimer's message were entirely forged, from the Received: to the From: headers, and then some. The message entered the Internet (despite five—count 'em—phony subsidiary Received: header lines) via a comcast.net customer computer, probably a zombie PC. Therefore, the actual sender is hidden well enough for government work, and has a near-zero liability on the spam-sending front.

Digging deeper, the URL for the spamvertised Web site (selling printer inks, wouldn't ya know) is hosted by an email marketer's system, on which the ink seller has a subdirectory containing both the spamvertised information and unsubscribe page. So, let me get this straight: An email marketer is doing the mailing (spamming) and hosting the sales Web site for the client, but the marketer disavows any responsibility for the actions of the "offer originator," presumably the inkster in this case. What a professional, trusting relationship these entities have. It also gives me, as a potential customer (not!), a lot of confidence in a vendor whose mailing company distances itself from the vendor from the get-go.

No thanks. I'll search out another source for my ink.

Spammer Stupidity #5: *Sending spam originating from Russia, Asia, and elsewhere in non-Roman languages to addresses harvested from English Web sites*

Example:

```
ÅóÓ£¬Çë¢Òâ£¬ÕâÊçÒ»·â¨ÀûÕÉÌÓÊ£¬»ÊÇÀ¬»øÓÊ£¬Èçû¶ÔÄãÎ
ÓÃÇëËæÊÖÉ£¬±«Ë±íÊÕæÏµÄÇ¸Òâ£¬ÕâÖÁÉÙÈÃÄãÁËâÁË¸ÏîÂÅÏ
¢¡£
```

Why It's Stupid: Well, duh! It's bad enough when I get spam in Spanish and Portuguese that I don't understand, although at least I can see the occasional word that makes sense. But when messages are sent with non-Roman character sets for languages such as Russian and Chinese, the source code in my Roman-character-based computer looks like the gibberish above. True, my MacOS X computer has support for several non-Roman character sets, allowing the characters to render as they were sent, but since I wouldn't recognize one Chinese character from another, I have no idea what the spammer is trying to sell me. And neither does almost everyone outside of his own region. Nor am I going to telephone Taipei to take him up on his offer (the phone numbers usually appear correctly).

For spam filters, these messages are easy to pick out if they are formatted correctly with their character set headers, like the following:

```
Content-Type: text/plain;charset="GB2312"
```

Most of the Asian language spam I receive is Chinese, using one of two character sets named GB2312 and BIG5. Content-based filtering can spot these distinctive strings and trash the mail before it gets anywhere.

By the way, when you get these messages and look at the source code, you can still make out the URLs to the spamvertised Web sites or links to images because, until recently, URLs have had to be in the "primitive" Latin character set. Don't be surprised to find .com domains in the addresses. You don't have to be a Westerner to glom onto a dot-com domain.

Spammer Stupidity #6: *Failing to fill in the blanks*

Example:

```
You are receiving this because of your registra-
tion with .
```

Why It's Stupid: The example is copied directly from a spam message that was an affiliate mailing for a vacation outfit. The message is obviously derived from a template supplied by the travel company. Unfortunately, the affiliate didn't fill in the blank that's supposed to assure me that I had signed up for mailings. Oops.

But that's only half the story.

Like a lot of spam messages, this one includes plain text and HTML copies of the message in separate blocks. The plain-text version is for recipients who don't use HTML email programs or have turned off HTML email (if that feature is available in their email program). The HTML template is slightly different. Here is the source code for the same portion of the message in the HTML part:

```
This email is being sent to you as a result of
your response to the <a ref="http://www.\x\.com/c
.html?rtr=on&s=3,se,g,810q,7ton,9ecl,m1ds">Florid
a Vacation Store</a> sweepstakes giveaway promot-
ed on <Market Program></a>
```

That placeholder at the end of the sentence (`<Market Program>`) is where the affiliate is supposed to fill in some a site or marketing program name where I supposedly registered for some sweepstakes. In HTML view, the placeholder is treated as a junk tag, so nothing appears in the message. Sheesh, the affiliate didn't even have the decency to fill in a plausible (although not necessarily credible) lie. Double oops!

Spammer Stupidity #7: *Forgetting to check forged header tactics before mailing*

Example:

```
Subject: Date: Thu, 15, Jan 2004 07:13:07 -0800
```

Why It's Stupid: For lack of either the correct mail-merging routine or a simple carriage return character, the message with the above Subject: line displays the contents of what should have been the Date: header line in the list of inbox mail. A lot of corporate spam filters would have added some extra spam points to this message because it lacked a genuine Date: field in the header, making it more likely to be deleted at the incoming server.

Spammer Stupidity #8: *Sending the same message with randomized variations in quick succession*

Example:

First message:

```
Received: from out007.verizon.net (out007pub.ver-
izon.net [206.46.170.\x\]) by dannyg.com
(8.12.10) id i0F6ZM14018949 for <\x\>; Wed, 14
Jan 2004 23:35:22 -0700 (MST)
```

```
Received: from creepers ([67.94.191.\x\]) by
out007.verizon.net
(InterMail vM.5.01.06.06 201-253-122-130-106-
20030910) with ESMTP id
<20040115063521.KBIE9064.out007.verizon.net@creep
ers> for <\x\>; Thu, 15 Jan 2004 00:35:21 -0600
From: "Marie Fanusie"<dan@att.net>
To: \x\
Subject: Re: Happy new years
Mime-Version: 1.0
Content-Type: text/html; charset=us-ascii
Content-Transfer-Encoding: 7bit
X-Authentication-Info: Submitted using SMTP AUTH
at out007.verizon.net from [67.94.191.\x\] at
Thu, 15 Jan 2004 00:02:47 -0600
Message-Id: <20040115063521.KBIE9064.out007.veri-
zon.net@creepers>
Date: Thu, 15 Jan 2004 00:35:21 -0600
X-UIDL: +gf"!LRY"!T#'"!4V*"!

<html>
<etuo5ad humerusexecutional>
<br>
<img src="http://plenary.position.amoco.\x\
.com/in/images03.gif"></b>
<p><a
href=http://excursus.tardiness.bergland.\x\.com/i
n/>This link will take you there.</a></p>
<BR><BR>
<p>Thanks so much,<br>
pornography ethically (brainstems)<br></p>
<BR><FONT COLOR=#FFFFFF>
gj8lxvnwryi1ps4fhk7zcbm0367kzcbm036792415qetuo
```

Second message:

```
Received: from out001.verizon.net (out001pub.ver-
izon.net [206.46.170.\x\]) by dannyg.com
(8.12.10) id i0GJUNac038165 for <\x\>; Fri, 16
Jan 2004 12:30:23 -0700 (MST)
Received: from hybrid ([68.41.114.\x\]) by
out001.verizon.net
(InterMail vM.5.01.06.06 201-253-122-130-106-
20030910) with ESMTP id
<20040116193020.CPO25581.out001.verizon.net@hybri
```

```
d> for <\x\>; Fri, 16 Jan 2004 13:30:20 -0600
From: "Jerald Phelps"<dan@hotmail.com>
To: \x\
Subject: Fw: Happy new years
Mime-Version: 1.0
Content-Type: text/html; charset=us-ascii
Content-Transfer-Encoding: 7bit
X-Authentication-Info: Submitted using SMTP AUTH
at out001.verizon.net from [68.41.114.\x\] at
Fri, 16 Jan 2004 13:29:38 -0600
Message-Id: <20040116193020.CPO25581.out001.veri-
zon.net@hybrid>
Date: Fri, 16 Jan 2004 13:30:21 -0600
X-UIDL: X=\"!Yn["!Pfp"!kTg"!

<html>
<uo5adgj americanaaccompanies> <br>
<img src="http://agricola.scarface.telemetry.\
x\.com/in/images03.gif"></b> <p><a
href=http://tenderness.hydrosphere.scrapped.\x\.c
om/in/>Please visit our website to learn the
facts about this quality health product</a></p>
<BR><BR>
<p>See You Soon,<br>
horseplay huck (expounded)<br></p>
<BR><FONT COLOR=#FFFFFF>8lxvnwryi1ps4fhk7zcbm
0367kzcbm036792415qetuo5a
```

Why It's Stupid: In their desperation to get past increasingly effective spam filters, the really high-volume guys do what they do best: crank up the volume. In the process, they can easily send multiple instances of the same offer to the same e-mail address, sometimes just seconds apart from one another. The example shows a case where two versions of the same offer arrived 36 hours apart. Aside from the stupid reuse of the same Subject: line (except interchanging Re: and FW: prefixes), with capitalization that is unusual for English (where "Happy New Year" would be the common greeting), by mid-January, it's getting rather old to get anyone's attention with that line.

But where the real stupidity sets in for the spammer is that by sending two variations of the same offer to the same address, the recipient can see how the spammer's template works. For instance, the From: line pulls plain-language names from other places, but sets the user ID of the bogus From: address to the first three characters of my email ID. The domains chosen here (att.com and hotmail.com) are probably pulled at random from a list of domains for use in this position in the template.

You can also see where the spammer builds in randomness as a hash-busting scheme to foil content filters. The junk tag after the `<html>` tag uses two groups of characters. The first appears to be a seven-character selection from some long gibberish string, while the second group consists of two words pulled from a dictionary. URLs for the image and spamvertised Web site link (the domains are all the same) lead with three random dictionary words—all ignored by the Web server anyway. The visible message varies, and is probably selected from a list of stock sentences. There is no identifier in the image or link URLs to tie to a particular sentence, so the spammer isn't tracking variations for market research purposes (a stupid omission as long as he's gone this far). After the parting words (also likely pulled at random from a list) come three random dictionary words (one in parentheses). Based on the comma after the parting words, I suspect the template originally called for randomly chosen names (first and last) and a title. But the spammer got his random flags messed up, and the signature is just a series of random words sure to make recipients scratch their heads.

Several more examples of this particular spam effort were reported to the news.admin.net-abuse.sightings newsgroup. Verizon customer machines were the chosen relay targets for this campaign. Same template, same tricks, same mistakes.

Another pair arrived recently that demonstrated not only Rule #3 but Rule #1 (Spammers lie) as well. Here are relevant parts of the headers of the two messages:

```
To: webmaster@dannyg.com
Subject: 18,697 Bottles sold daily - S1ZE MATTERS!
Date: Mon, 19 Jan 2004 09:48:59 +0000
```

and:

```
To: webmaster@dannyg.com
Subject: 45,195 Bottles sold daily - S1ZE MATTERS!
Date: Mon, 19 Jan 2004 09:51:38 +0000
```

Note that they were sent less than three minutes apart and arrived from two different hijacked servers. The offers and spamvertised URLs were identical, down to the affiliate ID numbers. Randomized junk tags were different, but I'd expect that. In any case, their "story" about how many bottles they've sold seems to have some, uh, inconsistencies. That happens when you use a random number generator.

Spammer Stupidity #9: *Sending local stuff around the planet.*

Example:

* Экскурсионный тур в Италию от 399 € , Заезды 24, 31 января и
Римини-Сан Марино-Рим-Ватикан-Сиена- Флоренция-Венеция-Бо
Включено: авиаперелет, проживание в отеле 3* с завтраками, медицинск
переезды по стране на автобусе класса „Люкс";

953-79-██, 953-76-██, 953-79-██

Why It's Stupid: Why would I, in California (or any English-speaking locale, for that matter), be interested in an offer written in Cyrillic, and with local phone numbers for someplace in Russia (Moscow)? This offer is for a bus tour of Italy for 399 euros. I guess you have to get to Moscow first.

The well-worn expression, adopted by ecologically-minded folks and big business alike, is "Think globally, act locally." Sending a Cyrillic message with local phone numbers to the world's spam targets is just the opposite: thinking locally and acting globally. Stupid.

Spammer Stupidity #10: *Registering gibberish dot-com domain names*

Example:

None. I don't want to advertise for them.

Why It's Stupid: There is ample evidence that most of the good names within the .com top-level domain (TLD) are taken. A "good" name is one that is easily remembered by a prospective customer because, as an e-commerce site owner, you want visitors to remember your site when they think about the product or service you offer.

High-volume spammers who also run spamvertised Web sites face a challenge when coming up with domain names for their numerous sites. It's not unusual for some of these guys to register hundreds of domains at a time. They can spam with groups of these domains, and keep the antispammers busy maintaining their filters that look for spamvertised domain addresses in links. When response drops off on some, they move on to other domains already registered and waiting.

I've seen some weird .com domains in my spam travels. You still find a lot of usage of hyphens to create domains that look like the established .com domains on the web. Phishers have used lots of these. Even a veteran doing a quick scan of a message's source code might not notice that the URL says http://secure-ebay.com, which has nothing to do with the real ebay.com domain, and is anything *but* secure. Unfortunately, the domain registration process is entirely automated. No one at the registrar sees the registration application of secure-ebay.com from India to question its legitimacy or potential trademark infringement. It's up to every trademark holder to uncover and pursue violators in the courts.

I'm also seeing lots of domains that are, indeed, gibberish, things like md30s4eh.com (if spammers can make them up, so can I). Perhaps it's utter frustration: After finding dozens of neat names you have in mind already registered, you just go berserk on the keyboard to come up with a combination that nobody else has.[1] Maybe the spammers are trying to make it more unlikely that recipients will see recognizable patterns in the repetitive spew and associate them with known spam gangs. It does demonstrate the power of the original .com TLD. So many new companies have flocked to the .biz TLD for their spamvertised Web sites that many email administrators flag as spam any message bearing a link to this TLD.

Spammer Stupidity #11: *Intentionally misspelling spammy words*

Example:

```
Genierc and Sepur Viarga (Caiils) available
online!
Most trusted online source!

Cilais or (Spuer Vagira)
takes affect right away & lasts 24-36 huors!
FOR SUEPR VAIRGA TOCUH HERE <http://www.acymf-
gopd.vmcipniej.com=www.dxnulhjfij.vsjora.\x\.com/
c/?AFF_ID=c1224&rzwm=bcaliy>

Genierc Virgaa
costs 60% less! save a lot of $.
FOR VIGARA TOCUH HERE
<http://www.ojhmb.qmvc.com=www.nzwrcra.rezmj.\x\.
com/g/?AFF_ID=v1224&xtuays=vmuvlgckzr>
```

Why It's Stupid: Maybe I'm just a literate snob, but not only do I not find this tactic clever, it makes me wonder how professional this outfit is with regard to handling my credit card info and other personal data if I were to order their "Spuer Viarga." Sorry, I don't conduct business with a clown.

---

[1] I find it amusing that lots of gibberish domain names use characters only from the left side of an English keyboard. Apparently, the right hand is occupied on the mouse while filling out bulk domain registration forms.

The URLs the recipient is invited to "tocuh" use various obfuscation tricks described in Message Trick #16 (Chapter 12). I'm supposed to be fooled by the initial "www" and ".com" at the beginning of each URL, but the real domain is the string before the last ".com" (disguised here as \x\) The domains for the two links are the same, but they go to different directories at the site, one named c (probably for the Cialis offer), the other named g (for the generic Viagra). This is an affiliate mailing (i.e., spamming by someone further down the food chain), and the affiliate's ID number (for the commission on the click-through) is 1224.

Oh yes, it doesn't help spammy's cause in building credibility that the spamvertised domain name is registered from Turkey and the site is hosted in Taiwan. That's just too far to send away for "Suepr Vairga."

Here's another intentionally misspelled gem. The message's subject was the (unfortunate) random word "gasoline." The heart of the message reads:

```
I finlaly was able to lsoe the wieght I have
been sturggling to lose for years!

And I couldn't bileeve how simple it was!
Amizang pacth makes you shed the ponuds!
It's Guanarteed to work or your menoy back!
```

I think he's got every spammy word covered there with a substitute. The domain for this offer is registered by the same Turkish company, and hosted at the same Taiwanese ISP, as the "Suepr Vairga" spam. Another message pointing to yet another domain, but using the same tricks, format, domain registration, and Web hosting service, offers various oils for various body parts. It's nice to know that this guy has a diversified portfolio of spam offerings. Grrrrr.

Spammer Stupidity #12: *Routing spam through a mail server with spam- rating software on it*

Example:

```
X-ACS-Spam-Status: yes
X-ACS-Spam-Score: 7.258 (xxxxxxx)
X-ACS-Spam-Tests:
FORGED_YAHOO_RCVD,HTML_30_40,HTML_FONTCOLOR_BLUE,
HTML_FONT_BIG,HTML_FONT_FACE_ODD,HTML_MESSAGE,HTM
L_TITLE_UNTITLED,INVALID_DATE,MIME_HEADER_CTYPE_O
NLY,MSGID_FROM_MTA_SHORT
X-ACS-Scanned-By: MD 2.37; SA 2.61; spamdefang
1.86
```

Why It's Stupid: The message that arrived with the above X-headers was sent by a clueless dial-up customer in Alaska, using his ISP's regular outgoing mail system to send the mail (as customers do with their regular mail). What this fellow didn't think about is that the ISP, who proudly advertises its spam-filtering system as an important selling feature to attract customers, applies the same spam rating to all mail that goes through its mail server, including outgoing messages. The spam-rating software inserted its findings in the form of X-headers fields, which travel with the message wherever it goes.

When this message left Alaska, it had already been analyzed by an anti-spam evaluator, finding numerous reasons to suspect this message was spam based on a variety of problems with the header forging, HTML formatting, and other problems. It scored a comparatively high spam rating (7.258 out of 10), and met the ISP's threshold for what it considers spam. Unfortunately, the ISP didn't block the spam going out; that would have been ideal. But it certainly made analysis on the receiving end easy, and greased the wheels of reporting the spammer back to the ISP. The account was closed. Woohoo!

Spammer Stupidity #13: *Fumbling with mail merging in the Subject: header field.*

Example:

```
Received: from seisrv08.ac.gov.br
([200.252.127.\x\]) by dannyg.com (8.12.10) id
i0I5vKoM089229 for <webmaster@dannyg.com>; Sat,
17 Jan 2004 22:57:21 -0700 (MST)
Received: from pop3.cnnb.net ([200.252.127.\x\])
by seisrv08.ac.gov.br (8.12.5/8.12.5) with SMTP
id i0I5v5hD020146;
Sun, 18 Jan 2004 00:57:06 -0500
Date: Sun, 18 Jan 2004 00:57:05 -0500
From: "Denniso" <tillo@cnnb.net>
To: "Davidt" <eerhz@yahoo.com>
Message-ID: <1074412558.0549828150@pop3.cnnb.net>
Subject: Fwd: Please reply by today Davidt
```

Why It's Stupid: I think the sender would really have preferred that my first name appear at the end of the Subject: line, to gain my confidence that we were already good buds. But he failed to align his merging program fields to put anything related to the message's envelope address into the To: field or placeholder in the Subject: line. Instead, he inserted some other name and address in the To: line, and repeated the incorrect name portion at the end of the Subject: line.

This guy had a real problem because four of these messages with the same envelope address arrived within a couple minutes (funneled through two different hijacked PCs). Computers, being what they are, rarely recover from these kinds of snafus on their own. Who knows how many thousands or millions of erroneously labeled messages went across the Internet.

Of course, even if this guy had used my real name in the Subject: line, I would not be responding to his promise to "make some extra ca:sh". Sorry, whoever you are. Now get lost!

Spammer Stupidity #14: *Boasting bogus compliance with the U.S. CAN-SPAM law.*

Example:

```
In compliance with federal law, you may end fur-
ther promotions<br>of this product to your e-mail
address with the above link or write us
at:<br> <br>
\x\.org, CX Postal \x\, Ingleses<br>
CEP: 88058 970, Florianopolis, SC, Brazil<br>
```

Why It's Stupid: The more a spam message claims to comply with some law or set of guidelines, the more suspicious I am of it. The message from which the above example came was sent through a hijacked server on a Roadrunner network node in upstate New York. So much for compliance with U.S. law. It's also incredibly odd (and stupid) that a spammer from Brazil, where U.S. law doesn't mean squat, would bother to comply with the law—unless it's to profess a tinge of legitimacy that doesn't exist. To the spammer's credit (as it were), the spamvertised Web site is hosted by the same Brazilian organization as the one whose address is shown; and the message's From: address also has the same Brazilian domain (whether the address is valid is anyone's guess). Of course, then the spammer runs afoul once more. The unsubscribe link doesn't work in some browsers, while in other browsers (especially Internet Explorer for Windows), it plays teenage JavaScript tricks to open an offscreen window that can lead to any amount of nefarious activities on unpatched systems. If they hadn't made such a big deal about their compliance, I wouldn't have bothered to explore further; but since they did, I did, and found them to be run-of-the-mill offshore spammers.

Spammer Stupidity #15: *Throwing the "hash-buster" book at spam content filters.*

Example:
```
Received: from dsl-80-46-199-\x\.access.uk.tis-
cali.com (dsl-80-46-199-\x\.access.uk.tiscali.com
[80.46.199.159]) by \x\ (8.12.10) id
i0U9Pkqo032864; Fri, 30 Jan 2004 02:25:58 -0700
(MST)
Received: from [234.17.133.59] by 80.46.199.\x\
with HTTP;
Fri, 30 Jan 2004 01:22:43 -0700
From: "Lawanda Harper" <mfrlhovr@lycos.com>
To: \x\
Subject: prudent albuquerque gigaherz
Mime-Version: 1.0
X-Mailer: cryptology eisenhower bipartite
Date: Fri, 30 Jan 2004 02:22:43 -0600
Reply-To: "Lawanda Harper" <mfrlhovr@lycos.com>
Content-Type: multipart/alternative;
boundary="540603348861356789"
Message-Id: <HGLXLCC-0009290334298@playroom>
X-UIDL: #pY!!UO1"!BIG"!~3O"!


--540603348861356789
Content-Type: text/plain; charset=us-ascii
Content-Transfer-Encoding: 8bit

amount dichotomous prelude ephemeral lippincott
majesty conjugate nucleant credo alkaloid island
decode eli chaperon chesapeake average dragon
aromatic concierge leatherneck consequent shuffle
indecipherable ineffable basket bibliophile

--540603348861356789
Content-Type: text/html; charset=us-ascii
Content-Transfer-Encoding: 8bit

<!DOCTYPE HTML PUBLIC "-//W3C//DTD HTML 4.0
Transitional//EN">
<HTML><HEAD>

<TITLE>Message</TITLE>

<META content="MSHTML 6.00.2800.1276" name=GENER-
ATOR></HEAD>
```

```
<BODY>
<DIV><!-- Converted from text/plain format -->
<FONT face=Arial size=2>
<p>Hi,<br>
<br>
Sufper chaarge your lorve licfe!<br>
Orrder your Vgiagkra and Scupber Vikagmra salfely
and securlely onlijne.<br>
<br>
<br>
Cigalais (Sufper Vicabgra) takes affcect rigoht
away and labsts for dajys!<br>
<A
HREF="http://www.ujksgz.bryu.com=www.mxwjk.tsapb.
\x\.com/c/?AFF_ID=c1224&sjtupxp=gagdxj">Epntker
Henre</a><br>
<br>
<br>
Gezneiric Viragera cozsts 60% lesvs, sakve lots
of cawsh!<br>
<A HREF="http://www.ggpbui.qmruzp.com=www.hud-
jzbkiq.rtcui.\x\.com/v/?AFF_ID=v1224&eszsqi=hakqu
nvci">Esntcer Hecre</a><br>
<br>
<br>
Both prodeucts shigpped discreetely to your
domor<br>
<br>
<br>
<br>
<br>
<br>
<br>
<br>
<br>
<br>
<br>
<A HREF="http://www.wlbubrvqk.akeq.com=www.nsdo-
tyoj.jtqzirr.\x\.com/homepage/?gxvjr=heerud">Not
itnreseted</a><br></FONT></DIV></BODY></HTML>
mcdowell morris cluj arson patch enid pedestal
quagmire schweitzer gotten since jig assemblage
explode confabulate fitchburg hipster foulmouth
fabian copy condition fungoid cromwellian
```

macrostructure equine jay doctor geminate
reticulate backorder chassis compound humid can-
cerous downey booth lull signor austenite dairy-
man bernstein heady cliff buyer plagiarist angry
dubitable betel
frey diligent marry immediate daybreak figurate
inability kelly charisma restful caribbean histo-
riography prohibit sidearm mustard powers
chartres preposterous daugherty dear dysplasia

magnanimous mere cushman insomnia keeshond
belfast hornwort matinal corpulent mcnulty octet
polka ellwood purgative gsa scandinavia customary
blockage denunciate hilt danube shard apace
effusion gazette chantry peek notary holster
knockout naval portmanteau scarves restaurant hal
langmuir cloudy driscoll revival dastard billiard
ifni auspicious haul expensive indwell coupe
grant coeducation rape beauty fatigue euphrates
scorch asher faceplate diffeomorphic preamble
quadrennial byword naomi accipiter dial
contributory decry gunplay coastline flagellate
capricious deus purchase alexis alps aggressive
freight homeland ruination
empiric jacobian limb bulge hungry pup furry
offshoot instead commendatory countrify quasi-
periodic grisly motherhood adsorb garcia amster-
dam bolometer cantor ineffable agate eighty chili
cart dean
gorky constituent cherubim liniment conakry cran-
berry frugal range anent chang augustus child
parquet bunsen pharmacopoeia humiliate altogether
pecan greenbelt himself estrange sinclair female
enigma feminism anxious achieve shipman hobo
dealt cogent nurse elusive gorton appleby brazen
hydrochloride descriptive heterocyclic
implicate intend ababa mrs nellie diction lesbian
armload doria occlusion bible carla cartel
gavotte afford haphazard domineer quote arteriole
mile ricochet adequate grass catalyst coruscate
electrophorus rate bivouac epilogue pepperoni
prentice burundi emplace besotted logician cake
pill griffith furtive barb
shackle forgive comeback bulldog hamlet corrupt-

```
ible absent gladys airfare gummy boatswain burn
hexadecimal dragonfly depository ethel fantod
marcello <br>
```

```
--540603348861356789--
```

Why It's Stupid: The full email shown in the example takes the cake. It has a combined content filter target, but fooling Bayesian filters is the apparent primary goal. Sent through a zombie PC connected to the European ISP tiscali.com (presumably from a node in the United Kingdom), this message starts the ball rolling by using dictionary-supplied random words and names for the Subject: line. Since this line is immediately visible in the recipient's inbox listing, I'm still puzzled why spammers think this is a good tactic. Perhaps the recipient is supposed to be curious enough about the gibberish to open the message. I'll grant that the trick may work on a lot of inexperienced users. Damn!

The message comes with a plain-text portion for non-HTML-capable mail readers, but the words are more random dictionary words. Text-only recipients are apparently not the targets for this spam offer. Next comes the HTML payload, which uses extremely wild obfuscation of spammy words. Not only are common words obfuscated, but those that appear more than once are spelled differently each time. Even the "Enter Here" link text is different in two places, and is barely intelligible. All link URLs go to the same domain name, but they're surrounded by random gibberish, different in each instance. "No statistical content recognizer's gonna see a pattern in this message," the spammer must be saying to himself.

After the closing HTML tag, another, larger stream of dictionary words attempts to weigh down the text with real, nonspammy words. I wonder if the mail reader is supposed to stop displaying content after the closing HTML tag. Mine doesn't, so I would see this huge list of nonsensical claptrap appended to the end of the mail.

Are people so desperate for Viagra that they'd respond to this message? Even if it's "shigpped discreeteley" to their "domor"? I don't know what the specific offer says (I didn't visit the spamvertised Web site), but the domain is registered to an address in Russia (although the registration data looks very fishy to me), and the spamvertised site is hosted in Malaysia. I think I'd want to keep my credit card info a little closer to home.

If there is any good news from this seemingly desperate attempt to bore through content filtering, it is that the spammer has to waste a lot more time per email message. I'm talking scarcely milliseconds here, but by having to double the number of characters (one character equals 1 byte) that each message contains, it means that the SMTP server doing the work can send fewer messages over a given period of time than if the hash-busting add-ons weren't there. Maybe it means that the spammer has to control twice as many zombie machines at a time to get the same "productivity" from his campaigns. More work for the spammer can't be all that bad.

Spammer Stupidity #16: Failing English

Example:

> Learn in your own home on a interactive media CD Rom. How to customize Cars, Motorcycles, Boats, Walls, Etc.
>
> You can make hundredth's even thousand's in just one day's work.
>
> **Offer valid until February, 25th 2004 - Limited Stock.**

Why It's Stupid: Sometimes I wonder how fluent in English some spam ad authors are. Anyway, I'm not drawn to some product that will help me earn pennies.

Fresh examples of spammer stupidity arrive daily. They provide the equivalent of battlefield humor to relieve the stress of dealing with the constant barrage.

CHAPTER 15

Technology as a Partial Solution

Ask a typical computer programmer or systems engineer how best to tackle spam, and the suggestions invariably involve technical solutions: software on PCs, software on servers, new email protocols, fee-for-sending systems, and so on. This is only natural, because to many computer folks, spam seems inherently like a technical disease in need of a technical cure.

It turns out, however, that just as there are different types of spammers, email recipients come in all shapes and sizes, and have various likes and dislikes. One technical system—at least of the ones proposed and implemented thus far—does not fit all. Antispam nerds have been pursuing this problem for over a decade, and we're no closer to a universal solution today than we were when spam first appeared. Some technical solutions work great for some email users, but others see those solutions as merely masking the symptoms of a more insidious disease that may need drastic surgery to cure completely.

Now that hundreds of spam-fighting products and services are available to individual users and system administrators, I'll leave it to others with testing facilities to evaluate and recommend some products over others. One Web site you can use as a starting point for your own software investigations is spamotomy.com. Also look into the Web sites and publications that produce independent comparative reviews of competing systems (infoworld.com, pcmag.com, computerworld.com, cnet.com).

Most spam-fighting products, out of necessity, employ a blended approach. One type of filtering or blocking is usually not enough to keep the spew at bay. What I hope to explain in this chapter is not any particular product's prowess at keeping spam out of your hair, but rather the basic types

203

of antispam technologies being hurled at the tidal wave of unwanted garbage. I choose this way to describe the technical approaches because I hear too many new recruits to the spam-fighting platoons say things like, "Why don't we just...?" as if one technique would solve the world's spam problem. While a particular idea may be a good one, it's important to understand why it might fail in other circumstances or contexts.

In case you're wondering, I use a home-grown variation of a long-available free utility program that I've tailored to the spam and ham (mail I want to get) that arrives at my server. Since I control my own mail server, I have the luxury of pinpoint control that most email users don't. I'm able to keep almost all spam out of my personal computer's inbox—my primary goal of spam control. And I don't offer my system to others because it is a custom fit for the way I run my email server; I wouldn't presume it would work as well for any other server or user.

This chapter presents the top technical solutions that have been proposed and/or implemented so you can see the range of ideas and activities ultimately aimed at eliminating spam from reaching every user's email inbox. The basic categories are:

- Server-side[1] content filtering

- Server-side IP blocking

- Server-side whitelisting

- Server-side authentication

- Upgrading or replacing SMTP

- Challenge-response systems

- Email fee systems

- Disposable email addresses

- Client-side content filtering

- Client-side whitelisting

- Individual spam reporting

- Electronic attacks

---

[1] "Server-side" means that the operation takes place either on the mail server that initially receives the mail (called a gateway in administration-speak) or on a server hosted by an outside service whose job is to perform the necessary filtering before the mail is passed back to the receiving domain for distribution to users' inboxes. Some commercial spam-fighting products work only on the mail gateway; others require forwarding all mail to the outside service.

For every great idea, however, there is at least one show-stopping problem that prevents it from making every antispammer happy. From most users' standpoint, the success of any system depends on three capabilities: how well it keeps spam out of their way; that it doesn't prevent legitimate mail from reaching them; and that it doesn't disrupt their existing email processing. Achieving this balance is tricky, especially if you do not have control over what your incoming mail server implements—a common occurrence if you get your mail through one of the giant providers (AOL, MSN, Earthlink, Hotmail, Yahoo!, and hundreds of others) or a server that is micromanaged by a corporation's or educational institution's IT department.

To best understand the technical side of spam fighting, if you haven't already, you should read Chapter 4 on how email works. Believe me when I say that I'm protecting you from a ton of email-geek (as opposed to email-chic) terminology here. As it is, most server-side solutions need to be installed and maintained by administrators or programmers who know how to fiddle with their servers securely; client-side solutions also need occasional attention, especially in the early days following installation. And, for each quasi-successful technical approach, spammers are hard at work to find ways around it.

Server-side Content Filtering

Content filtering attempts to computerize the process that the human mind is very good at: recognizing spam when it "sees" it. Just as true artificial intelligence has proven elusive in the computer lab, content filtering at best can simulate only certain analyses of an incoming message to determine whether it is spam or ham. This is particularly tricky on a server that needs to make such determinations for potentially thousands of users connected to a corporate or other institution's mail system.

Systems employing content filtering on the server generally accept all incoming mail with no questions asked (assuming, on most systems, that the addressee is a valid user on the mail server). Only after the mail has been received by an incoming server is the content of the mail analyzed. This means that the sending computer knows only that the message was accepted by the incoming email server, not whether the message actually reached the addressee.

Filtering systems also vary as to the way they handle mail identified as, or suspected of being, spam. To avoid the possibility of throwing away a legitimate message erroneously suspected of being spam, all suspects are quarantined, either in a separate folder that the user can download separately or in an area that the server software offers via a password-protected

Web interface. Users can scan the lists of suspects and inspect those that might be legitimate in a relatively safe environment. Legitimate mails can then be forwarded to the user's regular email inbox. More draconian handling deletes messages identified as spam before ever allowing them to enter into the user's realm. An advantage for deleting messages is that less mail storage is needed on the server; users are also spared from having to scan through lists of mostly garbage or succumb to time-consuming, largely worthless email downloads while traveling. Even so, the threat of a *false positive*—a legitimate message (say, from a potential new customer) that gets summarily deleted—always exists.

Numerous content analysis techniques are in use these days, ranging from the simple to rather sophisticated. It's rare that a product uses only one type of content analysis, but these are the types.

Word, Phrase, Pattern Lookup

The complete source code of the message (including header and body) is compared against a "laundry list" of words, phrases, and text patterns that have been previously identified as belonging to spam messages. Patterns are usually defined with the help of a special shortcut language called *regular expressions.* For example, the following regular expression rule (used in a content analysis program called Procmail) will find a match if the words "make," "money," and "fast" appear in sequence within a message. The instructions at the left of the rule specify that the pattern can be at the beginning of a line or be preceded by any nonalphanumeric character (like a space); the .* symbols mean that zero or more characters of any kind can appear between the words; and the trailing instructions mean that the word "fast" can be at the end of a line or followed by any nonalphanumeric character (like an exclamation point or period).

```
(^|[^0-9a-z])make.*money.*fast([^0-9a-z]|$)
```

However, using this rule by itself as an indicator of spam could lead to trouble. Imagine a business associate sending you an email with the sentence:

```
We can make a bunch of money on this deal if we
send them a proposal fast.
```

If the system is set up to divert to a "suspected spam" folder any message that contains matching words, phrases, or patterns, legitimate mail might be delayed or deleted. Pure text-matching lookup can work effectively for blocking words or URLs that you don't ever want to see in an email message—provided the spammer doesn't misspell words. It's tedious to load the list with patterns that will catch every variation of "Viagra" (like V1agra, Vigara, V1g@r@, and so on). Spammers use a lot of intentional misspellings on words that typically occupy lookup lists, caring more about getting past the filters than appearing literate to their prospective customers.

Unsophisticated text matching can work wonders with a list of spamvertised Web site domains. A list that gets updated with domains of recent link destinations can easily block future messages with the same domains in their links. The problem for spam fighters is that high-volume spammers who spend their lives covering their tracks register new domains daily, commonly with gibberish names just to get a dot-com top-level domain that isn't used by anybody else. Registration is comparatively cheap (about $5 each in bulk), and the registration can easily redirect Web browser requests to any existing server under the spammer's control. Registration name and contact information isn't verified at the time of registration, so it's no big deal for a spammer to provide fake data. Even if someone complains to the registrar (as if a registrar in China cares) and the International Corporation for Assigned Names and Numbers (ICANN, the international monitor of key top-level domains), it can take weeks to get a phony registration revoked. In the meantime, all it takes is a day or two after registration for the Domain Name Service (DNS) entries associated with a new domain name to propagate around the world's DNS servers. If the domain registration should be challenged, by the time it's revoked, the spammer has moved onto several other domain names for the latest spam runs.

Heuristic Analysis

Instead of just treating the presence of a text lookup match with a yes or no response, a program can assign a numeric score for the existence of a particular word, phrase, or pattern found in an email message. For instance, one of the trademarks of some spam is the overuse of the various disclaimer phrases that try to make you believe you registered with the sender or one of its "partners." The same message typically provides instructions for how to "unsubscribe" or "remove" yourself from the list, using language with those words in it. A heuristic analysis accumulates a score for each message based on points associated with each typically spammy word, phrase, and pattern. The administrator of the system establishes a threshold above which the score indicates that the message is likely spam. All messages above that score get flagged as spam, and are either marked up as such (by inserting customized X-header fields into the message) or are diverted to a suspected spam holding area.

I'm not fond of using "heuristic" to label this approach, because the term to me signifies a process of self-learning from experience. Instead, most heuristic spam filters rely on humans updating the pattern lists, the scores, and threshold value based on the human input, not the computer's "analysis" of the content.

Systems can employ more sophisticated pattern-matching techniques and still use the scoring. For example, if a message contains a base64-encoded body, a straight text analysis of the message won't find the blockable words or phrases that appear in the message when it is viewed in the recipient's email program. But there is nothing to prevent a content analysis program from decoding the base64 content, and then doing the text lookup and scoring.

Hash-based Analysis

Until recently, all messages for a particular spam campaign typically sent the same subject line and body, week after week, to however many millions of addresses were in the spammer's database. It's relatively easy for a computer program to generate a mathematical value based on the character values and other physical characteristics of the message. That value—called a *hash* or *checksum* value—is like a compact fingerprint of the message's content. Ideally, email administrators worldwide would participate in this system to report those hash values to a readily available database. A spam campaign to hundreds of thousands of addresses per hour would likely generate enough reports to increase the spamminess score of the associated hash value. Mail servers participating in this reporting network could compare computed hash values of temporarily quarantined messages from unknown sources against the values stored in the database, and flag the message as spam or summarily delete the message.

Spammers, as is their wont, tried to break the system by adding random character "hash busters" to parts of each outgoing message in the hope of preventing a given campaign from achieving too high a score. Of course, then the hash makers improved their analyses to be smarter about which characteristics of a message are evaluated for the calculation of the hash values.

Spam fighters using these techniques have organized around a variety of Open Source implementations, including ones known as Vipur's Razor and Distributed Checksum Clearinghouse, or DCC (www.rhyolite.com).[2] The DCC world is built around a network of more than 20 public servers (and many more

---

[2] Open Source is a process of software development that encourages public participation. All source code is freely available, allowing for peer review from independent sources during development. To learn more, visit opensource.org and osdn.com.

private ones) that receive and exchange reports from thousands of users around the world. As with any "real-time" reporting system, the effectiveness of the system depends on constant updating throughout the day. Also, because anyone can install a DCC query system on his or her own incoming mail server, spammers can use it to test new hash-busting techniques.

And the battle of bits continues.

Statistical Analysis

As described in Chapter 12, modern applications of Bayesian statistical techniques have achieved success in identifying spam.[3] The system uses a variety of content analyses to determine the statistical probability that a message is spam if an incoming message shares characteristics of previous messages that were identified as spam. As users classify suspects for their spamminess or hamminess, the routines improve their capability to more accurately predict the classification of a new message.

Bayesian analysis, however, works best on an individual level, because wording and other content of each email user's body of legitimate mail varies. An industrial engineer's mails will likely have quite a different vocabulary from mail arriving for the chief financial officer in the same firm. If a server-based system (operating either on the gateway or at an external service) can associate Bayesian rules with each incoming email account, then the statistical analysis stands a good chance of improving filtering—assuming the system is also wired in a way that makes it easy for a user to classify questionable mails and feed that information back to the server's area for that user.

As good as Bayesian filtering has been in its short life, two newer statistical analysis systems have been claiming even better rates of trapping spam with fewer false positives.[4] Still others are sure to emerge from the labs. Spammers, themselves, reveal that Bayesian filtering is doing its job. See Message Trick #8 in Chapter 12.

Server-side IP Blocking

An email administrator is in the catbird seat when it comes to determining which email message is allowed into an incoming server. Thanks to the

---

[3] The commonly used formal name for this approach is Statistical Token Analysis.

[4] One is called CRM114, whose letters stand for Controllable Regex Mutilator (crm114.sourceforge.net). The other is DSPAM, whose name means nothing more than "de-spam" (www.nuclearelephant.com/projects/dspam).

SMTP and TCP/IP standards, a mail server that intends to send mail to another server is automatically identified by the sender's numeric IP address. More than a dozen organizations around the world track the activities of spammers through the IP addresses used to send mail. Tracking is accomplished through reporting by recipients, as well as self-tracking when messages arrive at email addresses used for no other purpose than to trap senders who send to addresses that could be acquired only by harvesting from Web pages (so-called spam trap addresses).

From all this tracking activity come numerous blocklists (also called blacklists, blackhole lists, real-time blackhole lists, depending on the preference of the list creator). I use the abbreviation BL to cover them all. These lists contain IP addresses of known or suspected spammers (and sometimes even neighboring IP addresses, as discussed in Chapter 10). IP blocking focuses strictly on the sender's IP, not the domain name or content of a message.

Some spam fighters prefer IP blocking because when handled at the point of initial contact from a sending server, the incoming server can reject the connection before too many bytes flow through the Internet. All the receiving server needs to do is see if the sender's IP address is on a blocklist. If so, the connection is refused.

It's rare (and usually inadvisable) that IP blocking be done with only one BL source. As with so much spam blocking, a blended approach works best. Not all BLs are created equally or with the same emphases and reporting systems behind them.

Many administrators also maintain their own BLs tailored to their users' emailing habits. For example, because a lot of spam originates from servers in China and Brazil, some small business email server administrators take the position that no mail originating from IP blocks in those countries will ever achieve a successful connection with the server. I hope these folks have alerted the company management to these decisions, because it could mean that legitimate business inquiries from those countries will never reach the sales or publicity departments. Most companies and professionals cannot afford to block entire countries or regions of the world, but sometimes a myopic response to a flood of spam in Cyrillic can cause an angry email administrator to block all email from Russia. In my estimation, the Internet-connected world is too small to block geographical regions or countries arbitrarily. Even if 99.9 percent of messages from Lower Freedonia are spam, the 0.1 percent that makes product inquiries or requests product support could be well worth receiving.

Server-side Whitelisting

A whitelist contains addresses (domains, individual email addresses, and IP addresses) that are approved by an incoming mail server's administrator as being "okay" to enter without further filtering or scrutiny. In other words, the addresses in the list belong to senders who, metaphorically, wear white hats—as did the "Good Guys" in cowboy movies. For servers that handle a small number of users, it's conceivable for the server to maintain separate whitelists associated with each user. In other words, users submit addresses of senders for all mail that they want to receive. This is particularly useful for bulk mail in the form of confirmed opt-in newsletters and e-commerce weekly special mailings that might otherwise have enough spam signatures in their content to be flagged as spam by other means.

Some tech firms are working on mechanisms to produce whitelists of bulk mailers that not only swear to abide by the publicly acceptable definition of being spam-free, but are willing to put their money where their mouths are. The systems require that bulk mailers that use only confirmed opt-in subscriptions put up a surety bond, money that sits in a bank as a pledge to keep their mailing practices honest. If such a "bonded sender" is discovered to break that pledge (by sending an unsolicited mailing to a spam trap address), the sender may forfeit some or all of the bond and be removed from the list. As an added bonus to being a bonded sender, a mailer may receive some assistance in defending spam claims from recipients who really did confirm their opt-in request, but forgot they did so and reported the mailing as spam.

Keeping corporate or individual internal whitelists up to date is a pain for all involved. If a newsletter mailer changes the name of the server used for sending issues, that information may not reach a recipient's whitelist until a few issues go astray as spam fodder. Or if you need to receive automated confirmations from travel or e-commerce Web sites, you'll rarely know the address used to send such messages to add it to the whitelist ahead of time.

An extreme application of whitelisting would employ it as the sole filtering mechanism. Such a system would reject all messages except those that arrive from senders already known to the recipients. In other words, no mail from a stranger would ever be received or passed onto its recipient. I know lots of parents would prefer this kind of system for their children's email accounts, to limit incoming mail to known friends and relatives (some consumer-oriented Internet services offer this feature). Some employers might also like this notion to keep employees from abusing their email privileges for personal messages; but this kind of restriction could cause serious problems if the company wants to receive mail from "troublemaking" strangers: new customers and vendors.

Server-side Authentication

One of the hot buttons for future-looking spam-fighting technologists these days grows from a fundamental truism about the worst of the worst spam spew: It arrives with forged sender identities. One idea promotes a way to verify that a message is originating from not only a known place, but from a sender who is authorized to send mail from the originating server. Accomplishing this while staying within the confines of the existing (and well-entrenched) SMTP standard is no easy feat. It also has to be done in a way that is reliable enough not to be hacked. For example, if there were a directory or database associated with an outgoing mail server that contained references to all valid senders for the server, it would be quick work for a hacker to run dictionary-like queries to find out which user IDs were good ones, because all accepted test messages would be to valid addresses. You also want this kind of lookup to be independent of the outgoing server so that a zombie SMTP server on a PC wouldn't automatically authenticate any sender ID it wanted.

I won't bore you with the details of the ideas circulating among spam fighters, but the notions getting the most attention are known by names such as Sender ID, Sender Policy Framework (or SPF, merged in June 2004 with a Microsoft effort named Caller ID for Email), and Domain Keys (proposed by Yahoo Inc.). All are aimed at preventing a sender from hiding behind a false identity.

Blocking senders who fail to identify themselves accurately doesn't solve the problem of spammers who, buoyed by laws that allow them to send unsolicited mail legally, don't mind identifying themselves. Of course those senders are easily blocked by numerous other technical solutions being discussed here, especially if they have any record of sending spam from those identities in the past.

But what the various server-side authentication proposals emphasize is that the simplicity, mobility, and freedom that have allowed the current SMTP and related standards to become so entrenched—because users like those aspects—are impediments to deploying more restrictive systems that could help stem the spam flow. Will users be willing to give up, say, the ability to send and receive mail while sitting with their laptop computer at a wireless network "hotspot" at a Starbucks while on a road trip? Should anonymity on the Internet be outlawed? Do you want to prevent your teenage son from emailing his school principal using your From: address about an absence excuse? Oh, well, maybe some authentication could be good.

Upgrading or Replacing SMTP

The current document of record for the Simple Mail Transfer Protocol (SMTP) is RFC 2821.[5] Although it dates from a fairly recent year (2001), it was the first major updating of the specification that had held the Internet email system together since 1982 (RFC 821).

Various new proposals arise from time to time as ways to supplement SMTP (RFC 2821) and message format (RFC 2822) standards with features that attempt to work against spammers and spamming. Less intrusive proposals commonly add one or more new header fields to the message format, such as one that identifies the nature of a message as a solicitation, rather than burdening the Subject: line with government-mandated prefixes (ADV: and the like). If the standard treats such add-ons as optional (which would make them backward-compatible with existing servers and PC email programs), nothing prevents scofflaws from thumbing their noses at stuff that is designed to work against them.

More strident proposals not only extend the SMTP standard—after all, it has been a workable foundation for over 20 years (many Internet lifetimes)— but are quick to assume an attitude of conquering hero: Play by the new rules or we won't let you communicate with us! For example, the following excerpt from a proposal covering SMTP authorization through a reverse mail exchanger (RMX) server mechanism suggests how the transition to an incompatible system would work:

> Domains without RMX records must temporarily be treated the same way as they are treated right now, i.e. e-mail must be accepted from anywhere. But once the scheme becomes sufficiently widespread, mail relays can start to refuse e-mails with sender addresses from domains without RMX records, thus forcing the owner of the domain to include a statement of authorization into the domain's zone table.[6]

I giggle when I see wording like this in industry proposals, especially when some invisible peer pressure is supposed to change the way the world works. It reminds me of the way IP address blocklists include innocent bystanders within a blocked range, in the hope that the innocents will force

---

5　Help yourself to the gory details at www.faqs.org/rfcs/rfc2821.html.

6　Danisch, Hadmut. "The RMX DNS RR and method for lightweight SMTP sender authorization," IETF Internet-Draft, October 2003.

the ISP to mend its spam-friendly ways. While some ISPs eventually respond to this kind of pressure, the threat is not so widespread as to make all ISPs shake in their bytes. But think about how many SMTP servers are connected to the Internet and actively sending email—perhaps hundreds of thousands. And a number of those systems are no longer actively maintained by administrators who stay up to date on the latest email technologies. Some small businesses may not even have access to the systems administrators who set up the servers in the first place (they're away at college now). These firms could conceivably be cut off from email and not know how to upgrade or reconnect. Orchestrating a worldwide switchover to a new system, as occurred back in 1983 for ARPANET, is out of the question today.

But I fear that "it's my ball" strong-arm tactics will be tried by heavy hitters as ways to promise to protect their users from spam and viruses. The new service could entail wholesale replacement of SMTP with some cryptographically enhanced authentication scheme requiring new mail server software. Pulling off this kind of coup would be very difficult, and in the process it could muddy the email waters considerably. SMTP may not be the most modern way to get mail around the world, but changing it now would be like trying to change the North American road system to the British system overnight. Blood would be spilt.

A more likely scenario is a gradual phase-in of extensions to SMTP in a way that will coexist with the old system for awhile. The extensions will attempt to address the problems of forged sender identities (employing some kind of sender authentication) and unauthorized use of mail relays and zombie PCs. Numerous kinks have to be ironed out before such improvements can be deployed, but eventually it's conceivable that giant ISPs will require all mail servers to comply with the new extensions or have all messages from older servers tagged as "suspicious." All of the technical work will be on the server end, and we consumers may not even be aware of the damage except for some good mail being improperly labeled spam.

All I ask is that the design of the extensions be handled as an "open," similar to the way today's SMTP evolved. An industrywide campaign to design, test, and implement the protocol might gather the necessary support from those who would have to do the hardest work to implement it. One working group in the Internet Engineering Task Force (IETF) is aiming toward establishing an Internet Standard that uses the Domain Name Service (DNS) mechanism to provide a level of sender authentication.[7]

---

[7] If you're interested in following the progress of this activity, it is known as MTA Authorization Records in DNS (marid). MTA stands for Mail Transfer Agent, a piece of software that receives or relays email at the server level. Look for details at the IETF Web site (www.ietf.org).

Challenge-Response Systems

A challenge-response (CR) system operates like a combination of server-side whitelisting and a manual type of authentication. The incoming mail server maintains a whitelist of addresses from which mail passes without delay. Any message arriving from an address not on the whitelist is put into a holding bin on the server. A message goes back to the sender (at the address listed in the From: or Reply-To: header field) asking for confirmation that the sender is something other than a spam-spewing robot. This part is called a *challenge*. If the original sender responds correctly to the challenge, the sender's address is added to the whitelist, and the message is moved from the holding bin into the recipient's inbox.

To prevent robots from simply responding to a simplistic reply that needs nothing more than a click, the challenges typically include something more, um, challenging. There may be an image in the challenge message that displays some funky-looking numbers and letters the user must identify correctly; or there may be some kind of puzzle that requires a level of human thought to complete. The point is that the challenge task cannot be something that another computer can figure out based on the text or other kind of message scanning.

In spam fighting, however, no good idea goes unpunished. In the case of CR systems, there are three particularly thorny problems that can haunt recipients who put up the CR shields: (1) senders who don't wait for the challenge; (2) unexpected but desired automated senders; and (3) senders with visual impairments.

Ask any CR user, and you'll likely hear at least one story of an important piece of human-generated mail failing to reach its destination on time or at all. Here's a typical scenario: Tim is about to leave for a weekend outing with his family, but he needs to get some last-minute instructions to Janis about how to finish the sales presentation needed on Monday. Tim sends the email to Janis and bolts out the door. Unbeknownst to Tim, Janis had installed a CR system earlier in the day. Before Tim even gets to his car in the parking lot, the challenge message from Janis's system is in his inbox. Neither he nor Janis knows about the impending email exchange. Sunday night Tim checks his email and finds the challenge. It's too late by then, and Monday is ruined.

Another common story about a CR system snafu is the e-commerce order that gets confirmed or needs further input to be completed. When Ian enters his email address in the order form, he forgets about the CR system. And when the e-tailer sends an automated message to get more details, the sending computer doesn't respond to the challenge. Mayhem ensues when Ian blames the e-outfit for screwing up his order.

Not as common, but still troubling for a CR system is the case in which a visually impaired user, who relies on a text-to-speech system that "reads aloud" screen text through speech synthesis, sends a message to a contact address on a Web site. Unfortunately, the challenge message comes back with instructions to enter the numbers and letters displayed in the image embedded in the message. Even if the email reader can display HTML images, the coding for the image cannot contain any clues about the content of the image, because a spammer's robot could easily read the clues. The blind correspondent is completely cut off from communicating with the site's contact point.

Quite a few email administrators object to the concept of CR because of the excess Internet bandwidth it incurs. Each message from a new correspondent translates into three exchanges: (1) the original mail; (2) the challenge; and (3) the response. When a spam message with a forged, but working, address in the From: header line arrives at a CR system, the challenge goes to someone who didn't send anything to begin with. The challenge, itself, may get reported as spam by the miffed or befuddled challenge recipient. I receive a fair number of challenges to messages I never sent, and they are irritating to no end.

Despite these considerable disadvantages to CR systems, they can be useful if you micromanage your emailing behavior—meaning you'll have to reserve your CR-enhanced mailing address for people you know (or whom you can warn ahead of time about the one-time challenge). For all other activity involving a required email address, you'll need either another email account somewhere (one without CR) or a throwaway email address (described below).

Challenge-Response CAPTCHA

The goal of a challenge-response system is to substantiate as accurately as possible that a human being is the original sender of a message. To that end, the CR system sends back a message with some kind of test that supposedly can be solved only by a human. This type of test is called a CAPTCHA, for Completely Automated Public Turing Test to Tell Computers and Humans Apart. It is named after computer science and artificial intelligence pioneer Alan Turing, who devised requirements—the Turing Test—that would classify a computer as a "sentient being." Like almost everything in the world, CAPTCHA aficionados have their own Web site (www.captcha.net).

A CAPTCHA typically presents an image that is distorted or obfuscated to make it difficult for a computer to determine the meaning of the content. In the text-oriented test shown below (from captcha.net/cgi-bin/gimpy), the user is asked to type three of the words shown in the image. The twisty, overlapped text isn't too difficult for a sighted human to decipher, but more of a challenge for, say, an optical character recognition (OCR) program.

For every technical challenge, however, clever (and devious) folks seek ways to break the system. For instance, some University of California at Berkeley computer science students have achieved a level of success in programming a computer to solve text-based challenges like the one shown here. Although the success rate as of early 2004 was only 33 percent, repeated attempts to get through a CR challenge would land a large number of successes.

There are also reports that pornography Web site spammers have written programs that embed CAPTCHA images received from free email account registration challenges into their sites. Visitors can view some free porn by solving the puzzle. Of course the visitor doesn't really have to solve the puzzle (since the spammer's computer doesn't know the solution), but humans (and especially males) are goal-oriented, so they'll do their best to be right. In the end, the spammer gets another free email account from which to send spam until the account gets shut down from complaints.

Email Fee ("Sender Pays") Systems

Every couple of months it seems as though some industry "guru" gets 15 minutes of press coverage for a "unique" idea of charging high-volume email senders for their messages. The idea, which sounds good for the first few seconds the first time you hear it, appeals to the economic argument that works in the spammer's favor: that it costs next to nothing to send an individual email message, and only slightly more to send millions. Since spammers work in a system that has an extremely low breakeven point (with respect to orders received in return), proponents of the idea say it's time to get those who mail the most to pay for the privilege. Charging a fraction of a penny for every email message sent on the Internet won't hurt the everyday email user, but will grind cash out of the spammers and dissuade those who don't want to pay. Even Bill Gates offered this idea as part of a spam-fighting strategy described in early 2004.

I know that this sounds like a justifiable way to get spammers to start paying for their use of the Internet infrastructure. And you know what? The idea makes a sliver of sense, but only if spammers all operated in a world that forced them to identify themselves correctly and to mail from servers that they own or legitimately control. But anyone who receives a fair amount of spam (Yo! Over here!) can tell you that more and more spam can be traced back no further than a zombie SMTP server or open proxy server on some poor sucker's worm-infected computer. How would you feel when Comcast sends you a bill for your next month's cable modem connection, and it has an extra $500 charge for the 5 million messages your system sent last month, billed at one one-thousandth of a penny per message? Maybe *that* will teach ya to get some antivirus software and download the latest system software patches.

Oh please!

What really floors me about this fee business is imagining how the world's ISPs could ever agree on a system for collecting the money, especially since there are blackhat ISPs out there (on four continents I'm aware of) who willingly—no, eagerly—court the business of spammers equally eager to disguise the actual insertion points of spam (to evade the weak laws). Who would enforce the collections? Would the fees have to ripple through upstream Internet providers? Who would audit the whole mess? Would an email toll booth be erected in Redmond, Washington?[8]

Next, where does all this money go? To the backbone providers? To ISPs? As if they would share revenue with their customers, in essence to pay the "fees" for the everyday folks. Who's going to pay for the thousands or tens of thousands of messages that emanate daily from legitimate all-volunteer mailing lists?

Sorry, I simply can't fathom the world's Internet powers coming to agreement on how such a system would work. If substantial money were

---

[8] Okay, the last one is an exaggeration. Isn't it? Please tell me I'm exaggerating.

involved, the system, itself, will become a target for abuse, or worse. It could become a monster more troublesome than denizens of the ROKSO list, times ten.

Disposable Email Addresses

For everyday email users—meaning especially those who don't run their own incoming email servers—the one email address you are handed by your ISP, company, school, or organization becomes easy fodder for spammers. Once that address is exposed to the spammers' databases, you're hosed. To restrict exposure of your address to collectors—and still participate in Internet activities such as e-commerce, confirmed opt-in subscriptions, and a variety of "free" information and news sites—you have to take preemptive action. Your goal is to limit the possibility that your primary email address gets into the hands of anyone who could pass along that address to third parties.

One option is to create one or more accounts on free email services such as Hotmail, Yahoo!, and dozens of others. Use those addresses for Web site registrations where you need to supply at least a temporarily valid email address to sign yourself up to the site. If you find that the address you use for that purpose becomes burdened by spam, cancel that account and create a new one. This assumes, of course, that you either don't care about missing announcements from the sites you registered with the old name, or that you'll change your registration address on those sites you do care about. But having multiple email addresses and checking those accounts for incoming mail becomes a nuisance if you want to receive mailings from a variety of sites, such as newsletter subscriptions and newsgroup digests.

One solution to the problem is a service that lets you create disposable email addresses. Here is how one service, Sneakemail (www.sneakemail.com), works for someone already registered with it:

1. You obtain an address with the sneakemail.com domain and enter it into another Web site's registration form.

2. Mail from that site goes to the disposable address at sneakemail.com.

3. Sneakemail automatically forwards the message to your regular mail account.

4. A reply you send is coded in such a way that it goes first to sneakemail.com, and then to the actual destination, but only with your sneakemail address listed in the mail.

If you're suspicious that a site where you register might be less than honest with its "we won't share your address" privacy policy, you can create a sneakemail address just for that one registration. If you later discover that you're getting mail for all kinds of other garbage addressed to that address, you know that the privacy policy was a lie, and you can sever connections with all sites by deleting that address from your sneakemail account.

While disposable and free email accounts let the spam-weary potentially lower their involuntary contributions to the spamonomy, the micromanagement of your email life is a horrible price to pay. Spam fighters who live to catch privacy-claiming e-commerce and subscription sites red-handed in freewheeling partnership deals with spam slime love these services. But gee whiz, you have to keep a diary of what you use where. I mean, if you sign up as a customer at gizmos-iz-us.com with a disposable address and a password, you'll have to remember that combination for the next time you order or inquire about the status of a current order.

I'm glad these services exist, but I also deplore that spammers have driven so many people to such ends.

Client-side Content Filtering

Most modern email programs that run on personal computers have filtering built into them or available as third-party add-ons. They work primarily to separate the suspected spam from real ham after email is retrieved from the server. Suspects are placed in a separate folder within your email program, allowing you to manually scan the suspects for false positives. Virtually all of the recent filtering systems use Bayesian statistical analysis algorithms to examine the headers and content of the messages. This means that, in theory, the filtering gets better as it gets to know the characteristics of your "good" mail.

Server-side filtering doesn't always work as completely as you might like. But there is nothing wrong with supplementing server-side vigilance with client-side content filtering. A filter associated with your personal email program may be smarter or operate on a different baseline sampling of your good mail, thus providing a secondary shield against spam that gets past server filters.

If you choose to seek out a content filter add-on for your email program, first narrow your search by the email program you run. Each filter is usually built for a specific email program, including different versions or products for various incarnations of Microsoft's Outlook email program on Windows. Your choices on other operating systems are much narrower; and with less competition among the fewer offerings, improved versions of the filter of your choice may not arrive as quickly as on the hotly contested Windows email platforms.

The problem with client-side *anything* involving spam filtering is that you have to waste bandwidth (and perhaps connect time on a dial-up or commercial Wi-Fi hotspot account) as all the garbage downloads into your computer in the first place. Any technology that forces you to scan spam suspects for the occasional false positive is a personal productivity drain.

Transferring spam from your email server to your PC does not, by itself, confirm or deny the existence of your address with a spammer. Nor does it contribute to the spamonomy. At worst, it may impact metered connect time some users may encounter. The key, however, is treating all spam suspects with care, verging on dread. Your goal, remember, is to remain completely invisible—nonexistent—to the spammer, which means either summarily deleting the unviewed (and unpreviewed) message or performing an initial scan of the message in its source code form to prevent accidental triggering of Web bugs or script-driven nastiness.

Client-side Whitelisting

One of the earliest spam-fighting techniques built into personal email programs takes advantage of integration between the email program and your personal email address book. The basic notion is that if an incoming message's From: address doesn't match one of the addresses in your local address book, the message is visually flagged to let you see *in the list* of mail in your inbox that the mail is potentially spam.

As weak as this technique sounds, it can be effective for those who use email for nothing more than communicating with a small, closed network of family, friends, or colleagues. If Aunt Flo never—and I mean *never*—registers for anything at a Web site, participates in public online forums, registers a domain name, publishes a Web page, or buys anything through e-commerce, the likelihood of spam becoming a problem for her is very slim. Her email address is, however, still vulnerable to attack if it exists in an email address book of a regular correspondent whose computer becomes infected with an email-related virus or worm. Outside of that, a spam email would reach her only by way of a dictionary attack on her ISP, in which the attacker came up with the mix of letters and numbers of her user ID. In that case, she should trust her email program's whitelisting feature, and immediately delete any message that arrives from an unknown sender. Unfortunately, if she makes a mistake and views even one spam message, she may be confirming her address to the spam world. Get ready, Aunt Flo: Your email inbox is in for a heap o' trouble.

Spam Reporting

All of the technical solutions described thus far in this chapter are purely defensive. Their aims are to keep spam at bay or at least keep it out of your face as much as possible. But to a significant number of spam haters on the Internet, defending their servers or themselves against spam isn't enough. They want to do whatever they can to make the spammer's life difficult, ideally causing enough trouble to "encourage" the spammer to find another line of work. The two main weapons at the spam fighter's disposal are: (1) reports to ISPs through which spam is mailed or spamvertised sites are hosted; and (2) contributions to public blocklists (BLs).

Reporting to ISPs and upstream providers by way of the Luser Attitude Readjustment Tool (LART) is something that any user with sufficient knowledge can do. Doing a good job of tracking down the ISPs and determining which policies or terms of service the alleged spammer has violated is time-consuming. Sometimes even a lone LART from an independent reporter can succeed in getting an offending account or Web site closed. All too often, however, ISPs of the worst spam offenders completely ignore LARTs, no matter who sends them.

Effective LARTing is a science, especially when reports need to propagate to upstream providers or other parties whose affiliations with the offender - aren't obvious. One outfit that has automated a great deal of the LARTing process is SpamCop (www.spamcop.net). The organization, founded by Julian Haight, offers multiple ways you can submit spam messages for reporting purposes. When you report a spam message, the SpamCop system analyzes the header and links within HTML messages to present you with a choice of targets you want SpamCop to LART on your behalf. SpamCop's LARTs try to munge your address from the headers so that spammers who receive the LART can't simply wash you—a troublemaker—from their mailing lists.

While some participants might not mind being listwashed (to keep the slimeball from mailing them again), SpamCop veterans don't like listwashing because it doesn't do anything to dissuade the spammer from spamming. Moreover, if you let a spammer know your email address, the spammer could take temporary revenge by issuing a bunch of spam with your email address in the forged From: field. All bounce messages for undeliverable mail will flood back to your email address. In extreme cases, spammers have "joe-jobbed" particularly effective reporters by issuing phony pornography-related spam (particularly child pornography) that tries to associate the mail or spamvertised Web site with the LARTer. The spammer hopes that because such mail will be reported to law enforcement, the LARTer will get in hot water.

Simply removing your email address from a message header may not be enough to disguise your identity from a message copy sent along with a LART. Don't forget that some messages include identifiers—either the plainly visible email address or a numeric code associated with your address database entry—in the URLs for links and image retrieval. If you don't want to be listwashed, you can try removing parts of URLs after the domain names, especially the part starting with a question mark (a divider between a location and name/value data sent along with the URL).

Newcomers to SpamCop or any automated LARTing service need to carefully read the results of analyses of every spam message before blindly having the report(s) sent out on their behalf. There have been documented and unfortunate cases where the analysis program goofed in its parsing of the information in a sequence of Received: header lines, causing a LART to go accidentally to the reporter's own ISP. (See Appendix B for more about doing your own detective work to issue manual LARTs. Every fact-based, professionally-worded LART is for a good cause.)

Most spam-reporting services also gather information from user reports to contribute information to databases of known spam message content or blocklists. Because well-maintained blocklists keep the information refreshed and up to date, it's important that reporters keep reporting material from the same sources, thus assuring that the offending IP addresses stay in the BLs for others to block.

Occasionally a spam reporter will get discouraged that months of reporting does not seem to be stemming the flow of spam, as he or she had originally hoped when signing up to the service. Unfortunately, even getting your address listwashed by some spammers won't prevent your address from being passed around to others who have additional ways to get spam to you, even through your best defenses. The work of one reporter has little impact, but the combined effect of all reporters does have an impact. If reporting weren't so effective in getting some spammers booted from their connectivity, Web sites, and phony domain name registrations, the spammers wouldn't be jumping through the hoops they now do to disguise themselves through multiple relays of foreign Internet providers and occasionally launch distributed denial of service attacks on the Web sites that host reporting and BL services.

Electronic Attacks

Frustration with spam overload drives some recipients over the edge. The desire for revenge has led numerous programmers to respond with their own brands of electronic abuse against spam sources or spamvertised Web sites. A few antispam services use network attack tactics to flood spamvertised Web sites with hits to either overload spammers' servers or cause the site to pay click-through commissions for millions of hits that generate no business.

I disagree strongly with this approach, for a few reasons. For one, such attacks are typically set up in ways that are illegal in countries with laws against Distributed Denial of Service (DDoS) attacks. Second, treating abuse with more abuse is childish. And, third, even though such reverse attacks have been ongoing for some time, they don't appear to have had any effect on the overall spam problem.

As you can see, the wide range of technical solutions—already in place and proposed—indicates that no single solution is presently doing the job. Some solutions work better for certain recipient systems than others. Not every user or mail server can implement the technologies they'd like, either through lack of know-how or resources. And, for every new technology that comes along (like Bayesian statistical analysis that hit the Bit Time in 2003), spammers search with as much vigor and equal intellectual resources for ways to work around the blocks and filters.

While I encourage more geeks to get in on the spam-fighting act, I wish that those who rush to promote their be-all, end-all technical solution would do some research on the state of spam first. Even the biggest companies fall into the trap of claiming that their solutions will end spam within x years. Then they reveal their ideas (which rarely are new) that have so many potential problems associated with them that those who have been tracking spam for years simply roll their eyes in unison.

Vernon Schryver (rhyolite.com), who developed the Distributed Checksum Clearinghouse, has also assembled a list of ways you can identify an antispam "kook"—someone who steps up to a public podium (usually at a gathering of Internet nerds) and delivers a paper on the Final Ultimate Solution to the Spam Problem (FUSSP). Although Vernon ignored requests to let me reprint the list here, I recommend that you read it every time you think you've invented the way to end all spam. You can find the article at www.rhyolite.com/antispam/you-might-be.html. A few of the items assume a fair amount of technical knowledge, but I think you'll enjoy the piece just the same.

Because every email user has different requirements and receives a wide variety of legitimate email—some of which may intentionally include spammy words—no single technical solution will "automatically" solve the spam problem. Even blended solutions have to be mixed carefully and tailored to different types of users.

I believe that the current hype about sender authentication is raising false expectations that spam will disappear once authentication is universally deployed.[9] But that technology addresses only some segments of the spammers, scammers, and hackers on the Internet. Loose laws in the United States and elsewhere grant any spamming concern willing to identify itself the legal footing to keep doing what it has been doing. And if spam gangs should find ways to hack or spoof the authentication system, then we'll be no better off than we are today.

If you hear a claim that someone can develop an email system for the masses that cannot be hacked, run for the hills. As long as there is an economic incentive for spammers to spam, scammers to scam, and hackers to hack, no system will ever be safe. Until someone can demonstrate otherwise, technological solutions will continue to be one or one-half step behind the spammers.

We're playing defense. Full-time.

---

9 The U.S. Federal Trade Commission has even threatened to mandate an authentication system if the industry can't agree on a scheme quickly enough. In my opinion, that's an invitation to disaster.

CHAPTER 16

The Law as Partial Solution

Just as geeks turn to technology for the ultimate spam solution, politicians head for the legislatures of the world to enact laws that attempt to satisfy the demands of their constituencies. The job of lawmakers might be easier if it weren't for the fact that their constituencies consist of parties on both sides of the issue: those who send spam ("unsolicited email marketers") and those who don't want to receive spam ("solicited email marketees").

It sounds very pure and righteous to label some activity "illegal." The threat of committing an illegal act is not that you're going against the law, but that you might get caught and be punished for your illegal action. Even with those threats, I doubt in recorded history that the imposition of a law has completely prevented everyone from committing the illegal action after the law was enacted. Typically, a law is enacted to *stop* something that has been going on. I mean, look at all the "not" provisions in the Ten Commandments. Even the positively-worded one about honoring thy mother and father probably came to mind because for centuries kids were being kids. What that commandment is saying is: "Thou shalt *not* dis the rents."[1]

Enacting laws against spam activity in many parts of the world has been a tedious process, but started gaining traction in 2003 in places like the United States, the European Union, and Australia. The implementations are uneven (some would say "hollow" about the U.S. law), but there is an inkling that lawmakers in some parts of the industrialized world recognize that spammers who have exploited an unfettered system have gone too far in placing undue burdens on Internet networks, systems, and users.

---

[1] Translation for adults: "Don't disrespect your parents."

227

One overriding factor undermines even the most strident lawmaking efforts: Spam and the Internet operate on a global level, but laws so far have been limited in their jurisdictions. The global nature of spam and the local nature of laws seem to be rather difficult concepts for individual users afflicted by spam to comprehend or reconcile. Behavior of the worst of the spammers, who utilize offshore resources for mailing or Web site hosting, and who use multiple layers of redirection, relaying, and hijacking others' systems to disguise the audit trail, make it extremely difficult—at times impossible—to build a legal case that can successfully prosecute the offenders. Just because a prosecutor can look at the source code of a spam message and quickly identify a half-dozen apparent violations of a local law's antispam provisions doesn't mean that there is sufficient incentive or evidence to locate and convict the perpetrator. As you'll see later in this chapter, building a bulletproof case is much tougher work than hiring a bulletproof mailing or Web hosting service.

If I wanted to bore you to tears, I'd provide annotated versions of spam-related laws currently on the books. Instead, I'll simply run down the main issues that various laws have addressed (or ignored, as the case may be). Please note: *I am not a lawyer, nor a professional legislative analyst;* I'm just a regular guy trying to make sense of the laws that have been enacted. Some issues covered by laws are "no-brainers" in that they occupy a common ground in the fight against spam. On several other issues, however, various legislatures seem to be under the same misapprehension as lots of citizens: that making something illegal will inhibit the activity, so there's no need to make the laws very restrictive, lest the laws appear to infringe on other existing legal rights.

I'll be paying particular attention to three recently enacted laws that affect a large segment of the Internet population using Latin alphabets:

Name	Jurisdiction	Passed	Effective Date
The Privacy and Electronic Communications (EC Directive) Regulations 2003	United Kingdom	September 18, 2003	December 11, 2003
Spam Act 200	Australia	December 12, 2003	April 11, 2004
Controlling the Assault of Non-Solicited Pornography and Marketing (CAN-SPAM) Act of 2003	United States	December 16, 2003	January 1, 2004

The U.K. spam regulation (part of a broader privacy law) is what is known as a *transposition* of a European Community directive passed in 2002. Each member country creates its own transposition of such directives to write the specific law that applies to that country. The U.S. law explicitly overrides antispam laws enacted by three-dozen separate state legislatures. Of those laws, the ones from California and Delaware had significantly stronger antispam provisions than the U.S. law.

Now I turn to the hot-button issues that some or all of these laws address. And, please note, any "nerdity" in the rest of this chapter is predominantly of a legal, rather than technical, variety.

Definition of Spam

You have to read between the lines of the laws to deduce what they mean by "spam." By and large the laws apply to people, not email, and therefore outline what a person can and cannot do with email messages. In many cases, the laws proscribe what is not permissible, thereby implying that everything else is permissible. (This all-too-common way of writing laws leaves doors wide open for interpretation and litigation. It's like a naked man suing a restaurant for refusing him service because a sign on the door clearly stated "No shoes, No shirt, No service!" The man sues because he had carried his clothing in a bag, and the sign said nothing about *wearing* shoes and a shirt, and nothing at all about pants.)

The place to start, however, is to determine what the laws mean by "messages." In all three laws, constraints target email sent for commercial purposes (or simply "direct marketing" in the U.K. regulation). But there are also distinctions about how a message reaches its intended recipient. Both the U.K. and Australian laws take a liberal view that a "message" covers any text, voice, and sound message conveyed by a public communications network. Presumably, this includes Internet chat (IRC and IM) and even messages that can be sent to cellular telephones (cell phone or short message service—SMS—spam is a growing problem in many parts of the world). In contrast, the U.S. law covers only a message that is sent to an address consisting of a user name (i.e., mailbox identifier) and a domain name. I guess that leaves IRC, IM, and cell phone message spam beyond the scope of the law. Was that an opportunity lost or intentionally obscured?

The more you study the laws, the more you understand that a definition of "spam" is largely irrelevant within the laws. Instead, the laws cover what a sender can and cannot do with commercial email messages.

Consent

Just as consent is a primary antispammer test for spam, so does the concept play a role in some of the laws. The Australian law, in particular, devotes a substantial section to explaining what "consent" means. It must do so because it bases its primary constraints on consent and the "Australia-ness" of the spam:

16 Unsolicited commercial electronic messages must not be sent

(1) A person must not send, or cause to be sent, a commercial electronic message that:

(a) has an Australian link; and

(b) is not a designated commercial electronic message.

(2) Subsection (1) does not apply if the relevant electronic account-holder consented to the sending of the message.

Parsing the double-negative statements for Subsection (2), it means that sending a commercial message (with an Australian link) is allowed only if the recipient has given prior consent.[2] Of course, then you have to drill deeper to find out what the law actually says about consent.

On that subject, the Australian law comes up with "express consent" (no further definition supplied) and the potentially dangerous "consent that can reasonably be inferred." I say "potentially dangerous" because the definition leaves the door ajar to some spam if an email address is "conspicuously published." While saying no more would essentially allow flat-out Web site harvesting, the law gets more specific in that the only consent that a sender could infer is that the addressee consents to email relevant to the "work-related business, functions, or duties" of the individual. But before you get too excited, another extensive provision in the law prohibits the use of address lists gathered through harvesting. On balance, I read the provision about "inferring consent" to mean that if you list a contact email address on a Web site, an individual has legal standing to personally contact you with a commercial offer that relates to your business or position.

The U.K. law is fairly succinct in its application of consent with regard to spam. First of all, it's okay to send email to a recipient if the sender has an existing business relationship with the recipient, and the recipient agreed to be contacted thereafter. Other than that, however, no one can send "unsolicited communications" unless the recipient "previously notified the

---

[2] An "Australian link" means that the recipient's email address must clearly indicate that it is hosted in Australia or that the sender is in Australia.

sender" that it's okay to send. In other words, if the recipient does not explicitly request commercial email from a sender, anything the sender mails to that recipient is unsolicited—spam, in our lingo. Unfortunately for U.K. business, the entire law applies only to "individual subscribers," a provision that has bearing in the discussion later in this chapter about prosecution.

Although the U.S. law pays lip service to the notion of consent by defining it early in the text of the law, the idea of prior consent never arises in any of the proscriptive portions. As close to the consent idea as the law comes is the provision that prevents a sender from transmitting a message to any recipient who has requested to be removed from *further* mailings. In other words, the law assigns legal propriety to the opt-out method of email marketing, in which the sender can mail unsolicited mail *ad nauseam* until the recipient says "Stop!" This is why antispammers frequently refer to the law as U-CAN-SPAM, because it legalizes precisely the kind of activity that spam fighters have been battling for over a decade. The provision was a major coup for direct marketers and the organizations that peddle their influence in Washington, DC.

If there is a silver lining to this cloud, it is that the law explicitly allows ISPs to continue to filter, bounce, reject, delete, or forward to the Federal Trade Commission's UCE complaint address whatever email messages they want. Imagine if the law not only legalized opt-out mailings, but forced its citizens to receive them as well! I'm guessing there would have been rioting in the streets.

Opt-out Provisions

All three laws require that commercial email messages include instructions that the recipient can follow to discontinue receiving further messages intended for the recipient's address. The U.S. and Australian laws are more specific about opt-out mechanisms, requiring that the opt-out link or address be clear and conspicuous, as well as functional. And, in a modest acknowledgment of Rule #1 (Spammers lie), the opt-out address or link must be operational for at least 30 days from the transmission of the commercial message. Australia requires that the opt-out link address be "legitimately obtained," while the United States also requires the display of a "valid physical postal address of the sender" in the message, and that the unsubscribe request be acted upon within ten days.

Despite the comparative weakness of the U.S. law's predominantly opt-out leanings, an interesting provision prevents a sender from passing along to anyone else the address of someone who opted out of the sender's mailings. This is about as close to acknowledging my idea of email address "sanctity" as the three laws come. In a world in which spammers obeyed the law, it would mean not only that opt-out requests would be honored, but that your address would propagate no further to indicate that your address is alive. Unfortunately, we live in the real world.

The bottom line on opt-out provisions is that the feature is an easily legislated one that has a nice ring to it when you first hear it. Yet between the real evidence gathered by experienced antispammers and legends that grew out of that experience—not to mention the fact that computers make it so darned easy to abuse—modern wisdom discourages users from ever following an opt-out link from an unsolicited message, even when (or perhaps especially when) it works. Besides, even if every U.S.-based spammer obeyed the opt-out provisions of the law, it's nearly impossible for most spam recipients to know for sure that the sender of any particular spam is under U.S. jurisdiction. If you follow some of the sleuthing tips in Appendix B, you will certainly be confused when an opt-out link points to a site hosted in China for a domain registered in Belize for an offer selling an all-American product.

The limited natures of antispam laws—both the dullness of their teeth and short jurisdictional reaches of their arms—give spam recipients no reason to trust spammers, whether or not they obey the laws of any given land. At the same time, the history and predominance of spammers who validate Rule #1 by numerous deceits in their headers and messages invalidate even the "honest" claims of spammers who endeavor to play by the laws of their own countries. The well is poisoned beyond the point of reclamation.

Sender Identities

All three laws attempt to address one of the most egregious effronteries to the sensibilities of spam recipients: disguising the identity of the sender. As described earlier in this book, a lot of spammers, particularly the high-volume guys, have a history of using fictitious or "borrowed" email addresses for the From: and Reply-To: header fields of their messages. This prevents email system bounces due to incorrect To: addresses, or overstuffed inboxes from clogging up the spammer's incoming mail system. After all, the only time a spammer would want to know if a To: address were invalid is if the spammer really cared enough to clear the bad address from the database. Some do. Most don't.

From: addresses have also sometimes been set to fraudulently acquired addresses from ISPs that grant a new user Internet access long enough to get a sizable batch of spam out before the fake credit card causes the account to close. Earthlink successfully sued an upstate New York fraudster for this kind of service theft.

If your email address gets inserted into the From: address of a spammer's run, several things will happen.[3] First, you'll start getting bounce messages and alerts that you may not understand. The bounce messages will be from AOL or other ISPs that initially accepted the messages as sent by the spammer (probably through someone else's zombie PC). But because your address is in the From: or Reply-To: field of the header, the bounce message goes to you. If the bouncer sends the original message back, you obviously won't recognize the message because you didn't send it. You'll feel violated, then enraged that some idiot has dared smear your squeaky-clean reputation with spam fraudulently associated with your address. You'll worry that those who might have received the unbounced messages will report you as a spammer to your ISP. If you're an American, your first inclination will likely be to want to sue somebody for damage to your good name

Unfortunately, spammers who forge From: addresses do a good job of covering their transmission tracks by sending messages through relays or proxy servers (including zombie PCs) that are extremely difficult to trace (unless you have unlimited funds and excellent cooperation from ISPs). You'll have a link to a spamvertised Web site in the bounced message, but chances are good that the site will be hosted offshore from wherever you are, and the domain registration will be phony. The best way to try to figure out who is behind the spam would be to actually buy the product being spamvertised, and hope to follow the money paper trail through your credit card company during a lawsuit evidence discovery process. Lotsa luck!

As if this nonsense weren't enough, some spammers use a technique that relies on bounces to get their messages to the intended recipients. One scenario is this: the intended recipient is you, so your address is intentionally put into the From: field. The message is addressed to a known invalid address at an ISP that sends bounce messages with a complete copy of the original. The score is 15-Love, Spammer. When the message bounces, you get a copy, and, because you may think that the message is something you originally sent, you'll open the bounce message enough to see the original spam offer. 30-Love, Spammer. Because the message you received is an official bounce message, you are not allowed to report it to, say, SpamCop, which has a no-bounce policy with regard to spam reports. 40-Love, Spammer. You hit Delete. Game, Spammer.

Just as some recent virus email messages have been formatted to look like message bounces, some spam runs design their messages to look like bounces. All of the bounced message verbiage is completely bogus, inserted

---

3 It is also possible for a spammer to use your address in the normally hidden-from-view message envelope (Chapter 4), in which case the message header may not contain any mention of your address—yet the incoming mail server momentarily logs your address as the source of the message, no matter what the From: and Reply-To: header fields say.

by the spammer's transmission run. If the formatting is done well, a spam message content parser will skip over it because it has all the markings of an unreportable bounce.

Unsolicited bulk emailers are typically not fond of identifying themselves in traditional ways because those ways are easily blockable by content filters installed on incoming mail servers. Just because spammers may have the legal right in the United States to send such mail doesn't mean that ISPs will let it pass through to users who want spam filtered. The insistence on an honest sender identity in the laws assumes that senders will comply with the laws—a false assumption for a good chunk of spammers on the Internet. Since falsifying identities makes it very costly to track down offenders, I suspect the Rule #1 liars will continue to get away with it unless enough prosecutors spend enough money to identify the perps and build rock-solid cases against them.

While on the subject of accurate sender identity, of the three laws, only the U.S. law explicitly prohibits false or misleading message header information. The provision covers not only the From: field but also domain or IP address information that is bogus or disguised through the use of another computer, such as an open relay or proxy. This seems to mean that in addition to other laws being broken by using hijacked computers, every spam that reaches you by way of a zombie PC is outlawed if the sender is American. Of course, tracking down the "sender" may be difficult (or darned near impossible) because the infected PC likely gets its immediate instructions relayed to it from a computer located outside the United States or other untraceable source. That leaves prosecutors the task of searching for clues from the other end: the spamvertised Web site. If that site is also hosted offshore, and the domain registration is offshore and/or phony, the search becomes yet more difficult and costly. This law is unlikely to force any spammer to stop using relays and zombie PCs to hide his identity. Every new virus-spread worm infestation turns thousands more PCs around the world into zombies capable of anonymously relaying yet more spew.

Legitimacy of the Offer

Lots of countries have existing laws that cover fraudulent offers made to consumers. The CAN-SPAM law in the United States reinforces the fact that existing fraud and computer fraud laws on the books (numerous chapters of title 18 of the United States Code) apply to bulk commercial email. Moreover, the new law adds its own chapter to title 18 to include references to the new terminology that email brings into the realm—terms covering headers, domains, and IP addresses.

I have a theory why the U.S. law makes such a big restatement of fraud with respect to email. Are law-abiding bulk emailers supposed to be so dense as to believe that if it weren't for these specific restatements that it would be okay to defraud recipients by email? Are crooks defrauding recipients left and right because there has been no specific reference to email in existing U.S. law? How far would a crook's cartooney get with that defense in a court case before a judge slapped him or her upside the head? Frankly, all the verbiage in the law reads like window dressing to me—provisions that make it sound as though the law is doing all kinds of new things to protect email recipients. Trying to sound "hip" when in truth the old laws do the job just as well—if someone stepped up to apply them.

Tooth count for these provisions: 0.

Message Labeling

Of the three laws, only the U.S. one explicitly acknowledges that Subject: lines of headers can mislead recipients about the nature of the message body, and thus requires that Subject: lines accurately represent the nature of the message. This provision essentially "email-izes" the unfair and deceptive advertising provisions in the Federal Trade Commission Act (15 USC 45). Again, just a modern application of existing law.

Since the "P" in "CAN-SPAM" stands for "pornography," a subsection of the law is devoted to wording of the Subject: line of a commercial message that contains sexually explicit material. In particular, the law addresses messages whose content immediately displays such content in the message body. While the law does not provide the precise labeling to be used, it tossed the hot potato back into the lap of the Federal Trade Commission, which was tasked with devising such wording within 120 days of the law's enactment. The FTC settled on a Subject: line to include the string: SEX-UALLY-EXPLICIT. If porn spammers actually obey this rule, it will make such messages easy to filter. Users of unfiltered email accounts will certainly see the label and either delete the message immediately without being pummeled by the imagery contained therein, or, if the recipient is a teenager, open it before reading a different message from Grandma. Even then, the FTC wishes to go further by proposing that messages containing such material be formatted in such a way as to prevent any sexually explicit content from being viewable in the first view of such messages. They call it the "brown paper wrapper" idea, which means that even accidental opening won't display "naughty bits."

As further proof that the CAN-SPAM law is still a work in progress, one provision requires that the FTC study and report on the feasibility of requiring all commercial email to include the string ADV or some other readily identifiable label that the message is what it is. Labeling of this kind has some pretty hairy implications that have to be thought through very carefully before it can be implemented. If the requirement states something to the effect that every commercial email message's Subject: line must start with, say, "ADV:", then the basic inclination of most email recipients will be to use their email filtering software to block all messages bearing that label unless the sender is on a whitelist of allowed senders. But would this requirement apply to any commercial email message (as the law currently reads), including a personal message from someone offering to sell you something relevant to your company or job? A lot of legitimate commerce occurs through word of mouth: A friend of yours knows you're looking for a '57 Chevy to restore; your friend meets someone who has a '57 Chevy he's trying to sell; your friend gives the seller your email address. Since you don't know about the seller, he won't be on your whitelist. If he complies with the CAN-SPAM act, he'll have to label his first message to you with ADV:, which will cause your filter to block or divert it.

Address Harvesting

I pay a lot of attention to an email address as a piece of personal identity information. How do the laws view the sanctity of email addresses?

For the U.K. law, the fact that unsolicited commercial email is banned unless the recipient had given prior permission or had an ongoing transaction with the sender trumps the acquisition of an email address by any method other than explicit registration or subscription by the recipient. By implication, email harvesting is not permitted.

Down Under, the Australian law goes to great lengths to ban the sale or use of address-harvesting software. You also cannot supply or use an address list that was assembled through address harvesting. Their definition of address harvesting software is as follows:

> [A]ddress-harvesting software means software that is specifically designed or marketed for use for:
>
> (a) searching the Internet for electronic addresses; and
>
> (b) collecting, compiling, capturing or otherwise harvesting those electronic addresses.

That's a pretty general description, but I think, in this case, it works to the advantage of spam fighters.

Such is not the case in the U.S. CAN-SPAM law. Either the powers that be didn't understand what harvesting is, or the political action committees (PACs) that be did understand what harvesting is and made sure the true definition didn't make it into the law.[4] The law states that it is unlawful to cause a message to be sent if:

> [T]he electronic mail address of the recipient was obtained using an automated means from an Internet website or proprietary online service operated by another person, and such website or online service included, at the time the address was obtained, a notice stating that the operator of such website or online service will not give, sell, or otherwise transfer addresses maintained by such website or online service to any other party for the purposes of initiating, or enabling others to initiate, electronic mail messages...

This definition of automated address acquisition has nothing to do with the most common way addresses are ripped off from the Web: "scraping" Web pages for strings that contain the telltale @ symbol of an email address. Instead, the law refers to hacking of sites that may act as front ends to databases containing customer or other email address collections. That's not harvesting; it's outright theft. Bottom line: Traditional screen-scraping types of harvesting of email addresses from Web sites is protected by CAN-SPAM. Yikes!

As a bone thrown to those who object to this outlandish freedom to spam at will, an additional prohibition outlaws dictionary attacks with a reasonable definition:

> [T]he electronic mail address of the recipient was obtained using an automated means that generates possible electronic mail addresses by combining names, letters, or numbers into numerous permutations.

Unfortunately for my "sanctity" high horse, the final, confusing blow comes at the end of this section of the law:

> DISCLAIMER.—Nothing in this paragraph creates an ownership or proprietary interest in such electronic mail addresses.

I'm not sure if this admonition is aimed at the person who reads mail received at that address or other parties with access to addresses. If I read between the lines—including the lines missing from the address-harvesting definition—I take it to mean that users are denied the ability to claim their email address as property. Thus, if someone scrapes my address from

---

4 A PAC is an acronym for a Political Action Committee, a fancy name for a lobbyist, or, as described in the Dramatis Personae of Chapter 1, Direct Marketing Organizations.

a Web page or public forum archive, I cannot pursue the harvester for stealing my property.

Spammers appear to win again, dammit!

Applicable Parties

A lot of spam has multiple parties involved. Typically, the sender and owner of the spamvertised Web sites are different parties. While the true originating computer is easily concealed when the message is sent through open relays and proxies (including zombie PCs), the URL of a spamvertised Web site is usually an easy mark to identify when viewing the source code of the message.

From the legal point of view, then, a legitimate question arises whether the spamvertised Web site is in any way accountable for whatever violations occur in the transmission of the message. This turns out to be an important point of law, as evidenced by some previous cases that worked in favor of spammers who violated existing laws (including various fraud statutes and trespassing on the computer resources of the recipients and their ISPs). Some suits were brought against the spamvertising Web site owner, but the spamvertiser successfully hid behind a third-party subcontractor relationship to distance itself from the illegal activities of the company doing the actual mailing. If the product site hired a third-party direct marketing company to create an email campaign, and the marketing company swore up and down that it used only confirmed opt-in addresses, then the product site was able to deny any complicity or knowledge of the lies being perpetrated by the company performing the actual mailing.

The laws seem to be on top of this kind of evasion. The U.K. law (where unsolicited commercial mail to individuals is forbidden), says, "[A] person shall neither transmit, nor instigate the transmission of" spam. Presumably, a company hiring someone to do the mailing is instigating the transmission of spam. Provisions in the Australian law refer to the person or organization who sent the message or authorized the sending of the message. This applies equally (if not more so) to the spamvertised Web site as the mailer.

Unlike the occasionally weasel-like wording of various sections of the U.S. CAN-SPAM law, it is clear about what it considers a "sender" to be:

> [W]hen used with respect to a commercial electronic mail message, means a person who initiates such a message and whose product, service, or Internet Web site is advertised or promoted by the message.

Although the entity whose product, service, or Web site is being advertised seems to be the primary culprit, it will be interesting to see how the distances between advertiser and mailing house fare in litigation. How much due diligence is an advertiser supposed to perform on a bulk emailing service to assure that headers aren't forged or computers aren't hijacked to get the campaign into as many inboxes as possible? Perhaps the only satisfying point about this definition is that it provides prosecutors with a comparatively easy target to initiate a suit. Evidence gathered in the course of discovery will shine light on the bulk emailers and their practices. It will take some time, but the public may learn a few more details about the inner workings of both well-behaved and not-so-nice bulk emailers.

Do-Not-Email Lists

To my mind, one of the most preposterous provisions of the U.S. CAN-SPAM law is the suggestion that the email equivalent of a telemarketing Do-Not-Call list will allow users, in a sense, to opt out of spam universally. First of all, the law as enacted does not require this kind of system be implemented, despite what many ten-second television news blurbs would like you to believe. The law asks the Federal Trade Commission to report back within six months about how such a registry might work, detail what problems might be associated with it, and provide a timetable for implementing the system.

A Do-Not-Email Registry has a nice sound to it if you aren't aware of how the email system works and how spammers of various kinds operate. The nearest analogy in most U.S. consumers' minds is the Do-Not-Call Registry that began operation in October 2003—meaning that the idea of a one-time opt-out list was fresh in the minds of U.S. citizens. A poll conducted in mid-2003 by the ePrivacy Group and the Poneman Institute suggests that three out of four email users support the idea.[5] But the names of the two registries are the closest they come to having any relation to each other. Consider the following:

Telephone Numbers versus Email Addresses

In North America, there is a finite quantity of telephone numbers that can ever be supported by the current ten-digit system (three-digit area code, seven-digit phone number within the area code). That quantity is certainly huge, but a known quantity just the same. The potential number of email addresses—a combination of alphanumeric mailbox names and alphanumeric domain names—is astronomical. According to comments submitted

---

[5] Results of the poll are noted in the online article at http://www.informationweek.com /story/showArticle.jhtml?articleID=12803019019.

to the Federal Trade Commission in preparation for its June 2004 report to Congress, the computer system that would track a Do-Not-Email Registry would need to handle 300 million to 450 million addresses (perhaps growing to 1 billion addresses). In contrast, the Do-Not-Call list has grown to only about 60 million numbers. The task of comparing existing call lists against the Do-Not-Call database (a process called *scrubbing*) can take several days. Scrubbing an email address database against a much larger list becomes impractical. Moreover, each residential phone number usually applies to multiple individuals in a household, whereas it's not uncommon for one active Internet individuals to have multiple email addresses. Maintaining this registry and keeping it current would be a nightmare.

Geography

One valuable point about an area code and phone number prefix is that those two pieces of information reveal enough geographical information about the number to prove that it is for a phone line, not only in a particular country, but in the United States, down to the state, region, and city. Except for email address domains that specifically indicate a country other than the United States (for example, a top-level domain ending in .de means that it is in Germany), top-level domains for .com, .org, .net, and several others reveal no geographic trademarks. If the Do-Not-Email Registry is to be limited to U.S. citizens, then the registration will have to gather more information, and perhaps perform additional verification before allowing any address to be added. But then, what about U.S. citizens who have email accounts outside of the United States? Is the registry there to protect *citizens* or *accounts* from unwanted email?

Solicitation Sources

Due to the high cost of international phone calls, telemarketing on a mass scale generally involves callers and recipients being located in the same country. Thanks to other regulations, it is now also possible in the United States to identify the phone number (through caller ID services) of someone calling you to sell you something when you'd rather be eating dinner. Therefore, violators of the FTC's Do-Not-Call provision are easily tracked and very likely to be subject to the U.S. laws.[6] Such wouldn't be the case for the worst of the spammers, who would simply ignore the Do-Not-Email

---

[6] When international telemarketers start using the Internet to convey voice calls across the oceans (using a technology called Voice-Over-Internet Protocol—VOIP), antitelemarketing laws may have trouble keeping up with the technology.

Registry, and spam away from sources located outside the United States with impunity.

A Dangerous Collection

While it's true that some of the finite combinations of phone numbers are live and others not, it's an easily computerized task to try random or sequential numbers, and let the phone companies' networks advise you which numbers are not valid ("Beep...beep...beep. We're sorry, the number you dialed is not...."). If an automated dialer were allowed to run amok, it would eventually find every working number in your area code and prefix, whether you answer the phone or not. But for any given domain name, there may be no effective way of knowing which mailbox user names are valid in the system. Sure, you could try dictionary attacks and hope that the system is configured to reject messages directed to non-existent addresses, but you'd never know for sure that you're getting all the good addresses at that domain.

Now, consider that a Do-Not-Email Registry contains a list of valid email addresses. Except for perhaps a comparative handful of addresses that have become inactive since they were registered, the database contains pure gold for email marketers. If a spammer were to run a copy of his database of harvested, purchased, traded, and rented lists against this database—on the premise of wanting to remove those on the Do-Not-Email Registry—he could compare the list coming back against his original list. All those addresses *not* surviving the merge would be predominantly fresh and live addresses. Suddenly, the value of those names in his database increases, because he can now offer the list of live addresses to other spammers for a higher price. In a flash, the Do-Not-Email Registry becomes a Please-Email-Me Registry.

I was pleased to see in the FTC's final report to Congress that the agency unequivocally recommended against creating a Do-Not-Email Registry. Despite receiving several proposals describing ways in which such a registry could work, the FTC, in its wisdom, admitted that no power on Earth could force scofflaw spammers to scrub their lists. The exercise would simply be a huge waste of time and money, and would add no muscle to the CAN-SPAM law.

Prosecutions

Let's assume a best-case scenario for a prosecutor in Australia, the United Kingdom, or the United States under the laws and enforcement systems in place in those three countries. By "best-case," I mean that a spammer presumed to operate within one of these countries sends automated bulk commercial email to tons of recipients in the same country. In other words, no international borders are involved.

The primary piece of evidence would be a copy of the email message. To keep the playing field even among the three countries' laws, let's say that the message was addressed to a harvested email address (a spam trap) and that the From: address is a suspicious-looking address from a free email service, such as hotmail.com or yahoo.com. The recipient is angry, and wishes to hold the spammer accountable for violating laws against address harvesting and falsifying headers.

In Australia and the United Kingdom, prosecutions of antispam law offenses must be initiated only by a government agency. In Australia, it's the Australian Communications Authority (ACA); in the United Kingdom, it's the Information Commissioner. In the United States, the new law gives power to enforce the law to the Federal Trade Commission (FTC), an individual state's prosecutorial agency (e.g., attorney general), and ISPs affected by violations of the law.

California's Individual Prosecutions—Almost

The idea of individual prosecutions against spammers was frequently front and center in the creation of numerous U.S. state laws that eventually were superseded by the CAN-SPAM law. One of the most lawsuit-happy provisions was in the California antispam law, signed in September 2003. It allowed individual recipients to sue for damages up to $1,000 per spam message that violated the California law. This is strong stuff, especially when you consider that the California law declared *all* unsolicited commercial email originating from or sent to California to be illegal.

Proponents of individual prosecutions (for example, as written into the California antispam law of 2003) strongly believe that a large number of lawsuits brought by individuals against spammers will be a significant deterrent. I'm not sure, however, that it will be so easy for individuals to make a killing this way. As you will read later in this chapter, it's one thing to trot out a supposed spam message, and quite another to prove that the message is genuine, passed through the Internet, wasn't a forgery (or joe-job), and the like. For Californians, however, it's now a moot point because the CAN-SPAM act supersedes all state antispam laws. States and individuals, however, can still pursue cases for alleged violations of other state laws, such as trespass, theft of service, and so on.

The hard reality is that bringing cases against even the most blatant transgressors is time-consuming, frequently technologically challenging, and—worst of all—expensive. The U.S. CAN-SPAM law has a placeholder for a possible system that rewards anyone who provides the FTC with information about the identities of violators, and supplies additional information that leads to the "successful collection of a civil penalty by the Commission." Details have yet to be worked out.

Despite mechanisms in place in other countries to report violations, the "long arm of the law" can sometimes look like a tiny stub. Take, for instance, the case of a fellow who identified himself on the SpamCop mailing list as Reg Flobert. He reported how he tried to work within the U.K. system, whereby individuals who receive spam can file a report with the Information Commissioner's Office. The form (available in Adobe Acrobat format on the Web) is five pages long, and must be submitted by postal mail, along with a copy of the email message. Reg relates that he did just that to report a spam message he received from a U.K. spammer, and specified that his email address not be revealed to the alleged spammer (the form lets you indicate what information is to be kept from the spammer).

Two weeks after submitting his report, he received word back that the commission had contacted the spammer, asking the spammer to remove Reg's email address from the database (perhaps violating other privacy laws in the process), while reminding the spammer about the spam regulations. In the end, the spammer was able to listwash Reg, so he'll never know if the spammer is still mailing. The spammer also knows that Reg's address is "live." And the spammer escaped a possible £5000 fine.

Gee, I wonder where cynicism about "the system" comes from.

The first legal actions taken against alleged violators of the U.S. CAN-SPAM Act are not by the government, but by ISPs. One small California ISP brought the first suit, soon followed by a coordinated batch of suits by AOL, Earthlink, Microsoft, and Yahoo, each targeting different senders. In April 2004, the U.S. Federal Trade Commission filed its first formal complaints against one spamming group in Michigan, and another in Australia. If my spam logs are any indication, the loud publicity noise of the lawsuits did nothing to frighten spammers. Will convictions from these early suits deter other established spammers from being caught in the next roundup? I have my doubts, unless there is a steady stream of high-visibility prosecutions, convictions, and penalties against the best-known spammers in the United States. Then again, the knowledge and visible proof that highway patrol cars routinely ticket speeders doesn't dissuade everyone from speeding.

Penalties

Ask any fervent antispammer about penalties for spamming, and you'll hear suggestions about corporeal punishments of varying kinds. The word "criminal" is also frequently mentioned.

The U.S. CAN-SPAM law offers two levels of penalties, depending on which provisions the spammer is convicted of violating. Outright fraud in the form of hijacking computers, intentionally falsifying message headers in a bulk mailing, creating fraudulent outgoing email accounts, or falsifying multiple domain registrations can land the convicted perps in the Gray Bar Hotel for one to five years and require forfeiture of not only the computer gear used in the spamming, but also any goodies acquired with the money made from their activities. Less severe deceptions and violations (e.g., using a misleading Subject: line or failing to provide an unsubscribe address) are treated as civil violations, and are subject to monetary penalties (to a worst-case maximum of $2 million).

Australia's spam law violations are strictly civil affairs. The maximum fine for the worst of the worst convicted offenders is approximately $853,000.

Penalties serve as deterrents only when they are imposed on others as examples of what could happen to you if you're caught and convicted. Even before trials begin, prosecutors seem to take great joy in leading indicted and handcuffed suspects in front of television news cameras—the "perp walk" it's called. Because it takes so long to build a good case against spammers and bring it to court, it will be awhile before we know if perp walks, hefty fines, and prison terms will drive U.S. spammers out of business, out of the country, or simply underground.

Jurisdiction

Clearly, the weakest point of any national law against spam or fraudulent emailing practices is that jurisdiction rarely extends beyond the country's borders. At least some laws recognize this limitation.

Wording of the provisions within the U.K. version of the European Community Directive is directed toward senders within the United Kingdom. There does not appear to be any limitation as to the nationality of the recipient, because it is the sender (or instigator) of unsolicited messages who violates the law. This characteristic is likely intentional so that recipients in other European Union countries (and perhaps elsewhere) would be able to initiate a valid report (hah!) against a verified U.K. spammer. In fact, wording on the Information Commission's reporting form explicitly states the following:

- If the sender is based outside the United Kingdom, he is not subject to this legislation.

- If the sender is based outside the European Union, he is not subject to the EU Directive on which this legislation is based.

Australia's spam law bans unsolicited commercial email messages that have what the law calls an "Australia link." This means that the message must be sent to an obviously Australian recipient (e.g., one whose top-level domain ends in .au) or the message is either sent from a mail server or advertises a Web site hosted within Australia (and territories). In theory, this means that the ACA could attempt to prosecute a spammer from outside Australia for every message sent to an address ending in .au. It remains to be seen whether the ACA would prosecute such a case, and whether a defendant from another country and with no other business ties to Australia would even bother to respond to a suit of that nature. Would a civil penalty judgment against someone in another country ever have a chance of being collected? I'll leave that to the lawyers and diplomatic staffs to decipher.

The CAN-SPAM law is, for the most part, silent about its jurisdiction. An intriguing section of the law (Section 12) modifies a phrase in the Communications Act of 1934 (47 U.S.C. 227(b)(1)) to include "any person outside the United States if the recipient is within the United States." But this section doesn't yet appear to have any direct application to email messages. Instead, it applies to telephone and fax solicitations. Perhaps it is simply laying the groundwork for eventually broadening the law's apparent reach to email in the future.

Of course the U.S. law can make all the claims it wants about its jurisdiction when a violation outside of the United States has an effect on U.S. interests. That's one basis that the FTC cites regarding jurisdiction in the April 2004 complaint against alleged Australian spammers *(FTC v. Global Web Promotions Pty et al.)*. Four out of the six counts in the complaint focus on alleged deceptive advertising practices, rather than spam-related issues. Enforcement, however, comes down to the usual cross-border stickiness of one country digging into the affairs of another country. Even FTC Chairman Muris acknowledged in a 2003 speech the importance of improving the reach of consumer protection laws internationally.[7] So far the few successes they've had dealt with outright fraud. But if there is no universally recognized definition of spam activity, prosecution of U.S. laws in other countries could be hampered by the inability of other countries' laws being enforced in the United States. In the meantime, any spammer

---

[7] You can read the full text at www.ftc.gov/speeches/muris/030819aspen.htm.

who feels threatened by the CAN-SPAM law has many ways to use the global Internet to evade detection and avoid prosecution.

In the rest of this chapter I examine the anatomy of a late-2003 lawsuit brought against alleged spammers in the United States for their violation of laws separate from, but akin to, some provisions of the CAN-SPAM law. I'll let the attorneys and court evaluate the merits of the case as it progresses. My purpose here is to convey a sense of how cumbersome, time-consuming, and expensive it can be to bring a case against an alleged violator. All information is derived from public records filed with the Supreme Court of the State of New York by Attorney General Eliot Spitzer on December 17, 2003.[8]

The suit was brought against a bunch of individuals and companies, as follows:

- Synergy6, Inc. (doing business as synergy6.com, american-give-aways.com, and hotfreesamples.com)

- Justin Champion

- OptInRealBig, LLC (doing business as optinrealbig.com)[9]

- Scott Richter[9]

- Delta Seven Communications, LLC

- Paul Boes

- Denny Cole

That there are so many respondents in this case is not surprising given the common arrangements that exist among direct marketers, lead generators, and bulk emailing companies (the individuals are or were principals of the companies named in the suit). It also demonstrates the business relationships that need to be ferreted out by anyone building a case in the bulk email world.

So that you understand the reasons behind the case, I'll summarize the charges levied against the respondents. The bulk of the charges are based on alleged actions between May 13, 2003, and June 13, 2003, as derived from evidence collected by Microsoft Corporation's Hotmail service and submitted to the N.Y. Attorney General's office. Hotmail maintains hidden but harvestable spam trap addresses, which it uses to validate compliance with the

---

[8] The complaint is downloadable at www.oag.state.ny.us/press/2003/dec/syn1.pdf, and the large set of exhibits can be obtained by contacting the New York State Attorney General's office (www.oag.state.ny.us).

[9] These parties settled the case out of court in July 2004.

company's Terms of Service (TOS). The body of evidence collected during this one-month period consists of 8,779 email messages arriving at Hotmail spam trap addresses. The suit claims that all these messages were sent by one advertiser through two affiliate emailing firms.

Of the total number of messages, 7,559 were identified as having false From: field names (the name-only portion of the From: field; we'll get to the address in a moment), using no fewer than 2,990 different identities. A large percentage used the recipient's user ID (or slight variation) as the sender's name. Over 1,500 of the messages used sender names that also were the user ID portion of a phony email address in the From: field. Another bunch used the word "Confirmations" as the sender name, while another sizable group simply plugged in the domains of several large ISPs, such as AOL, Earthlink, Yahoo, Hotmail, and others.

The next charge focuses on the email address part of the From: field, which managed to use an address other than the sender's true address for every message in the batch. The senders' computers managed to create 7,030 different combinations of user IDs and domain names for the 8,779 messages. If nothing else, it proves that the respondents' randomizers are pretty good. Of course, sometimes a randomizer assembled an address that really blew its cover. For instance, 808 messages claimed to originate from a Hotmail spam trap address. Oops. Some combinations also belonged to real people. If the To: address was bad, then the spam bounced back to the unsuspecting users with those addresses. One evidence exhibit is a copy of a consumer complaint to two of the respondents about using that person's Earthlink address in the From: field of one of his messages.

We move onto the server names used in Received: header fields. The claim is that every one of the 8,779 spam trap messages had falsified server names in the header chain. In all cases, the header chain shows the entry point of the spam to be the same domain as the fake address in the From: field. The final tally was a total of 123 email servers spread across 108 domains, all inserted into the header by the bulk emailer, and none of their true email servers.

Next in the list of charges comes a false originating IP address. While the Hotmail incoming mail system correctly recorded the IP address of the email server sending the message, the suit claims that none of those IP addresses in the 8,779 messages belonged to systems registered to the senders. The claim is more specific, indicating the use of 514 servers across 35 countries (and 6 continents, in case you're counting). One of the servers used for these relays happened to be in New York City. A total of 77 spam trap-addressed messages were relayed through the New York computer without the knowledge or permission of the computer's owner. Among the pieces of evidence were copies of SpamCop complaints to the computer owner's ISP about spam being sent through this open proxy server.

The last part of the complaint against the header information focuses on the Subject: line, which the suit alleges was loaded with false information to trick recipients into opening the message. Of the 8,779 spam trap message, 3,596 began with Re:, 2,830 started with Fwd:, and over 1,000 used the name of a big ISP in the Subject: line.

When the final accounting of header-related offenses was done, the suit claimed over 40,000 instances of deception, forgery, or misleading information. With an extra little jab, the suit adds:

> Moreover, this number reflects only the number of fraudulent emails that happened to have been sent to Microsoft's spam traps, and is a miniscule fraction of the total violations committed by the Respondents. (Verified Petition Par.26)

One more bit of fuel for this bonfire is the charge that the respondents received complaints about the fraudulent activity from consumers, but continued sending the mail anyway.

Despite the focus on email activity, the New York state laws to which the suit applies are related to deceptive acts or practices and false advertising. The suit seeks, among other things, injunctions against the fraudulent activity, posting a $100,000 bond to reimburse the state for possible future fraudulent activity, and a fine of $500 "per each instance of a deceptive or unlawful act or practice alleged or discovered" to have been sent to an email address of a New York consumer. The burden of finding which recipients are New York consumers falls on the respondents.

Admittedly, there is a lot of stuff going on here. The work needed to assemble the evidence for these charges ranged from tasks as simple as printing out a Web page with domain name registration information to visiting the New York City company whose server had been hijacked to analysis of the 8,779 spam messages for numerous factors and patterns to issuing subpoenas for internal email messages of the respondents.

A packet of evidence submitted to the court with the case comprised 619 pages and 48 exhibits. Some of the exhibits are as follows:

- Affidavit from an investigator of the Internet Bureau of the New York State Attorney General's Office describing the sources of many other exhibits

- Copies of incorporation authority for Synergy6, Inc. from the state of Delaware

- Printouts of Web home pages and domain registration records for synergy6.com, american-giveaways.com, hotfreesamples.com, and offerstream.com

- Email transcripts among the respondents during the one-month period of the messages sent to the Hotmail spam traps (131 pages)

- A copy of correspondence from a Synergy6 Inc. attorney in response to a September 2003 subpoena from the New York Attorney General, pointing a finger at one of its affiliates, OptInRealBig LLC

- Copies of business papers (certificate of authority) for OptInRealBig.com LLC from the Colorado Secretary of State, and incorporation certificate from the Nevada Secretary of State

- Copies of emails and funds transfer requests between OptInRealBig.com and its subcontractor, Delta Seven (Texas)

- Printouts of search results about Delta Seven from the Texas Comptroller of Public Accounts Web site

- Bankruptcy petition for David Boes (former Delta Seven principal)

- Affidavit from a MSN Hotmail project manager regarding the capture and transfer of emails its spam traps received from the New York-based Synergy6 domains to the attorney general

- Three-page chart analyzing the alleged fraudulent components of the email campaigns received in the spam traps

- Printouts of the email message and spamvertised Web page for each of the campaigns sent out during the one-month period to the spam trap addresses (14 separate exhibits)

- Printouts of email message source code (including headers) and HTML-rendered versions of messages that were relayed through the New York City proxy server

- A copy of recipient complaint about fraudulent use of his address in the From: field of a message

- List of 123 allegedly false email server names extracted from spam trap mail headers

- Over 13 pages of IP addresses (and the reverse DNS lookup names) of open relays or proxy servers through which the reported messages were allegedly relayed

- Affidavit of a vice president of the New York City company whose system was allegedly used as a proxy server without its permission

- Reverse DNS lookup for the allegedly falsified IP address inserted in the relayed message (pointing to a block of IP addresses hosted in China)

- Reverse DNS lookup for the proxy server IP address, showing the New York City ISP for the company whose system was allegedly hijacked as a proxy server

- Copies of SpamCop reports (email messages) to the ISP regarding suspected spam messages appearing to originate from the hijacked proxy server

- Copies of spam abuse complaints (during the one-month tracking period) to Synergy6 and OptInRealBig, some of which also highlight allegedly forged From: header information

- Copies of subpoenaed invoices and checks between OptInRealBig and Synergy6 for mailings during the one-month period

- Copies of notices of proposed litigation mailed to respondents on December 8, 2003

Your eyes may be glazing over by now, but I believe it is instructive to see how much effort goes into assembling a case. While a spam recipient with even a little bit of experience (e.g., having read this book) would be able to spot phony header information and a hijacked proxy server within seconds, it takes months of hard work to put the offenses into a form that has any chance of passing muster in the courts. At the January 2004 Spam and the Law conference (run by the Institute for Spam and Internet Public Policy, isipp.org), California Attorney General Bill Lockyer quoted a figure of 20 subpoenas being needed to trace a spammer.

Even if one highly publicized case succeeds—whether you measure success by the accused changing their ways, paying a big fine, or shutting down completely—it is only one case, affecting a tiny fraction of the individuals and organizations worldwide who ignore the laws while flooding the Internet with the worst kinds of spam.

Laws, prosecutions, and convictions may deter wannabe spammers from going too far with the typical lies and deceptions. That's certainly good. But just as severe punishment fails to deter "career criminals" from repeating their offense or offenses of their convicted peers, all the truly antispam legislation in the world won't stop serial spammers from finding ways to work around the system to avoid detection and prosecution. Successful enforcement of antispammer laws makes for a feel-good news story for a few moments and may do some good by bringing the spam problem into greater public view. Unfortunately, the public may treat the stories as proof that antispam laws work, when in truth they are at best a tiny contribution to the total antispam effort.

CHAPTER 17

An Email Manifesto and To-do List

Let me begin this final chapter by saying that you won't find any earth-shattering revelations or recommendations here. Most of what I have to say has been stated or written before in one form or another. I've also covered most of these topics in more detail earlier in the book. But I don't believe all of these items have been gathered together as a comprehensive list of tasks we must all follow if we hope to reclaim the email system for ourselves and prevent its complete collapse. My only assumption is that you've reached this point in the book because you care about email, whether to manage a far-flung enterprise, to extend two-way communications with customers and clients, or simply to stay in touch with your family and friends.

Outside forces—spammers, scammers, and hackers—threaten a medium we have come to rely on. If these types of forces were to wage the same level of attacks on our other communications media, such as the telephone, the postal mail, or face-to-face personal conversations, would we fight for the restoration of those media? Sure we would. We must do the same so that email returns to the safe and reliable medium we expect it to be.

That fight takes the form of some simple automated precautions and—the hardest part—changes in the way you think about and act on the mail arriving in your inbox every day. You may have to break old and bad habits. You'll definitely need to change your attitude about unopened email until the new ways become second nature. Comfortable rhythms and processes that you now follow will likely have to change, making the job of reading your email slightly more cumbersome. The attackers assume you follow the easy way, and exploit that weakness. You have to be stronger than that, and make sacrifices in the name of a guerilla war to take back email.

253

I'm not asking you to do anything that I haven't already done. I've already checked off all of the items on the to-do lists in this chapter. But if it's just me doing these things, it won't make a dent in the war to reclaim the email system. Even though I've personally gotten some small-time spammers thrown off their ISPs, and uncovered small business Web servers that had been hijacked by phishing criminals, my actions represent scarcely a drop in the ocean. But if enough email users adapt to the ways I suggest here, we can quickly outnumber and outsmart the forces working to rob us of email without waiting for new technologies or law enforcement.

Let this be our Email Manifesto:

- We will suck the spam economy—the spamonomy—dry with a Zero Response policy to all bulk mail sent to us without our consent.

- We will not let our PCs be hijacked by others who want to steal our personal information or relay spam.

- We will not permit a virus, worm, or other foreign intruder to enter our computers via email.

- We will train our nontechie friends and family to join our side of the war.

Fulfilling the manifesto requires action on your part—immediate, near-term, and ongoing. Use the following to-do lists as guides to reaching the manifesto's goals.

To Do—Right Now

These items should be your first priority. Most are free; some require a purchase that is so important it should rank as the number-two necessity for your computer—right after the power cord.

Update Your Operating System

You need to pay the same level of attention to the security of your PC as you do to your home, car, and bank account. The first step in building your defenses against Bad Guys is to make sure your computer's operating system, email program, and Web browser are up to date. Every modern operating system—Windows, MacOS, Linux, or any of the flavors of Unix—receives updates and patches from time to time. Various versions of Windows get the most publicity with the frequent releases of "critical updates" that patch newly found security holes. But all operating systems receive patches if vulnerabilities are located. If you fail to install the latest patches, you may be leaving your computer open not only to virus infections, but to more disastrous hijacking of your machine through open ports on your IP address. Hackers continually probe random IP addresses for open ports or other vulnerabilities as entry points to places that these patches try to block.

If you buy a brand-new computer, do not be lulled into believing that it has the latest operating system patches. More than likely, the operating system is *not* equipped with the patches. The instant you connect a new computer to the Internet for the first time, visit the operating system update site to get the latest security revisions.

If you are not connected to the Internet via a high-speed connection, downloading frequent patches through dial-up connections can be laborious, problem-prone, and tedious. Patches tend to be multimegabyte affairs, which can take literally hours to download at dial-up speeds. Despite such disincentives, you *must, must, must* grab the latest critical updates for your operating system. Here's how to go about it:

Windows 98 or Later

1. Launch Internet Explorer and choose Windows Update from the Tools menu.[1] This action visits Microsoft's Windows Update web site.

2. If you are prompted to install a program called Windows Update, first click the More Info button to verify the security certificate associated with the program.[2] If you're satisfied with the certificate info, then let the program install itself.

3. Once downloaded and installed, the program looks through your system software to find what it needs. You'll get a list of critical and other available updates. Install the critical updates. If the download process is interrupted, you can go through the process again, and the download will pick up where it left off. If you haven't downloaded critical updates for awhile, you may have to perform these in stages, restarting after each stage.

4. Repeat these steps 1 through 3 until Windows Update reports no more critical updates for today.

---

1 Sometimes the browser visits the update site automatically. But if your system is infected, you could conceivably be taken to a bogus site. Use the menu option to initiate the process manually.

2 Confirm in the Certificate window that the certificate was issued to Microsoft Corporation by VeriSign Commercial Software Publishers CA, and that the certificate was *not* issued on January 29 or 30, 2001 (when two Microsoft certificates were erroneously issued to somebody else).

MacOS 9.x

1. Choose Software Update from the Control Panels menu item in the Apple menu.

2. Follow directions.

MacOS X

1. Open the System Preferences application, and click on the Software Update icon in the System row.

2. Click the Check Now button.

3. Install at least any update labeled as security-related.

If your email programs or non-Microsoft browser offer online updates, also get those now. Spammers, scammers, and hackers rely on users not updating their machines to exploit whatever weaknesses the current patches address. Spit in their eyes by updating your system now, and keep it updated frequently.

Close the Preview Pane

If the email software you use on your computer is set up to preview messages when you click on them in the inbox list, you must close the Preview Pane to prevent Web beacons from accidentally reporting back to the spammer's server that you are viewing the message. You can either drag the divider bar to the bottom of the program window, or navigate through the program's preferences (or View menu) to turn off the feature.

You can bypass this item if your email program lets you disable images in email views and you have updated all operating system and email software with the latest patches. Even so, I like the idea of viewing only those messages you believe to be legitimate email, to help you resist the temptation of clicking on a spamvertised Web site link.

If you've grown accustomed to the convenience of quickly managing your incoming mail with the Preview Pane, you'll resist following this directive, because it will force you to change the way you work with your email: you'll have to double-click each incoming message to read it in a separate window. This will slow you down and make you whine with frustration. But keep in mind, spammers are taking advantage of everyone taking the easy way out. I strongly urge you to keep the Preview Pane closed forever, even if you've cleanly deleted any spam in your inbox: You'll forget to close it before looking at your next incoming batch, and you'll be back where you started.

Close Each Email Window

Here is another instruction you'll dislike but need to follow. Once you close the Preview Pane, you'll be opening up each message in its own window. Some programs provide Next and Previous buttons in the window that let you work your way through the inbox listing in the same window. In some programs, even deleting the currently viewed message automatically opens the next one. The software designer is trying to help you be more efficient, but this is precisely what spammers exploit. Instead, close each window before deleting or filing its message.

If, however, clicking the Delete button on your software both deletes the message and closes the window, you can use that. The goal is to prevent any email message from opening "by itself"—it could be deadly.

Disable Email Images

Most modern email software programs and email systems you access via a Web browser (e.g., Hotmail, Yahoo, and so on) allow you to turn off automatic loading of images that may be in an email message. Turning off images is vital because plenty of spam messages still include tracking Web beacons that let the spammer know you've both received and opened the message—in the process usually verifying your email address as being "live." Spammers can also use unbeaconed images to count how many times a particular spam message campaign has successfully gotten recipients to view the message. Each retrieval of an image increments the "hit" counter on the server where the image is hosted. It's possible that the spammer is getting paid by the hit, and you don't want to contribute to that fund if the mail is unsolicited. Look for a "disable images" choice in preferences or user settings associated with your email program or Web-based email service.

In fact, if your email program provides a preference to turn off HTML mail entirely, choose that option. You'll immediately become immune to numerous HTML and scripting attacks buried in email messages.

Buy a Quality Antivirus Software Program and Subscription

This to-do item isn't free, but it may be one of the most important pieces of protection you can add to your personal computer, regardless of operating system. There are several brand-name antivirus products on the market today (Norton, Sophos, F-Secure, Trend Micro, and McAfee are among the more visible brands). Some products work better than others, but since the horse race among vendors and products changes from time to time, I'll leave it to a few reliable independent testers to steer you to the latest product versions that will work best. Here are a few Web sites to check for reviews for Windows users:

www.cnet.com

www.pcmag.com

www.pcworld.com

Be sure you search the Reviews sections of these sites, rather than the shopping areas. Comparison reviews are best. Do not, under any circumstances, buy or install any antivirus product that is advertised in an unsolicited bulk email message. No-name free products are more than likely spyware programs. Brand-name products sold via spam at unbelievably low prices are pirated copies, for which you will not be able to receive technical support or continued updates (if you receive the package at all).

More important than buying and installing antivirus software is keeping it up to date. Most packages offer an initial period of free online updates. Even after the free period ends, you must subscribe to continue receiving updates if that is necessary for your package.

Outbreaks of new viruses can occur at any time, and recently have infected numerous users *in advance* of the antivirus product being updated to catch them. Virus writers do their best to beat antivirus products to the punch in the perennial cat-and-mouse game. A brand-new virus will circulate through email many hours before the antivirus companies can decipher it and issue an update. During those first few hours, everyone is extremely vulnerable, especially if the virus is wired to disable known antivirus and firewall programs running on your computer (as most recent ones do to facilitate the computers being taken over by outsiders). Because your system is at risk of being exposed to a brand-new outbreak, think of antivirus software as being more of a backup to otherwise safe email behavior covered in other items later in this chapter. In other words, your vigilance and good operating practices should never allow an email-borne virus to take hold in your system. But accidents can happen. Let your antivirus software catch those accidents. Your true first line of defense is you.

De-zombie Your PC

I haven't heard of significant outbreaks of non-Windows PCs being taken over by spyware and adware, so the advice in this item applies predominantly to Windows users. This isn't a slam against Windows; it's a genuine measure of the real world.

If you or any users of your computer have installed freeware on your machine, especially things like music-downloading programs, browser add-ons (various toolbars, cursors, smileys, and so on), media players to view electronic greeting cards, or some self-proclaimed "cool" application, your computer is likely running spyware and/or adware.

Fortunately there are software products that you can download and install that have built good reputations of finding and deleting this malware from your system. These products are free (although premium versions are also available for some, and they welcome donations to help keep the programs up to date) and have been tested by plenty of independent sources. Experience by lots of users indicates that while neither product catches every piece of malware, the combination of the two does an excellent job. Visit these sites, download their products, and run them *now:*

- Ad-aware by Lavasoft (www.lavasoft.de/software/adaware)

- Spybot-Search & Destroy (www.safer-networking.org)

After you've made the first run with these programs, run them every week or so. Also use the updating mechanisms of these two programs to grab the latest malware definition files to catch the newest malware forms uncovered by the developers.

Under no circumstances should you ever investigate software programs offered via unsolicited bulk email for the eradication of spyware. Avoid at all costs the "free spyware scan" advertised in spam. Even a number of products that don't use spam for their propagation may entice you from banner ads and the like. Be aware that many of these programs have been found to delete some spyware and then install their own spyware on PCs. Never use a spyware or adware zapping product without first investigating independent reviews of the products, to make sure they don't install further malware on your system.

Install ZoneAlarm (Windows)

As one more insurance policy for Windows users, I strongly recommend downloading and installing a software utility program called ZoneAlarm from www.zonelabs.com (and lots of shareware download sites). You can choose from a well-endowed free version or even more powerful paid versions.

You will be amazed at how much Internet traffic occurs on your computer behind your back. ZoneAlarm alerts you to every instance of a program on your computer that attempts to connect to the Internet, and every instance of hackers trolling your computer's IP address for open ports or other ways to invade your machine (and local or home network). When you first start ZoneAlarm, it takes a little bit of training to tell it not to bother you again the next time your Web browser or email program reaches out to the Internet. You can also allow a program to access the Internet during one session, and then query you the next session. For instance, if you use RealAudio's RealPlayer to listen to downloaded music, video clips, or media stream, you obviously want to let the player access the Internet. But you'll be amazed the next time you start your PC and suddenly a background process started by RealPlayer wants to talk to the Internet, probably "phoning home" to either look for an update or grab a new ad to show you. ZoneAlarm lets you block that kind of communication.

Tighten Your Email Program's Security Settings

Email software preference settings vary so widely from one program to the next, it's difficult to give specific advice. Some programs, like Outlook Express for Windows, are rather mysterious in precisely what kind of security settings you get with its choices. In the Security options window, I select the Restricted Sites zone. Then I go to Internet Explorer and choose the Tools→Internet Options→Security item. Clicking on the Restricted Zones icon, I next click on the Custom Level button to inspect individual settings for that zone. Make sure that all settings (especially ActiveX, IFRAME, Microsoft VM, and Scripting choices) are set to Disable or Prompt. The goal is to eliminate the chance of a Bad Guy sneaking something onto your system via an HTML message without you knowing it.

For other personal computer email software, look through all the preferences (or options, as they may be called). If you have the choice of disabling JavaScript for email, do so immediately. Take this advice from someone who has been writing about and programming JavaScript since 1995. It has no place in email messages, where it is typically used for evil rather than good. If choices are presented to you about disallowing objects to load or execute, preventing executable files from executing, or anything else you don't understand, disable it all.

To Do Very Soon

I can't expect you to do everything at once, so the next group of to-do items should be your next priority after carrying out all the preceding items. Some of these items take time and thought to implement successfully, so you'll need to put your thinking caps on.

Take Advantage of ISP Spam Filtering

If your ISP or email provider offers spam filtering as a service option, you more than likely want to take advantage of it. That said, one potential problem with ISP spam filtering is that you have little, if any, control over the filtering techniques employed on your mail. As described throughout this book, a blended approach of blocklisting and content filtering is best, but even then, the quality of the processes varies from vendor to vendor and changes over time as spammers and filter makers play leapfrog. The ISP (or mail server administrator at your company or school) may also add some homegrown filtering of its own. Or, the ISP may rely on just blocklisting with a limited number of BL providers, some of which may be too severe or too lenient. To protect the effectiveness of their systems, it's unlikely that your email provider will tell you precisely which techniques it uses for filtering and blocking. In fact, it will probably be suspicious that you even ask (lest you be a spammer hoping to find weaknesses in its systems).

The one aspect of spam filtering you need to guard most closely is the *false positive:* mail you want that doesn't get into your inbox. False positives are, unfortunately, inevitable. Murphy's Law also dictates that the most important email message of the day is the one that gets thrown into the spam bin or forwarded to the server bit bucket.[3]

Not all spam filtering ISPs let you see the dross that is culled from the incoming flow. Some of the biggest email services, such as Hotmail and AOL, destroy billions of messages each day. Is your invitation to a job interview in there? You'll never know. But if your ISP lets you set up spam filtering so that suspected spam is diverted into a separate folder, elect that option. It still means that you'll have to check that folder periodically for the presence of false positives—using techniques described later in this chapter. But that's preferable to missing a vital message.

Eventually, however, you want the server to do the bulk of the filtering so that the mail you need to download to your PC (especially while traveling or using a dial-up or wireless connection) is predominantly the good email you want.

---

[3] Murphy's Law (www.murphys-laws.com) applies to every aspect of life: If anything can go wrong, it will. It's why an open-face sandwich lands on the floor face down, completely negating the Three-Second Rule for Food on the Floor.

Use Spam Filtering on Your PC

Even if your ISP provides spam filtering as part of the email service it provides, spam will likely still slip through. As an extra filtering level to prevent accidental opening, turn on filtering that your email software offers. If your program doesn't have its own filtering facilities (or does a poor job of it), look into favorably reviewed third-party add-ons to popular programs, such as varieties of Microsoft Outlook. You can find many reviews of add-ons for Windows and Mac software at www.spamotomy.com.

Some of the earlier spam-filtering facilities in email programs are extremely lame, relying on the From: address of the message to identify suspected spam. Spammers' tactics have changed, and you need more sophisticated weapons in your arsenal. Statistical sampling content filtering (often using Bayesian techniques) is currently favored for its capability to distinguish spam from ham. Antispam software running in your email programs usually separate spam into a special folder, which you can view in batches. In the case of Bayesian-type filters, your guidance on how to treat spam and ham will improve its capabilities to do so on its own in the future. Give the software about a week to get to know your ham patterns.

Design an Email Account Strategy

People use email in so many different ways that it's perhaps impossible to recommend an email account management strategy that everyone should use to limit their exposure to the potential harvesting of email addresses for spamming. There are folks who use a single work or home email address as their one-and-only address for all business and personal email; others have one address handed out by their IT departments where they work, and another handed out by the ISP that provides connectivity at home; others have active accounts through their ISPs and many free email systems; still others manage their own domains and email servers, giving them the opportunity to create literally one unique email account for each form they fill out on the Web. Some users change email addresses as often as they change socks (and then send out incessant notices to their address books); others have the same address they've been using since, um, 1995, and are loathe to change.

For lots of users, maintaining multiple email accounts is a royal pain in the neck. In other connectivity aspects of our lives, it seems we long to make things simpler, like having one telephone number that works for the home phone and cellular phone, depending on where you are. But the problem with having only one email address, especially if you are active on the

Internet as a subscriber to newsletters, public forums, and e-commerce, is that the more places you spread that address, the more likely it will reach the hands of spammers. And, as described in Chapter 6, once an address gets into one spammer's database, you have lost control of that address; it'll spread like influenza through a second-grade classroom.

Allow me to present some guidelines to help you decide how you may want to use one or more email addresses in a variety of situations. The main goal is to protect at least one primary address as much as possible from exposure to spam. But be aware that until everyone you communicate with practices safe computing with regard to virus and other hacker-induced infections, even your most secret address can get into spammers' databases if it exists anywhere on another user's computer.

1. Make one email address your primary address.

This is the one you give out to your most trusted family, friends, and colleagues. It is the address to which, if given one chance to check your email per day or per week, you'd go for truly important email. Unfortunately, this is the address that is vulnerable to exposure by your correspondents if their machines are hijacked by virus programs that lift addresses from email program address books (the Window-based Outlook address book is the primary target). Unfortunately, there isn't much you can do about that, except to educate your correspondents about the subjects covered in this book.

To minimize exposure of this address to potential spammers, you should not use it for any online subscription or e-commerce registrations until you use a different address for those purposes, and, after a month or two, you feel that you can trust the site with an address. At that time, you can log in to the registration information pages of those accounts, and change the email address to your primary address.

2. Sign up for one or more alternate email addresses.

You have several options to accomplish this. For example, some services, such as AOL, let subscribers create multiple aliases that they can use as they please without any extra cost to their monthly fees. You always have the option of signing up for free email accounts at places such as hotmail.com, yahoo.com, and dozens of others. You'll have to put up with their advertising, but that's the cost of "free." You can use these addresses for Web site registration forms, where you want to be able to receive messages back from the sites, either in the form of registration confirmations, e-commerce order confirmations, or newsletter subscription mailings.

Be aware that some sites do not accept registrations from free email hosts. In that case, you can register with services that provide disposable email addresses and forwarding services, such as sneakemail.com. If you had all the time in the world, you would ideally use a different address for each registration so you could track whether the site gives away its registration addresses. If you find that a unique address you used to sign up with Site A triggers spam from Site B (and C and D and...), then you know not to change that account over to your primary address; but if the address isn't propagated elsewhere after a couple of months, then you might trust Site A with your primary address.[4]

If you use multiple email addresses for registrations, keep a separate log of your activity. You want to be able to recall which site(s) had a particular address so you know when you receive email from a site that isn't in that collection—spam!

3. Use a separate email address for public forums and newsgroups.

If you contribute to public forums (newsgroups and others) where you submit your comments via email and your email program, be sure to use a return address that is not your primary address. Set up a separate email account in your email/newsgroup software, and send messages to the group via that separate account. Newsgroup archives are a prime harvesting source for spammers. In particular, they use the subject area of the forum as an indicator of your personal interests, and thus turn your messages' return email addresses into something they can sell as a "targeted" address for other spammers. They'll claim you opted into receiving messages about the subject merely because your address is visible in the archives.

Remember that there is no requirement that you provide a valid return address in the message. Good netiquette does recommend it, so you can disguise your address in a way that those humans who want to reach you directly can do so. For example, I might modify my address from:

```
dannyg@dannyg.com
```

```
to:
```

```
dannygR_E_M_O_V_E@R_E_M_O_V_Edannyg.com.
```
[5]

Then, in my automated signature line, I could add further instructions, such as:

```
delete R_E_M_O_V_Es from my reply address.
```

---

[4] Remember that if a site sells out to another company, you may regret skipping over the privacy policy clause that equates your email address with an asset that can be transferred to the company's new owner. The new owners do not necessarily have to live up to the privacy policy of the original company.

[5] You must avoid using a domain that is or could be someone else's real domain. Using illegal characters as placeholders is one way to guarantee that.

Cumbersome, yes. But it lets humans reach you while directing to oblivion email messages aimed at the harvested address.

Establish a Password Management System

Ask most computer users about their biggest hassles, and right up there with spam is keeping their passwords straight. Different systems have different requirements for the length or makeup of passwords. Very secure systems require that you change your password regularly. Similar problems exist for user IDs. Some registration pages let you (or require you) to use an email address as the login name, while others want some other string that hasn't been used by a previous registrant. Naturally, this causes you to come up with a whole slew of user IDs and passwords that are scattered around various sites.

At the same time, you are warned against writing down your user IDs and passwords anywhere that could fall into the wrong hands. Plenty of user ID and passwords can be found on Post-It notes stuck on computer monitors in cubicles and homes around the world (yikes!). How many of your passwords are stored in an address book entry in your PDA?

Keeping your user IDs and passwords straight is a tough job. Frankly, I don't know of a good system to recommend. That's not what I'm here to help you solve, anyway. But here is my big security concern: that you might reuse an important user ID and password combination on a site that shouldn't be trusted with it. Take this scenario: You are a Paypal user, for which your user ID is an email address; you also use a password that you commonly use for your accounts, such as for your ISP login and home banking. Next, you sign up to a Web site to download some free software gizmo, where you need to register with your email address and password. If you supply the same pair as your Paypal account, and the software gizmo site is a scam, the scammer now has a copy of the keys to one or more of your financial accounts or accounts with your credit card and banking information. They could make the rounds to eBay, Paypal, and various online banks to see if that combination works.

Just as with the email address strategy, you need to generate multiple passwords. Reserve one or more supersecret passwords for trusted accounts that provide access to financial information, especially banking and credit card data. These passwords should be no fewer than seven characters, contain numbers and letters (preferably with numbers interlaced between letters), and some letters uppercase while other letters lowercase. Do not use a password consisting of a name or single word, unless you also sprinkle numbers inside the name/word, and change the case of some letters. With a seven-character password of this nature, a hacker would have to happen upon one of over 3.5 trillion combinations to find your password; an eight-character combination yields over 218 trillion combinations.

You should also create a series of what I call "throwaway passwords." Use these for any password-controlled registration that is not guarding significant personal information. For example, a newspaper that requires a login to access its free archive might have, at most, some (possibly bogus) demographic data that you supply to get the access. Or any other site you register for free stuff would be the place for another throwaway password.

So, how can you remember which user ID and password you used for all these registration sites? It's definitely a hassle, and you'll have to record them somewhere—unless you have a photographic memory (I don't). Whether you do it on paper or computer, I don't recommend recording the actual passwords (at least your supersecret passwords) in their normal form. In the case of passwords with numbers and letters, you will quickly get to know the combination; in fact, you may have an easier time typing them than recalling them character by character, as the physical keyboard sequence becomes etched in your mind. What you need is some reminder of which password you used. Devise alias code words that remind you of the supersecret ones. Perhaps just the first couple characters; or the characters in a different order and case structure—something that a passerby (or crook) happening upon your piece of paper or file on a stolen laptop computer could not use immediately to enter your account.

One more tip about passwords: If you use a laptop computer, do not check the box on supersecret registration forms that lets the computer automatically log in to the account for you. Force yourself to enter at least the password into the form for entry to sites with your personal and financial information. Should your laptop be stolen, you don't want the crook to simply visit eBay, Amazon, Paypal, or your bookmarked stock-trading account and gain unfettered access to those accounts. The damage would likely be worse than having your wallet stolen. I recommend this behavior for deskbound PCs, too, because unless you live on a desert island, someone else in your home or office could have access to your computer. A stroll down your browser's bookmarks will provide instant access to places you don't want them to go.

To Do—All Day, Every Day

This last, long group of to-do items will reshape the way you respond to all of your email, including the messages you want. The primary goal is to help you appear invisible to spammers, scammers, and hackers. It's hard work, and you may feel discouraged after awhile if your spam load doesn't diminish despite your hard work. But it's vital that we all keep up the fight. It's we humans against the computer-enhanced enemy. We're the smarter ones; they're the more persistent and durable ones. That's what we have to overcome.

Suspect Every Email Message

I got a little chuckle out of a technology news story that suggested email filtering shouldn't be on the lookout for spam, but rather on the lookout for ham—the good messages we want to receive. But in a sense, that's what you should be doing at all times. Despite your natural inclination, you should be suspicious of literally *every email message* you see in your inbox until you can safely ascertain that a message is ham and not spam.

You've learned that you cannot automatically trust every message that shows the sender to be someone you know and trust. Such messages may have been sent by someone else's virus-infected machine using your friend's email address lifted from an Outlook address book. Even a good friend can forward a virus that is disguised as something cool. Or a phony instant message sent from a friend's infected computer could lead you astray. Heck, there are even services on the Web that will deliver an "e-card" to a friend or family member that, in turn, installs spyware into the unsuspecting recipient's computer. The spyware reports back to the "friend" logs of keystrokes and visited Web pages. To your friend, it's a practical joke; to you, it's a massive invasion of privacy.

The point is to exercise care before opening any piece of mail, with or without an attachment. If you don't receive a lot of email, you may be eager to open every precious piece that arrives. Resist the temptation. Be on the lookout for message subjects that provoke you when you don't recognize the sender in the From: column.

Delete Obvious Spam First

If something doesn't look right by reading just the From: and Subject: columns of your inbox list, delete the message without opening it. If your email program's spam-filtering system wants you to identify spam, do so to help train the software to filter similar items in the future.

The reason you should delete obvious spam first is so that you don't accidentally open something you don't want to. You may be viewing a good message and accidentally click the Next button, which opens the next unread message. The more trash you can eliminate without viewing, the less likely you'll see a message that doesn't deserve to be read.

Admittedly, the spammer tactic of using one or more random words in the Subject: line makes some messages look so squirrelly, it's difficult to resist opening them. But do resist. Instead, follow the advice in the next to-do item.

View the Source Code of Spam Suspects

This is one of the harder habits to get into because most email programs make it so darned laborious to read the source code of a message. For example, in Microsoft Outlook Express for Windows, you have to right-click on an item in the inbox listing, choose Properties, and then click on the Details tab and Message Source button to see the source code.

Viewing the source code of a message is the safest means of getting an idea of the message content. It's not important at all that you understand the HTML code that comes with most messages. A nonspam message, including commercial bulk mail that you sign up for via confirmed opt-in systems, will either not be formatted in HTML or will have a clearly readable text-only portion as the first part of the message body (beneath the header section). What you're looking for is something that lets you know a message is something you want to receive.

Dead giveaways to spam mailings are a profusion of HTML tags that break up words. More recently, spam messages endeavoring to trick content filters also include long lists of random words at the beginning and end of messages. Check Chapter 12 for examples of the spammers' message tricks. You'll be able to spot them quickly with only a little practice. Close the Source View window, and delete any spam message without opening it.

Suspect Every Attachment of Being a Virus

If a virus attachment should manage to elude your antivirus software (perhaps it's a brand-new virus), you must do everything in your power to resist opening the file. When you scan the list of unread messages, the ones with attachments usually stand out with the help of an icon denoting the file.

A lot of corporate email systems automatically delete email attachments (or attachments of certain file types) before recipients even have a chance to see them. If you were to do the same, especially from senders you don't recognize, you'd be joining the club. But with the ways viruses spread themselves, you'll also likely receive attachments with messages having From: addresses you recognize.

The best, albeit most cumbersome, way to treat attachments that might be legitimate is to check with the sender before opening the attachment. Make sure that the sender did, in fact, knowingly send you the thing. Also ask what it is. If it's some "cool" software gizmo, your friend may not be aware of what dangers lie within.

One of the problems with looking at attachment information in an email program is that, depending on how you have your preferences set (especially in Windows), the file name extensions of dangerous files are hidden from immediate view. The file name may be listed as neatPic.jpg, but the actual file is neatPic.jpg.exe, an executable program that could have free rein within your system to do all kinds of nasty things.

A source view of the message will reveal the true file name, regardless of your system preferences. At the start of the section that holds the file, you'll find some content-type information as well as the complete file name. Any file name that ends with one of the following extensions should be highly suspect:

.bat   (Windows/DOS batch file)

.cmd   (Windows NT or DOS command file)

.exe   (Executable application)

.html   (Web page file)

.pif   (Windows shortcut)

.scr   (Screen saver)

.zip   (Zipped archive file)

These aren't the only file types that can contain viruses, but they tend to be the most common, especially because their files or file-name extensions are hidden by default in Windows file listings. It's more proof that the hackers try to take advantage of the neophyte or nontechnical user who typically leaves default settings as they are.

I strongly suggest changing your Windows folder options so that normally hidden files and file name extensions are always visible. In Windows XP, do the following:

1. Open Windows Explorer.

2. Choose Tools→Folder Options, and click on the View tab.

3. In the Hidden Files and Folders section, click the "Show hidden files and folders" radio button.

4. Uncheck the "Hide extensions for known file types" checkbox.

5. Uncheck the "Hide protected operating system files" checkbox.

6. Click the "Apply to all folders" button.

7. Click OK to activate the settings and close the dialog window.

In sum, treat all attachments as if they were bombs. Trust only those that you are expecting or have verified were intentionally sent by someone you know or trust. Handle all others gently while deleting the messages that contain them.

Don't Be Fooled by Tricksters

Believe me when I reveal the following secrets to you:

- You did *not* win a Dutch (or Spanish, German, or any other country's) lottery.

- Paypal, eBay, your financial institutions, and government agencies do not send emails with links to empty account information forms: They know your data when you visit their sites, so they can fill in most, if not all, form fields for you from their databases.

- You *cannot* opt out of all spam by registering anyplace, for free or for a fee.

- You will *not* receive an email warning about pending government litigation, especially a message that contains attachments of the "evidence."

- *No one* received email addressed to you by mistake, so the attachment does not contain messages intended for you.

- You do *not* have a secret admirer.

- Lisa did *not* just move into your area.

- The free gift for which you're supposed to register is *worth less* than the value of your "live" email address.

- *No* order for anything will be shipped to you if you haven't placed the order.

- You have *not* received an e-card from anyone you know (and if you did, the payload may be deadly).

- Pay-per-view TV is *not* free.

- Anonymous stock tips are for *suckers*.

- You will *lose* money without ever having a chance to stuff envelopes at home in your free time.

- You do *not* have a check waiting from a stranger.

- Filling out surveys is *not* a road to riches.

- You need a *prescription* for legal prescription medicines.

- Excess fat *doesn't* burn—except during exercise or on a barbecue.

- *No* stranger is holding a highly valued "position" open just for you in a network marketing plan.

- Eventually, you'll be caught having a *phony* degree from an unaccredited college and be fired.

- *No* self-respecting developer or marketer of antispam and antispyware software would have the gall to sell his products via spam.

- Genuine new and upgradeable copies of multi-hundred-dollar Symantec, Adobe, and Microsoft software products cost *a lot more* than $30 to $60.

- The form embedded in an email does *not* submit the information over a secure connection.

These and thousands more outrageous claims clog the spam and scam buckets of the world every day. Some of these tricks are tough to resist, so you must remember to destroy all bulk mailings sent to you without your consent. Do not visit the Web sites linked from the message (each click-through might earn money for the spam's sender). Do not open the attachment, no matter how serious or threatening the email message's claim is. Anything involving a real legal matter requires notification by postal mail or some other verifiable tangible medium. And if you are concerned about a security warning from a Web site you visit, instead of following the link in the email (which likely takes you to a phony page made to look like the real Web site page), use your bookmarks or type the URL of the site, and then check your account information. If there are any real problems, you'll learn about them at that time.

Resist Spam Offers

An effective spammer is usually an effective marketer. An effective marketer knows that some keywords are difficult for consumers to resist. The two words most difficult to resist are "free" and "save." Who doesn't like free stuff? And who doesn't want to save money on something they want or need? Either of those single words is capable of undoing the tens of thousands of words in this book.

Keep reminding yourself that very little of value is completely free, especially if you learn about it from spam. The cost may be hidden from you, as when you are asked to register your email address to receive a free gift (the tactic used, for example, by the emailings involved with the New York State prosecution detailed in Chapter 16). You may receive some low-value trinket for your trouble, but others will be making much more from the sale, rental, and lease of your live email address and any other demographic information you provide in the form. And that means your spam load will increase, with whatever costs are associated with your spam fighting and management.

Some offers should sound too good to be true—because they are. One offer I received was selling Adobe Systems' high-end products (retailing from $550-$650) for prices under $45. The chance that these were genuine copies of the programs was zero. I would not be able to get customer support, nor would I be able to upgrade the packages to the next versions. Symantec's Norton product line (especially SystemWorks) seems to be offered a lot through spam. If you buy such products (and haven't simply had your credit card information ripped off), you are not only encouraging software pirating, but you are also simply delaying the inevitable moment when you have to pay the real street price for the next versions of the pirated products you buy.

Keep telling yourself that our combined goal is ZERO RESPONSE!

My mother used to tell me how to get back at someone who confronts you like a screaming maniac in order to goad you into a shouting match: Ignore him. The less you react, the more maniacal the screamer gets, while he makes an even bigger ass of himself and eventually flames out. Likewise, a spammer hates being ignored by his intended audience. If a spammer realizes that not only is a huge chunk of his spew being blocked but that the rest isn't even being looked at, he'll eventually find another line of work.

If You're Tempted, Investigate Domain Registrations

Okay, a spam message arrives offering a genuine product you want or need for a substantial (but not pirate-level) savings. Savings are especially attractive to U.S. citizens who pay a lot of money for prescription medications. Or maybe you simply can't resist the offer for some hot toy product that is being promoted in a spam mailing.

First of all, shame on you for opening the spam in the first place. But if you do, and you are tempted to visit the Web site, first look into the sources of both the email message you received and the Web site you're asked to visit. This takes a bit of effort, and wading through some technical business, to get the information you're after. Use Appendix B as a guide to locating the true pieces of information about the mail server used to send the spam and the Web address associated with a clickable link in the mail. If you were an American consumer, how safe would you feel about ordering from a site that is running on a Web server in China with a domain name registered by someone showing a Uruguay address; and the mail message arrived from a server in Russia? What if the domain were registered only a few days ago? Is this the kind of organization you'd want to give your credit card information to? I wouldn't, even on a dare.

If you think that your click-through to visit a spamvertised Web site, or placement of one order, won't have any impact on spam one way or another, remember that some spammers may receive only a handful of orders for each spam spew, yet it is enough to break even. If we stop enough of those click-throughs and orders, the revenue can fall below the breakeven point, and eventually drive the spammer into other lines of work.

What was that I said? Oh yes: ZERO RESPONSE!

Know How to React to Spam Bouncing to You

If you find that email messages come bouncing back to your email address, and you didn't send the mail in the first place, the culprit is a forged From: header field that used your address. Assuming you are not a spammer, you will feel violated that someone dared sully your good name and reputation. Will a phony spam spew in your name go on your "permanent record?"[6]

It's hard not to take this effrontery personally. It's possible that someone who actually received a message with your address in the From: field will be an email newbie, and flame you back for suggesting that he or she needs to enhance a particular body part dimension. You may even pull out the "joe-job" term on the belief that a spammer is deliberately targeting you to make you look like a Bad Guy.

But take heart. The spammer likely doesn't know your address from adam@eden.god. A lot of spam with a forged From: field doesn't knowingly use existing email addresses. In fact, spammers would rather the addresses be totally false so as not to raise more eyebrows than necessary to get past various filters and suspicious recipients. But the tactic of assembling From: addresses from user IDs and domain names chosen at random from their databases will certainly find working addresses from time to

---

6 The threat of bad marks on one's "permanent record" is a myth—propagated by parents and school disciplinarians—that haunts most school-aged children. If only I hadn't been caught throwing that blackboard eraser across the room in the third grade, I'd have a real job today. What they don't tell kids is that your permanent record doesn't start until you're an adult. Just ask the cops. And Equifax.

time. If the To: fields contain addresses that are no longer active, some mail systems will send a bounce message to the From: field address (rather than doing the correct thing, which is to reject the message immediately before it can be sent to an invalid address). The bounces will raise no alert level anywhere along the way. They're simply something you can delete, or save in a separate archive as possible evidence for a future ISP law suit against a spammer.

Don't Forward Spam to Friends or Family

No matter how much you may believe that someone you know is interested in the latest spamvertised product, do not forward the message to anyone else. A lot of spammers already use the facilities of zombie PCs around the world to issue their malarkey. Do you want to help the spammer spread his message wider?

If you do forward a spammer's message, two potentially negative outcomes may accrue to you. First, if the message has Web beacons or coded links to a Web site, your friend will be validating your email address when viewing the message or clicking a link. Second, if your friend should report your forwarded message as spam, *your* IP address in the message header may get reported as a source or relay of the spam. Not such a hot idea, now, is it?

You may, however, forward your spam to a special address at the U.S. Federal Trade Commission. The newly updated address is:

spam@uce.gov

Spam samples received at this address are stored in a database known as the Refrigerator. The FTC's Michael Goodman (no relation to me) reported in early 2004 that the agency receives hundreds of thousands of forwarded spam messages every day. I didn't think such a huge volume of data could be of much value, but FTC court documents for CAN-SPAM violation complaints state that the agency uses samples from the Refrigerator as evidence. Now that's a good cause.

Don't Unsubscribe from Mailings You Didn't Subscribe To

The hallmark of the opt-out system of unsolicited email—now legalized in the United States—is the ubiquitous unsubscribe instruction. A lot of other spam sent by less law-abiding netizens, who violate other provisions of the law by forging headers and disguising identities, also contains unsubscribe links or instructions. Unfortunately, over the years, the majority of spam messages that provide unsubscribe links have supplied either bogus links (they lead to nowhere) or links that lead to pages that capture your live email address for resale, rental, and lease to other spam campaigns by the same mailer (under different identities) or other spammers. Instead of getting your name off one list, you essentially offered it to dozens or hundreds of lists. Wham, bam, thank you, spam!

The reputation of unsubscribe links is so tarnished that all such links are now suspect. A lot of law-abiding bulk emailers (but still spammy in the eyes of true spam fighters) use unsubscribe registrations as a way to wash their lists of recipients who might cause trouble with spam reports. But you know what? Despite the U.S. legality of opt-out bulk emailing, spamming violates the Terms of Service and Acceptable Use Policies of most honest ISPs, including the connectivity points for the bulk emailers' outgoing servers. Thus, even law-abiding mailers can still get in trouble with their ISPs—something that spam reporting services count on.

I keep coming back to the consent issue. When I read dictionary definitions of the word "subscribe," they all indicate that some specific action must be taken to give assent to receive something in return. It goes beyond logic to assume that I can *be subscribed* to something against my will, yet these spam messages insist that I can unsubscribe from something I didn't subscribe to (and puh-leez, don't give me that "partner" garbage). In a sense, by unsubscribing, I'd be admitting that I subscribed in the first place. But I didn't. And I won't unsubscribe from something I never subscribed to. Period.

By the same token, if I really did subscribe to a newsletter or regular mailings from a public forum, I will honor that commitment, and gladly accept the mailings without complaint or reporting it as spam. If the volume of the messages gets annoying, I look to see if the mailing offers a digest version, which groups together 25 or one day's worth of messages into just one mail. When I wish to discontinue receiving these mailings, I will unsubscribe in the ways indicated on each mailing I receive. And I expect to be removed from the list at that point.

Avoid "Cool" Downloads Until Declared Safe

Most of the spyware and adware that robs your computer of its power, and perhaps robs you of your personal information (e.g., a keylogger that grabs your user ID and password entries for Web sites), arrives as a hidden payload along with some other free software download. As described in Chapter 13, "Beware Geeks Bearing Gifts," neat animations, browser toolbars, email smileys, dancing cursors, and even well-known music-sharing service software have been known to bring all kinds of unwelcome goodies with them.

Sometimes the extent of the hidden activity is described in the End User License Agreement (EULA). I always encourage users to read those things, or at least scan for the parts that state the rights you yield to the software developer. Better still is to wait until you can research independent sources (online and magazine reviews) to verify that the software does not contain any malware. Also be sure to update and run Spybot-Search & Destroy and Ad-aware at least once a month, if not once a week, if you are, or another user with access to your computer is, an active downloader.

Beware of Social Hackers

A so-called social hacker has one major goal: to get you to leak your computer system's network user name and password. They target workers at companies, especially nonmanagement employees, who might not be too suspicious while trying to be nice to a telephone caller. A social hacker may identify himself or herself as another new-hire employee of the same company working in the IT or some other department—someplace the real employee wouldn't have a chance to know the staff.

Knowing that a lot of employees use children's or pets' names for passwords, a social hacker will not only try to gain the trust of the hapless employee through casual conversation, but will ask questions about whether the employee has any kids or pets. Then, sharing bogus information about non-existent children and pets, the hacker asks what the employees' children's names are. Within a few minutes, the hacker has enough information to log in to the company's system and run amok.

If you follow the to-do list instructions above about selecting and managing your passwords, and your dog's name isn't fR7o2D1o, the likelihood of an inadvertent slip drops to near zero.

Spread the Word to Friends and Family

You and I can't fight spam alone. We have to educate more nontechnical friends and family members about the threat that spammers, scammers, and hackers pose to the email system and our privacy. Lend this book to everyone you know. Buy them all copies for Christmas. Get this information in front of as many email users as you know.

We have to use *all* the powers available to us—technology, legislation, and personal responsibility—if we are to have any hope of deflecting this corrosive activity from the Internet. It's ironic that we have to work so hard to appear invisible and nonexistent to spammers, scammers, and hackers. But that's the best way we can convince them that they're wasting their time.

That's my plan, and I hope it becomes yours, too. The original idea of a connected network of computers and the messaging that travels around the network was to enhance sharing and communication among individuals. It was not meant as a place to fear for your privacy or sanity.

Despite my length of service in the email ranks, I'm not so nostalgic as to want to return to the "good old days." The technology was crude, speeds were slow—those old days weren't necessarily that good. I don't expect the Internet and email to become the equivalent of a town where you don't have to lock your doors. But maybe we can eventually reach a stage where a simple lock will do the trick, while we dismantle the three extra bolt locks, two chains, and alarm systems; where we don't have to continually look over our shoulders while walking down the street; or worry that someone is listening in on a private conversation.

What power it would be to regain control and declare victory in the spam wars.

All about Email Message Headers

In Chapter 4 I introduced you to a few high points of the email message header. In this appendix, I dive deeper into a typical message's header in case you're curious about what the gibberish means. Understanding every header field other than Received: fields is not crucial to dealing with spam, or even for getting into the hobby of investigating spam sources covered in Appendix B. I find, however, that many newcomers are either confused by header information, or come to their own incorrect conclusions about what the various codes and numbers mean.

To assist in the ensuing discussion, I repeat the sample message from Chapter 4, complete with artificial line numbers.

```
(1) From freddiej@example.com Thu 7 Aug 2003
    16:15:54
(2) Received: from smtp.example.com (jimbo.exam-
    ple.com [192.168.1.101]) by dannyg.com
    (8.12.9) id h77MFrGx025158 for <dannyg@dan-
    nyg.com>; Thu, 7 Aug 2003 16:15:54 -0600
    (MDT)
(3) Received: from freddiej (dhcp-172-24-30-
    238.north.example.com [172.24.30.238]) by
    smtp.example.com (8.11.2/8.11.2) with SMTP id
    h77MFm326503 for <dannyg@dannyg.com>; Thu, 7
    Aug 2003 15:15:48 -0700 (PDT)
(4) Message-ID:
    <004d01c35d30$ff50bac0$ee1e18ac@north.exam-
    ple.com>
```

```
(5)  From: "Freddie J Muggs"
     <freddiej@example.com>
(6)  To: <dannyg@dannyg.com>
(7)  Subject: Available for lunch next week?
(8)  Date: Thu, 7 Aug 2003 15:12:31 -0700
(9)  Organization: Examples, Ltd.
(10) MIME-Version: 1.0
(11) Content-Type: text/plain; charset="iso-8859-
     1"
(12) X-Priority: 3
(13) X-Mailer: Microsoft Outlook Express
     5.00.2314.1300
(14) X-UIDL: a<!#!Od~"!+A~"!YAe!!
(15)
(16) Hey Danny,
(17) Just got back from a week in Bermuda. Let's
     get together next week so I can show you the
     photos.
(18) Freddie
(19)
```

Here is a line-by-line analysis in plain language (I hope).

Line 1—Return-Path:

You may not see this line, or at least in this form, if you view a message header in your email program, but this is what it looks like in the message's raw form as appended to your email server's mailbox file. This piece of information is the last bit of information that incoming mail servers add to a message after it travels from sender to receiver. Some email programs assign a label—Return-Path:—to the address part, dropping the date and time.

The address inserted into this line of the message is derived from the return address of the message's envelope. In a typical email message, the outgoing mail program fills in the envelope's return address by copying the Reply-To: field (if present) or the From: field. It is possible, however, for a sneaky outgoing server to insert a return address for an envelope that doesn't match any other address in the header. For example, if a spammer's server inserts your address in the envelope and a different one in the From: field, you might receive a "bounce" message even though your address doesn't appear in the header. This is because the incoming mail server uses the Return-Path: info to report any problems while processing the mail. You'll likely be completely confused because not only do you not recognize the bounced message, but you don't even see your address in the From: field of the bounced message, and you'll wonder why you received the bounce.

Lines 2 and 3—Trace Information

This message had a fairly typical direct route between sender and receiver. Each time an SMTP server receives the message to be passed along, the server adds the current trace information to the top of the list. Therefore, the most recent transfer line is the one that your own receiving email server made. It received the message from some other mail-oriented server, and, because it is the destination server (dannyg.com in this example), the message gets passed onto the rest of my server's email processing (over to the POP server, which stores my incoming mail in a mailbox and from which my personal computer retrieves the message).

Each Received: header line indicates a transfer from one point in the journey to another. Not recorded here are the travels of the individual packets that make up the entire message, as routers fling the packets around the hidden Internet infrastructure. Thank goodness, because we have enough on our hands with just the mail server transfer parts.

Let's look more closely at the topmost Received: field (line 2) to see what it tells us about the most recent transfer point. The field is written by the receiving mail server, the dannyg.com mail server in this case. To receive the message, my mail server had one of those "conversations" with a server that identified itself as smtp.example.com, along with an IP address of 192.168.1.101 (I show a reserved IP address here for demonstration purposes). Upon receiving the request to accept mail from smtp.example.com, my mail server performed a quick lookup (using a Unix utility command called nslookup) of the IP address to see if it resolved to a domain of any kind. In this case, it found that the name of the server associated with the IP address is jimbo.example.com. While the two names don't match, my incoming mail server (like most such servers) passes no judgment on the validity or honesty of the identification made by the server passing along the message. That both the original identification and the name associated with the IP address have the same domain probably means that no one is playing games (but see more about this later).

The numbers in parentheses after my server name refer to the version of my mail server software program running at the time this message was received. This server assigns a unique ID number to each incoming message, and posts that identifier as part of the trace information. Information about the recipient's email address (the "for" part of the field) is derived from the message's envelope. (Recall that the envelope is deleted after the message arrives at its destination.) While this message has one recipient, and the address happens to be the same as the To: field (line 6), that isn't always the case. A mailing list message, for example, might use some other data in the To: field (frequently the address to which submissions to the mailing list are to be mailed), but each of the outgoing messages has the actual recipient's email address on the message's envelope to help it reach its destination.

Each Received: record receives a timestamp of the transaction. Industry standards have determined the format for the date, down to the three-character day name, followed by a comma, and then the date and time in the order shown. Although not required, it is good practice for the time to be designated in the local time zone of the mail server receiving the message. In the case of our example, the mail server is located in a time zone six hours behind Coordinated Universal Time (essentially the same as Greenwich Mean Time), in the North American Mountain time zone (during Daylight Saving Time—MDT).

In line 3, the next previous transfer point in the message's route is recorded, inserted into the header by the smtp.example.com server. As the lowest Received: record, this is the point at which a legitimate message started its movement through mail servers and the Internet. The originator is a mail account named freddiej, and Freddie's personal computer sent the message by way of a router somewhere within the example.com corporate computer system (a router that generates its own internal IP addresses within a host system called north). Freddie's machine identified itself by the IP address 172.24.30.238, and the north.example.com mail server software validated the address as, indeed, belonging to that IP address assigned by one of its routers. While the notation of the computer at the end of the lookup process is slightly different (dhcp-172-24-30-238), the numbers line up with the IP address numbers.

As indicated by the timestamp, the north.example.com server (running a slightly different software version from my mail server) appears to be located in the Pacific time zone, one hour earlier than mine. Thus, the elapsed time between north.example.com receiving Freddie's message and my email server receiving it is approximately six seconds.

Some messages may have more or fewer Received: records in their headers. A single record is generally evidence of an automated transmission generated directly by a mail server. Legitimate mailing lists frequently send mail this way, as do experienced spammers who have their own mail servers. More complex trace records can indicate a complex mail processing system behind a corporate firewall; or it can mean that the spammer assembled a phony set of Received: lines (all but the topmost one following the sending server's claimed identity) to make the message look legitimate. In other words, the number of Received: records is not a satisfactory predictor that a message is spam.

Line 4—Message-ID:
A message identifier is optional in an email header, but it is traditionally added to the header by one of the first (if not the first) mail servers to handle the message. The number can be used to isolate the message within a sequence of messages handled by the server if someone needs to dissect a problem with the server. The specific number used is of little consequence to humans.

Line 5—From:
The From: field of the header usually gets its information from the email program that the user employs to create the message. In the Preferences or Configuration dialog boxes, the user fills in his or her name and email address. If the name is left blank, then only the email address appears in the From: field. At the receiving end, the recipient's email program inspects the From: header to figure out what information about the message it displays in the list of inbox message. Usually, if both a name and email address are in the From: field (in which case the email address is inside angle brackets), then only the name is displayed in the column. But if no name is in the field, then the email address appears in the column for that message.

I should note that a user could put any name and mail address—real or bogus—into the Preferences panel for the email program. You could name yourself the president of the United States, and insert an email address of prez@whitehouse.gov, and the email program would fill in that information for the From: field of the outgoing message. Of course, if the recipient hits the Reply button, then the response is addressed to the commander-in-chief, not you. The point is, unless some new authentication enhancements are added to SMTP, there is no validation or verification that the information in the From: field is accurate or true.

Line 6—To:
Most of the legitimate one-to-one email you receive has your email address listed in the To: field of the header. The sender either typed your address manually into the blank message while writing the new message, or the information came from the sender's local address book containing your email address (and perhaps your name, too). In such legitimate mail, the SMTP server initially forwarding your message reads the address from the To: field to assemble information for the message's envelope, in which case both the envelope and To: field point to the same address. But that's not always the case, even in legitimate mail.

When a message goes out to a long list of recipients, the sender has some options that impact the data in the To: field. The clumsy and rather impolite way is to list each recipient in a long list of names and addresses in the

To: or CC: fields of the message. This is impolite because it bloats the overall size of the message and exposes all recipients' email addresses to everyone on the list. Not all recipients may appreciate that.

Another possibility, used commonly by mailing list software, is for the To: address to be filled in with such placeholders as an address that identifies the list, or an indicator that the recipient list is purposely hidden from view ("Undisclosed Recipients"). The originating software uses the equivalent of a blind carbon copy (BCC). What you don't see is that, upon receiving the list of BCC addresses, the SMTP server addresses each message's envelope individually with the destination address so that the To: field need not be inspected to address the envelope. It also means, however, that as long as an automated sender fills out the envelope address correctly, any name and address—real or imaginary—may go into the To: field.

Line 7—Subject:

The content of the Subject: field is the sole responsibility of the software that initiates the mail message. From the standards point of view, the only restriction is an absolute limit of 998 characters and a recommended limit of 78 characters. While email programs that list and read incoming messages can accommodate long subjects, the typical column arrangement on a personal computer screen doesn't encourage long text strings for this field.

Line 8—Date:

Inserting the date and time that the message was sent is the responsibility of the sender's email software program. Surprisingly, the accuracy of the time-stamp is solely dependent on the accuracy of the internal clock settings in the sender's personal computer. If the clock has the wrong year, or if the time zone setting in the clock control panel is incorrect, the time and date of the message will represent those incorrect values. Email programs that list incoming messages tend to list the messages by default in the order of the dates and times indicated in the Date: header field. That's why you sometimes receive a message that appears in the list well out of sequence from the normal flow. This might even be an intentional spammer ploy to plant the message at the top or bottom of your inbox list, calling extra attention to it.

Standards govern the format for the date so that computers around the world, regardless of native spoken language, interpret the value the same way. Values for these dates are in the same format as those use in the Received: header fields.

Line 9—Organization:

The Organization: field is one of many optional fields specified in the email message format standards. The field and a value for it are inserted into the message header only if the sender's email program provides that information. Figure A-1 shows the Microsoft Outlook Express dialog box that users fill out to configure the software. If the Organization: field of the dialog box has anything typed into it, the outgoing message header includes the Organization: field (the Reply: address field forces the addition of the Reply-To: header field).

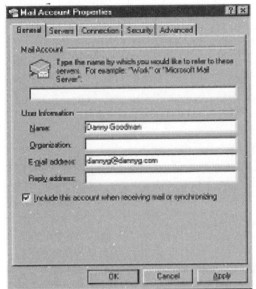

Figure A-1. An Outlook Express dialog governs several header fields.

Line 10—MIME-Version:

Email messages today can contain a variety of types of information beyond just the simple text that mail used to contain. You have certainly received messages that include attachments. Back in the days of teletype printers and text-only video terminals, attachments and embedded images far exceeded the capabilities of the equipment. But today's highly graphical personal computing environments and high-capacity transfer rates (especially with DSL, cable modem, and local area network access) have plenty of horsepower to allow more sophisticated kinds of data beyond straight text.

To help standardize the way such additional content is embedded within a message, a series of standards were developed under the technical heading Multipurpose Internet Mail Extensions, abbreviated MIME.[1] These extensions (published in 1992 as RFC 1341) were designed to build on the existing RFC 822 standard for the structure and headers of an email message. Although RFC 822 was written in the days of the ARPANET, the formats specified in that standard were well entrenched in the public Internet by the time the MIME standards became carved in stone. Even by then, the extensions had been employed informally by email programs.

---

1 There have been numerous discussions about how to pronounce this acronym. The natural inclination is to pronounce it like the word "mime," even though the technology has absolutely nothing to do with silent acting or a face-painted street performer. This is the way MIME-related RFC authors I know say it, so it's good enough for me. Some followers of the technology, however, vehemently prefer to speak it by articulating each letter: m-i-m-e. L-o-o-n-y.

The header field for MIME-Version: signifies nothing more than which generation of MIME standard is being used by the message. The version associated with the first series of published MIME standards was 1.0, and is the version used by most email programs today.

Line 11—Content-Type:

In most cases, when the MIME-Version: field is specified in a message header, the Content-Type: field is also present to provide instructions to the receiving email program about how to process the message content. Syntax for content-type specifications is spelled out in a variety of RFC documents. Most of the types are easily discernable from their description. Regular text messages, like the example shown earlier, typically also specify a character set that the message uses. The specific character set specification is of little value to humans.

If the message includes an attachment, the content type indicates something called a multipart type. This Content-Type: field value can look like gibberish because it includes a further label consisting of letters and numbers. For example:

```
Content-Type: multipart/mixed;
boundary="--7bee2baa6b9e6139"
```

This designation means that the content includes two or more parts, each of which may be of different content types. The boundary designation is a string of characters that is inserted into the message content between the sections corresponding to each attached file. Boundary identifiers have only one requirement: that they begin with at least two hyphens. In the body of the message, you will find the boundary identifier along with specifications about that particular section's content type.

To demonstrate how a multipart message uses the boundary number, the following is an abbreviated message body section that includes a regular text portion and an attached Microsoft Word document.

```
This is a multi-part message in MIME format.

----7bee2baa6b9e6139
Content-Type: text/plain; charset=us-ascii
Content-Disposition: inline
Content-Transfer-Encoding: 7bit

Dear Steve,
Here is the Word document I promised you.

Karen

----7bee2baa6b9e6139
```

```
Content-Type: application/msword
Content-Transfer-Encoding: base64
Content-Disposition: attachment;
filename="Project Specs.doc"

OM8R4KGxGuEAAAAAAAAAAAAAAAAAAAAAPgADAP7/CQAGAAAAA
AAAAAAAAAABAAAAJwAAAAAA
AAAAEAAAKQAAAAEAAAD+////AAAAA-
CYAAAD////////////////////////////////////////
[ lots more base64-encoded material here ]
AAAAAAAAAAAAAAAAAAAAAAAAAAAAAAAAAAAAAAAAAAAAAAAAA
AAAAAAAAAAAAAAAAAAAAAAAA
AAAAAAAAAAAAAA==

----7bee2baa6b9e6139--
```

When the receiving email program reads the content of the message, it knows that the pieces are going to be divided by the boundary numbers. The first section is text that is to be displayed like a regular text message (as indicated by its text/plain content type). The second part is to be listed as an attachment to the message, with the name of the file as it will appear in the list of attachments. The encoding of the attached file—a format called base64—is described in Chapter 12, but it is the way most nontext attachments are formatted for sending across the Internet. Finally, the boundary number appears at the very end of the message to signify the end of the multipart portion.

Don't confuse attachments, such as images, with the kinds of images that appear in HTML-formatted mail. HTML content usually arrives as plain text (although with a more specific content type of text/html), and does not include any data other than the body text you see in the message and angle-bracketed tags that mark up the text. Among those tags may be ones that go out to the Internet (a Web site) and load an image into a place within the message. The image is loaded separately (just as it would be in a page displayed in a Web browser), and is not delivered with the mail message. The recipient's email program must be connected to the Internet for the image to be downloaded from its Web server. As described in Chapter 12, an image tag also allows a sender of automated email (both wanted and unwanted) to validate the recipient's email address.

Lines 12-14—X Fields

The SMTP mail standard could not possibly envision all pieces of information that a mail message might want to convey in the header. To make way for custom fields, the standard allows any nonstandard header field to be preceded by X-. Custom fields may be added at any point along the transport path from sender to recipient. For example, it's not uncommon for a sender's email program to insert one or more custom fields into the header to identify the name of the email program and its version. Some of this is pure ego on the part of the software maker, but if the program inserts additional fields, those fields can have a special meaning that enhance the message on the receiving end if the recipient happens to be running the same email program. For instance, the program may have special ways of signifying a message's priority. Other email programs ignore the custom field for this, but the program that knows about this field can perform some special highlighting or coloring to the message when listed in the recipient's inbox.

A fairly common custom field you will see if you view the source code of an email message in your inbox is the X-UIDL: field.[2] A mail server known as a POP3 (Post Office Protocol Version 3) server, commonly used to queue incoming mail, and from which your PC's email software downloads your mail, adds this custom header field to help it and your email software keep track of messages that you may have read but that have not been deleted from the server (in case you set up your mail preferences to act that way).

Line 15—A Blank Line

Believe it or not, a blank line has genuine significance in an email message. One such line is required between the message header and body. In other words, a header must not contain any blank lines between the fields. After encountering the first blank line, the recipient's email program begins rendering the content according to the content-type instructions in the header. If this seems rather simplistic, it is. But, then, so is having a batch of header lines identify themselves by nothing more sophisticated than their text labels at the beginning of a line up to a colon. Recipient email programs perform crudely simple text-matching tasks to find things such as the subject of the message and the sender's email address to place into the list of messages in your inbox. If the sender's email program had a bug in it, causing the Subject: header label to be accidentally misspelled as Sujbect:, your email program would leave the Subject column blank for that message in your mail list.

Lines 16-19—A Text Message Body

Following the blank line after the header comes the body of the message. Text messages are clearly readable even from the source code view of the message. If you understand HTML tags, an HTML-formatted message would also be meaningful in source code view if it didn't have spammy junk tags thrown into the mix. You wouldn't see any images or colorful text because the HTML needs a browser-like rendering engine to translate the markup into pretty text and formats.

---

[2] UIDL stands for "unique-id listing," essentially a message number on the server.

Some email programs, such as those supplied by AOL and MSN, send a message both in plain text and HTML-formatted versions. In other words, two copies of the message are embedded in each message. Not everyone likes to receive (or is able to view) HTML-formatted email. A message arriving both ways allows text-only email readers to see the words without the HTML tags cluttering up the screen; those who elect to view HTML-formatted email can see the fonts, colors, images, and other specifications that the sender puts into the design of the message.

Other kinds of content, especially messages containing attachments and those that are intentionally disguised from source code view (usually, to bypass spam filters) will be unintelligible in the source view. The content will be familiar characters, but they'll be jumbled. You can, however, decode the disguised messages (they are plain-text or HTML messages put through a base64 encoder on the sender's end) with the help of a utility described in Appendix B. Even though you can see the contents of base64-encoded attachments in a safe environment, you won't be able to tell whether the attachment is a file containing a virus or something harmless.

If you've reached this point in the discussion, you now know more about email headers than 95 percent of the world's email users. Congratulations.

An Introduction to Spam Sleuthing

The source code listing of an email message is a gold mine of pointers to various Internet destinations that can reveal more about the sender or advertiser than you'd ever deduce by simply reading the spam message. You'll need some extra tools to get your personal investigation underway, but fortunately those tools are available for free (or for, at most, a requested donation) on the Internet.

Before you start poking around for clues about a spam message, you should have a clear idea about what you want to accomplish. The kinds of things I like to know about a spam message without viewing it the regular way are:

- The ISP (name and location) from which the spam message arrived

- Whether the sender's IP address is on any major blocklists

- Details about the owner of the spamvertised Web site's domain name

- The ISP (name and location) of the spamvertised Web site

- The plain-language version of any encoded link URL

- What any base64 message content really says

- Whether the link to a spamvertised Web site would redirect me to another site

- Whether this message has been reported by other victims

By obtaining information tidbits about a spam message from its source code, I can determine where to direct LARTs about this message, evaluate whether the sender or spamvertiser is hiding behind offshore Internet services, and confirm that a suspicious message is really spam without ever hitting the spammer's Web site. Spam detectives with more notches on their magnifying glasses also look into a spammer's primary Domain Name Server providers to look for additional spam abetters. For this introduction, however, I'll stick with the more popular investigation tools, which will reveal quite a bit to you.

Extracting Domain Names and IP Addresses

Your first job in investigating a spam message is to dig through the source code to find the IP address of the sender and the domain name of the link(s) to spamvertised Web sites. Sender information is in the message header; the spamvertised site URL is in the body.

The Sender's IP Address

Your success in obtaining the IP address of the actual sender depends on whether your own incoming email server is configured to record the sender's IP address in the Received: header line. The only Received: header lines you can completely trust are those entered by your own incoming mail system. If your email system is not complex, the topmost Received: header line is the one added by your own email server, and is easy to read (it may be the only Received: line in the header). More complicated email environments, including those that use extensive firewalls and external spam-filtering services, add more Received: lines to the top of the headers as the message wends its way through your own system on its way to your inbox.

To help you decipher complex Received: header sequences, study the headers of two or more messages that arrived from outside sources (spam or ham, it doesn't matter). Look through the first several Received: lines to see which ones are the same in all messages. Those are the ones that your own system is adding through additional internal processing. Eventually, you'll reach a line that has the same "by" address (likely with a familiar domain name of your company); in contrast, the "from" portions are different with each message.

If your incoming email server is configured in a helpful manner, you will find the IP address of the sender's computer in parentheses and square brackets after the "from" portion, as in the following:

```
Received: from mdi-ger.de (adsl-67-125-157-
\x\.dsl.irvnca.pacbell.net [67.125.157.\x\]) by
mail.example.com (8.12.10) id hB4MYkm5011107 for
<\x\>; Thu, 4 Dec 2003 15:34:48 -0700 (MST)
```

Your server may have also performed a reverse DNS lookup on the IP address. The results of that search appear within the parentheses and in front of the square brackets. The reverse lookup reveals how the Domain Name System reports the identity of the IP address of the sender. Note in the above example that the identities of the actual IP address and the way the sender identified itself (as being mdi-ger.de) do not match. The "from" identity (supplied by the sending server) was forged by the sender in this case, while the spam message got "inserted" into the Internet via a DSL connection at a pacbell.net customer. Not all IP addresses report reverse DNS information, so you may find only the IP address in square brackets. That number is what you need to begin your investigation of the sending computer.

The Spamvertised Domain Name

Down in the message body, you typically find HTML-coded content, sometimes with a plain-text version appearing above the HTML. In the case of the HTML version, you need to do some digging to find the URLs that link to the spamvertised Web site.

HTML messages typically contain two different kinds of tags that contain URLs: the <a> and <img> tags (in upper- or lower case). I tend to ignore the <img> tag URLs unless the images have Web beacons associated with them (see Message Trick #9 in Chapter 12). For unbeaconed images, it's very common for the clickable links and images to be hosted on completely different systems. Images may come from a kind of "image bank" not under the direct control of the spamvertiser. It's the spamvertiser I want to know about.

In a link (<a>) tag, look for the attribute called href. The link might look like the following:

```
<a href="http://example.biz/bizop1.asp">CLICK
HERE</a>
```

Recall from Message Trick #23 (Chapter 12) that sometimes the HTML content is inside a "quoted-printable" section, in which case the equal sign will be represented as =3D. Also be on the lookout for spammers who introduce deceptive additional attributes in <a> tags, mostly to trick spam content analyzers. Ignore all URLs except the one assigned to the href attribute. You'll occasionally see bogus attributes intended to trip up spam-analyzing software that might be programmed to look for patterns of characters. For example, a `ref` attribute inside an `<a>` tag is meaningless. So are long ones that look like `hrefhwemohref`.

Consult Message Trick #2 in Chapter 12 for additional hints about extracting the true URL from one that has additional login strings (valid or otherwise) before an @ symbol in the URL. The domain you are interested comes after the @ symbol and before the next slash (/) or question mark (?) character. Look for familiar top-level domains, such as .com, .net, .biz, and .info. Occasionally the URLs will contain two-letter country designations at the end, such as .cn for China or .br for Brazil. In still other cases, the spammer uses an IP address instead of a domain name.

Decoding Obfuscated URLs

As described in Message Trick #18 (Chapter 12), some spammers try to conceal spamvertised URLs by encoding them with character references (characters represented in the form &#n; where n is a decimal number representing the character in the ASCII table). Another kind of encoding is called URL encoding, in which each character is represented in the form %n, where n is the hexadecimal value associated with a particular character. Table B-1 presents an abbreviated list of typical URL characters with their decimal and hexadecimal ASCII equivalents. For example, the character represented by . or %2E is a period.

Table B-1 Typical URL Character Decimal and Hexadecimal ASCII Values.

Character	Decimal ASCII Value	Hex ASCII Value	Character	Decimal ASCII Value	Hex ASCII Value
-	45	2D	8	56	38
.	46	2E	9	57	39
/	47	2F	?	63	3F
0	48	30	@	64	40
1	49	31	A	65	41
2	50	32	B	66	42
3	51	33	C	67	43
4	52	34	D	68	44
5	53	35	E	69	45
6	54	36	F	70	46
7	55	37	G	71	47

Character	Decimal ASCII Value	Hex ASCII Value	Character	Decimal ASCII Value	Hex ASCII Value
H	72	48	e	101	65
I	73	49	f	102	66
J	74	4A	g	103	67
K	75	4B	h	104	68
L	76	4C	I	105	69
M	77	4D	j	106	6A
N	78	4E	k	107	6B
O	79	4F	l	108	6C
P	80	50	m	109	6D
Q	81	51	n	110	6E
R	82	52	o	111	6F
S	83	53	p	112	70
T	84	54	q	113	71
U	85	55	r	114	72
V	86	56	s	115	73
W	87	57	t	116	74
X	88	58	u	117	75
Y	89	59	v	118	76
Z	90	5A	w	119	77
a	97	61	x	120	78
b	98	62	y	121	79
c	99	63	z	122	7A
d	100	64			

Before you can perform any lookups of domain names or IP addresses, they must be in unencoded form. You can find decoders for both types of encoding at spamwars.com/tools. Copy the encoded text from the message's source code view and paste it into the form text box for the conversion type you need. If the entire message body is encoded in base64 characters, copy the entire base64 text and paste it into the base64 decoder at spamwars.com/tools.

Command-line Tools

Most operating systems that provide connections to the Internet include several tools that perform different types of queries about domain names and IP addresses. Access to these tools is via a command-line prompt, not the friendly graphical user interface of, say, Windows or MacOS X. You need to open the command window to take a step back in time.[1] In Windows XP, look for the Start→All Programs→Accessories→Command Prompt program; in MacOS X, open the Terminal application.

Each tool is a small utility program that you typically run by typing the name of the tool, a space, and a domain name or IP address on which the tool is to act. The tool does its job either by sending some data packets or by going out to various sources on the Internet to make queries on your behalf, looking up things like domain name registrations and lists of ISPs that provide service to a particular domain. Results appear in succeeding lines until you either stop the action (by typing Ctrl+C) or all returned information appears (see Figure B-1).

Figure B-1 Issuing the ping command in Windows XP's Command Prompt window and stopping the returned values after a couple of packet transmissions.

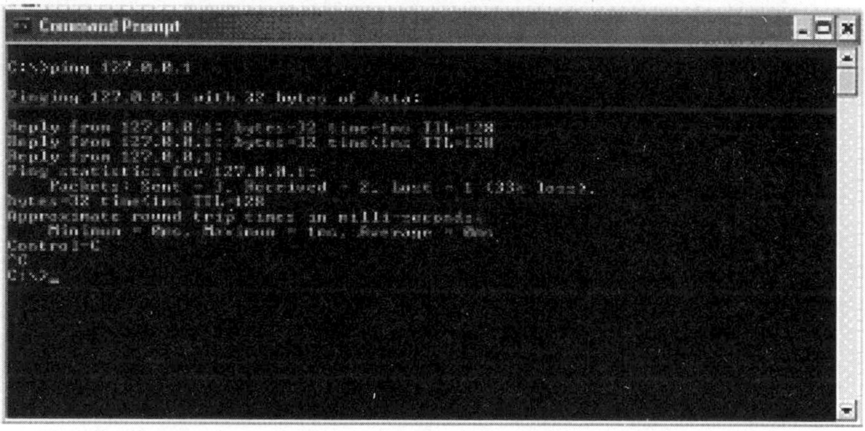

Table B-2 lists the primary command-line tools used in spam research and what information they produce. All four commands accept either a domain name (example.com) or an IP address as a parameter. Most of these tools have additional parameters and switches you can invoke to access advanced features.

Commands such as `nslookup` are easy to use. For example, if your incoming email server doesn't perform the reverse DNS lookup for the captured IP address of the sender, you can do it yourself. Simply copy the IP address from the square brackets, and supply it as a parameter to the `nslookup` command:

---

[1] Unix and Linux users tend to be more comfortable with command-line interfaces than with graphical user interfaces. Since most of these IP tools started their lives in the Unix world, their "old-fashioned" ways prevail to this day.

Table B-2 Popular Command-line Tools for Investigating Spam Addresses.

Tool Name	Description
nslookup	Looks for the opposite information of what you supply as a parameter: the IP address for a domain name; the domain name for an IP address (a reverse DNS lookup).
ping	Lets you know if a domain name or IP address resolves to a working system connected to the Internet.
traceroute	Reveals the Internet node routing between your system and the target system, often revealing the target's upstream ISP(s).
whois	For a domain name, returns a domain name registration data on file; for an IP address, returns information about the ISP that controls the block containing the IP number.

```
nslookup 192.168.1.101
```

If DNS has a record for the IP address, you'll receive the domain name of the computer associated with that IP address.

The whois command, which is the main one to use to locate domain name registration info, can be more difficult to work with if the domain is not one of the main generic top-level domains. To get the most accurate information, it helps to supply a specific whois server address to query with the command. If you don't know which server is the most likely to give you what you want, it could take some searching. Fortunately, as described in the next section, there are free automated services on the Web that do the hunting for you.

Spam Research Web Sites

Several free services are available to anyone who wishes to investigate spam domains and IP addresses. But be aware that these sites, many of which are completely volunteer efforts, occasionally get overloaded or, worse, stormed by a Distributed Denial of Service (DDoS) attack, presumably by spammers. Therefore, it's a good idea to put the following URLs into your browser bookmarks so you can rotate their usage or find help when your favorite site is out of commission:

Site	URL
DNSstuff	www.dnsstuff.com
Network-Tools	network-tools.com
Open RBL	openrbl.org
Sam Spade	samspade.org
Spamhaus	combat.uxn.com

My personal favorite is openrbl, simply because it presents the most information with the fewest steps (RBL stands for Real-time Blackhole List, another way to reference a blocklist). From openrbl, you can get not only comprehensive whois information, but also spam abuse reporting information and the existence of an IP address in the top block lists.

To demonstrate the kind of information that openrbl provides from the whois and Domain Name Service Block List (DNSBL) queries, I'll start with the domain of a Web site advertised in a message that arrived at one of my spam trap addresses. (Note: To keep cartooneys away from my door, I substitute example.com for the actual domain under analysis and I use XXX for the final portion of the IP address.)

Step 1. Conduct a domain name whois lookup

Click the Whois radio button. Then type only the domain name (no preceding www. or directory stuff after it) into the top frame of the openrbl page, as shown in Figure B-2. Click Submit.

Figure B-2 Openrbl.org entry field for domain or IP query.

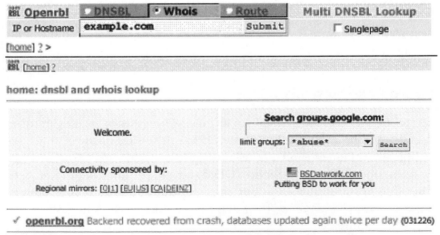

The bottom frame switches to show the results of the whois search and other lookups. It's a lot of information, so I'll discuss it in segments.

Figure B-3A reports the IP address of the domain name, as well as a URL you can use for future reference to retrieve this record from openrbl.org. Next comes a listing of up to two upstream providers under whose control the IP address lies. Although the order may flip-flop from one listing to the next, each provider manages a block of IP addresses that encompass the address of your query. One provider's block is large enough to contain the smaller provider's block.[2] The provider of the smaller block is usually the ISP that provides service for that IP address. In the example shown in Figure B-3A, the relationships between the two firms is more complicated than most, in that the firm with net identity CQNET (in Chongqing, China) is a joint venture with China Netcom Corp. (in Beijing). CQNET is the company offering service to the spam's advertiser.

Figure B-3A IP address and upstream provider IP address allocation blocks

Whois/NS-Delegation **211.158.15.XXX** http://openrbl.org/ip/211/158/15/XXX.whois.htm

```
Address: 211.158.15.XXX resolved to example.com
AS: 211.158.8.0/21 AS9929    China Netcom Corp. Beijing
Net 211.158.0-31 CQNET    Chongqing, Sichuan @cqnet.com.cn
```

After a section that includes pointers to the DNS servers, and provides email addresses where abuse reports can be sent to the site and DNS providers, comes information about the IP space provider closest to the target (see Figure B-3B). Details presented in this IP-Whois section vary, but you can always determine the size of the IP block controlled by the ISP. This is the information that some blocklists use to include all IPs of a provider if two or more numbers within that block show evidence of spam activity.

We can tell from information in Figure B-3B that CQNET offers IP addresses in the range between 211.158.0.0 and 211.158.31.255, a total of 8,192 address (32 times 256).

The final portion of the openrbl.org record is the whois information about the domain name originally queried (see Figure B-3C). I had to block out a lot of identifiable information here, but veteran spam trackers will immediately recognize various other trademarks of a domain registrant of hundreds of domains in China and elsewhere. Spam hunters attribute this registrant to a well-known American bulk emailer. How much, if any, of the registration information is accurate is anyone's guess.

---

[2] IP address notation (shown as 211.158.8.0/21 in the figure) is a shortcut indicator of the precise contiguous IP block that the provider controls. The smaller the number after the slash, the larger the block represented by the notation.

Figure B-3B Provider's IP-Whois information.

```
IP-Whois 211.158.15.XXX: (APNIC/CQNET)
[Cached]
[whois.apnic.net]
% [whois.apnic.net node-2]
% Whois data copyright terms    http://www.apnic.net/db/dbcopyright.html

inetnum:        211.158.0.0 - 211.158.31.255
netname:        CQNET
country:        CN
descr:          Chongqing CNC BoardBand Networks Co.,Ltd.
admin-c:        IPAS1-AP
admin-c:        PF20-AP
tech-c:         PF20-AP
status:         ALLOCATED PORTABLE
changed:        pengxm@cqnet.com.cn 20030815
mnt-by:         MAINT-CNNIC-AP
source:         APNIC

role:           CNNIC IPAS CONFEDERATION
address:        No.4, Zhongguancun No.4 South Street, Haidian District, Beijing
country:        CN
phone:          +86-10-62553604
fax-no:         +86-10-62559892
e-mail:         ipas@cnnic.net.cn
admin-c:        LW152-AP

tech-c:         LY220-AP
nic-hdl:        IPAS1-AP
mnt-by:         MAINT-CNNIC-AP
changed:        ipas@cnnic.net.cn 20020910
source:         APNIC

person:         Peng Frank
nic-hdl:        PF20-AP
e-mail:         pengxm@cqnet.com.cn
address:        21/f Dushi Plaza,No.39 Wusi Road Yuzhong Dist. Chongqing
phone:          +86-23-69089900-616
fax-no:         +86-23-63782270
country:        CN
changed:        pengxm@cqnet.com.cn 20021128
mnt-by:         MAINT-CNNIC-AP
source:         APNIC
```

Intentional falsification of domain name registration is a common offense by spammers. Some spam fighters exert substantial effort in investigating registrant addresses and phone numbers to see if the information is real or phony. Getting a registrar (or the grand overseer of generic top-level domains) to take action against a false registrant can be a difficult challenge.

Even if the registration information is phony, the date information about the record is accurate. You'll be amazed at how recently most deceptive spam domain names have been created within a very short time prior to the spam message being sent. The spamvertiser doesn't expect to build too much brand awareness for that domain.

Figure B-3C Domain registration record.

```
 Domain-Whois example.com: (example.com)
[Querying whois.internic.net]
[Redirected to whois.paycenter.com.cn]
[Querying whois.paycenter.com.cn]
[whois.paycenter.com.cn]

Domain Name:example.com


Registrant:
zzz jun
        P.O. box 000
        118000



Administrative Contact:
zzz jun
        zzz jun
        P.O. box 000
        dan dong Liaoning 118000
        China
        tel: 86 415 616xxxx
        fax: 86 415 616xxxx
        mailbox*2004#126.com

Technical Contact:
zzz jun
        zzz jun
        P.O. box 000
        dan dong Liaoning 118000
        China
        tel: 86 415 616xxxx
        fax: 86 415 616xxxx
        mailbox*2004#126.com

Billing Contact:
zzz jun
        zzz jun
        P.O. box 000
        dan dong Liaoning 118000
        China
        tel: 86 415 616xxxx
        fax: 86 415 616xxxx
        mailbox*2004#126.com


 Registration Date: 2004-03-18
       Update Date: 2004-03-18
   Expiration Date: 2005-03-18

    Primary DNS:  ns2.network-dns.biz          200.210.167.XXX

    Secondary DNS:  ns1.network-dns.biz        211.158.15.XXX

12 Lookups done in 9.066 Sec, Average 0.756sec
```

The bottom-line lesson from step 1 is twofold: We know the spamvertised Web site (or at least the initial destination of the link in the spam message) is hosted on a server in China, and that the domain registration is also listed as coming from China. There is no restriction that requires the domain registration and Web site hosting to be in the same country or hemisphere, but you at least can get an idea of where parts of the operation may be working.

The spam message that carried the spamvertised URL we've been looking at arrived from a broadband network in Sweden. It was most likely transmitted through a zombie PC, making further exploration of the insertion point of the spam futile. But you could still alert that broadband provider that spam originated from one of its IP addresses. If the provider is concerned about its customers' security, it would contact the customer and help cleanse the computer of its infection.

Step 2: Find out the blocklist standing of the IP address.

For the next stage, click on the DNSBL (Domain Name Service Block List) radio button in the top frame of the openrbl.org page. If you are continuing from step 1 on the domain name, then the IP address is already inserted for you. If, after you click Submit, you receive an alert about having just made a request for the same URL, force the request to go again—you're performing a different kind of search this time.

Figure B-4 shows the results of the search for the spamvertised URL's IP address. At the time I ran the search, openrbl.org was tracking 31 different blocklists, and found either the particular IP address or a block containing it mentioned in nine of them.

Not all blocklists (BLs) are created equal, so the sheer number of positives isn't always a call to arms. For example, some of the ones mentioned in Figure B-4 list the IP block simply because it is in China or has been reported by multiple other BLs. Moreover, many BLs list only email sender sources, not spamvertised URLs, causing this particular domain to come up negative because no mail originates from the IP block. If you find listings for Spamhaus, you can follow links provided here to review the records that Spamhaus has amassed for the IP or IP block.

I find this aggregate listing useful to locate links to SpamCop, Spamhaus, and Spews information gathered for the suspected IP address. It also provides a sense of how spam filter services that use blocklists might be treating incoming mail from large IP blocks, including those that contain innocent bystanders.

Figure B-4 Openrbl.org-aggregated blocklist report.

Multi DNSBL Lookup 211.158.15.XXX http://openrbl.org/ip/211/158/15/XXX.htm

Lookup 211.158.15.XXX (example.com) in **20+11 Zones**
AS: 211.158.0.0/21 AS9929 **China Netcom Corp. Beijing**
Net 211.158.0-31 CQNET Chongqing, Sichuan @cqnet.com.cn
Results: Positive=9, **Negative=22** (2004-03-24 00:05:49 UTC)

- @COUNTRY/country: 211.158/16: 553 COUNTRY CHINA - http://hatcheck.org/google?china; http://hatcheck.org/sbl?china
- @DYNAMIC/dialup: 211.158.15/24: 553 SORBS DUL
- @SPAM/spamsource: 553 SBL http://www.spamhaus.org/SBL/sbl.lasso?query=SBL15082; 211.158.15/24: 553 SBL http://www.spamhaus.org/SBL/sbl.lasso?query=SBL10264; SPEWS [1] Supabill/porncash/pzest, see http://spews.org/ask.cgi?; SPEWS [1] guide2grants/pharmacourt, see http://spews.org/ask.cgi
- SBL/spamhaus.org: 553 SBL http://www.spamhaus.org/SBL/sbl.lasso?query=SBL15082; 211.158.15/24: 553 SBL http://www.spamhaus.org/SBL/sbl.lasso?query=SBL10264
- SORBS/sorbs.net: 211.158.15/24: 553 SORBS DUL [Remove]
- SPEWS/spews.org: 211.158.15/24: 553 SPEWS2 [1] Supabill/porncash/pzest, see http://spews.org/ask.cgi?S343; SPEWS2 [1] guide2grants/pharmacourt, see http://spews.org/ask.cg
- BLARS/block.blars.org: INET 127.1.0.17
- SPAMBAG/cqnetcomcn: Blocked - see http://www.spambag.org/cgi-bin/spambag?mailfrom=cqnetcomcn
- FIVETEN/china.spam: added 2003-06-28; http://www.herbalpillsonline.biz on 61.131.62.58; added 2003-04-09; http://www.coolstats.com on 218.246.33.55, moved to 211.99.203.213; added 2003-06-21; http://red.ecablenetwork.com on 61.129.70.183, moved to 211.98.112.186; added 2003-06-07; http://www.ehostz.org on 218.28.3.188; added 2001-04-19; china does not seem to care about spam; added 2003-08-16; http://www.shop321.com on 218.80.151.1; added 2003-08-16; http://www.bearch11.com on 61.232.226.3; added 2003-08-16; http:/www.great12ssa.com on 61.174.153.41
- **Negative 22:** @ISP AHBL BOGONS BONDED BOPM CBL DRBL DSBL INTERSIL JIPPGMA LNSG NJABL NOMORE ORDB PSBL PSS REYNOLDS RFC_IPWH SPAMCOP SPAMRBL SPAMSITE UCEPROT

Hints for 211.158.15.XXX: (external, use BACK or ALT-LEFT when done)

- Track "example.com" at [Whois & Abuse|SpamCop*]
- Search "211.158.15.XXX" at [Google|SpamCop*|SenderBase] [MAPS|Schlund]
- CHECK: Nominate Relay-Test at: [ORDB] [Add Comment]

Step 3: Find identical spam incidents.

Numerous spam haters post examples of their fresh spam to one of the newsgroups you can access at groups.google.com. An even easier way, again, is through the openrbl.org home page, which includes a field in the lower frame in which you can enter a string of characters to search the newsgroups. If you followed step 1 to look up a spamvertised Web site domain, that domain name will likely already be entered for you in that field.

You have a choice of searching various newsgroups whose names include "abuse" or "email." Spam examples generally appear in the group named news.admin.net-abuse.sightings. The spamvertised URL domain name is usually the best string to search for because it is likely the most constant part of the messages that get spread to the masses. Other parts can have a variety of randomized features in the subject and body.

The resulting list comes from the groups.google.com site, showing all matching spam messages during the previous three months. You might find a flurry of activity spread over several days, and then nothing. This is common when high-volume spammers rotate their domain names.

If you're ever wondering whether a message you get is a truly personal message or a spam sample that used mail merging to insert your name, this is the place to go. Other reports of a spam message will appear within minutes of being received elsewhere.

Step 4. See if the spamvertised URL redirects you elsewhere.

You must use extreme care with this step; in fact, I generally recommend against it because I don't like to hit spamvertised Web sites with any traffic if I can avoid it. Remember the Email Manifesto cry: Zero Response. I rarely apply this step to spam, whereas I might investigate a phisher's link to find out what kind of skullduggery he may be up to.

The tool I use for this step is available on the Sam Spade page at samspade.org. You'll find lots of text boxes here where you can perform the same kinds of whois search as in openrbl.org. The text box to look for is the one next to the Browse button. Because it may be necessary to enter more than just a domain name, you may be tempted to copy and paste the complete link URL from a spam message. But because you don't want to convey any identifying information, try lopping off any name/value pairs following a question mark symbol in the URL.

When you click the Browse button, Sam Spade captures the content returned by the Web server at that address, and shows the results to you in source code form. Not only does the request conceal your IP address from the target's Web site log, but the content is returned in a completely safe environment. If you had visited that URL with your own browser, and the URL redirected you to a different site, you probably wouldn't realize it unless you viewed the Address bar in the browser when everything settled down. By looking first at the Sam Spade request results, you can see if there are any JavaScript or `<meta>` refresh tags. If there are, you may be able to see quite readily the URL to which you would be redirected. Now you can go back to step 1 and reach closer to the real spamvertiser's identity—or at least find out on which continent this stage of the redirection scam is located.

Step 5: Send a LART.

Not many spam recipients submit LART complaints to ISPs because it can be a lot of work. One avenue to follow is to subscribe to SpamCop (spamcop.net) and let them do the LARTing for you. Responsive ("white hat") ISPs have come to know and trust SpamCop's LARTs, and assign them quite a bit of credibility.

If you hope to earn the respect of an ISP, prepare to make your reports professional and unemotional. Most ISPs have an address reserved for reports of this kind:

```
abuse@<theISPDomain>
```

It is also a good idea to do your homework before submitting a LART. By that I mean, visit the ISP's Web site and make sure the published Acceptable Use Policy (AUP) or Terms of Service (TOS) document explicitly prohibits the activity you are reporting. Just because a hosted domain is the spamvertised Web site, you cannot automatically assume without other evidence that the same ISP is being used as the source of the mail.

Compose your LART as a report of possible violation of the company's AUP or TOS, *not* as an accusation. Abuse desks are so accustomed to receiving strident, accusatorial spam reports, that your polite, informational message will likely get more attention. Cite the section number of the policy you believe the spam message violates, and include a copy of the message. The only portions of the message you should modify (if at all) are parts that identify your email address. Check the Received: and To: headers for the presence of your address, and substitute an indicator that you have "munged" your address (simply replace your address with <munged>). Also look for your address in Web beacons or link name/value pairs.

After you submit your LART, you may receive a standard reply; or you may never hear another word, even if the ISP takes action; or you may receive a description of the outcome many days later. You may also hear from the sender you're accusing of spamming, so arm yourself with facts (not hypothetical suppositions) and be prepared to fend off or ignore a cartooney threat.

If you intend to research the origins of spam that arrives in your inbox, you'll have much to learn. Those who have been doing it for a long time know all of the IP and domain search commands and options inside and out. When you follow discussions in some of the antispam newsgroups, you'll be amazed at the depth some researchers go to track down a spammer and his activity. Pace yourself on your climb up the learning curve. Knowledge really is power over the tricks and scams that seek out the unwary.

APPENDIX C

Online Resources

Enter the word "spam" into the Google search box, and you'll get more than 7 million hits. A lot of those destinations are old pages that haven't been updated in years, while others are, indeed, valuable resources. There are only so many hours in a day, so if you're like me, you'll want to hit the high points, especially those sites that are innately reliable information sources or act as aggregators of information from a wide range of other sites. Here I list those high points, where you can find information not covered in this book as well as continuing news about the attacks on email. Many of these sites have further links to equally deserving destinations.

Support for This Book
> www.spamwars.com

Spam News

> ComputerWorld's Spam Coverage
> www.computerworld.com/news/special/pages/
> 0,10911,2105,00.html

> ComputerWorld's Spam Coverage RSS Feed
> www.computerworld.com/news/xml/coverage/
> 0,5451,2105,00.xml

> Marketing Vox
> www.marketingwonk.com/archives/categories/spam_antispam

SpamNews
spamnews.com/blog/spamNEWS/

Virus/Worm/Trojan News

F-Secure Virus News Page
f-secure.com/virus-info/virus-news

Sophos Virus Information
www.sophos.com/virusinfo

Sophos Virus Information RSS Feed Registration
www.sophos.com/virusinfo/infofeed/rss_index.html

Symantec Corporation Security Response
www.symantec.com/avcenter/index.html

Antispam Organizations

Coalition Against Unsolicited Commercial Email (CAUCE)
cauce.org

SpamCop
spamcop.net

Spamhaus (and ROKSO list)
www.spamhaus.org

Spam Prevention Early Warning System (SPEWS)
spews.org

Direct Marketing Organizations and News

The Direct Marketing Association
www.the-dma.org

DM News
www.dmnews.com

Opt-in News
www.optinnews.com

Email and the Law

Complaint Addresses (compiled list)
banspam.javawoman.com/report3.html

Institute for Spam and Internet Public Policy
isipp.org

Spam Laws (David E. Sorkin)
www.spamlaws.com

U.S. Federal Trade Commission
ftc.gov/spam

Antispam/Antivirus Product Reviews

CNet
reviews.cnet.com

Spamotomy
spamotomy.com

ZDNet
reviews-zdnet.com.com/

Spam Sleuthing Tools

DNSstuff
www.dnsstuff.com

Network-Tools
network-tools.com

Open RBL
www.openrbl.org

Sam Spade
samspade.org

Spamhaus
combat.uxn.com

Email Abuse Newsgroups and Mailing Lists

Newsgroups (via news reader or groups.google.com)
news.admin.net-abuse.email
news.admin.net-abuse.sightings

SpamCop Mailing List
news.spamcop.net/mailman/listinfo/spamcop-list

SPAM-L (mailing list; registration required)
www.claws-and-paws.com/spam-l/spam-l.html

GLOSSARY

AUP (Acceptable Use Policy) An ISP's written guidelines for acceptable behavior of its customers. Customers agree to the AUP as a condition of becoming a customer, and risk being kicked off the system for violations of the policy. Not all ISP AUPs prohibit spam. AUP and TOS are different names for essentially the same document.

base64 encoding A system of converting characters and symbols from any language to a lowest-common-denominator set of 64 characters that can be sent, relayed, and received by virtually any Internet software. The character set consists of a–z, A–Z, 0–9, plus sign (+), and equal sign (=). Email and Web browser software automatically converts base64-encoded content to its original form.

bounce An email message that is returned to the address in the message's From: or Reply-To: header field if the message cannot be delivered. Antivirus server software is sometimes configured to send a bounce when a virus is found, even if the message was composed with a spoofed From: header field.

cartooney A lawyer—real or imaginary—who threatens (or threatens to threaten) an antispammer with legal action. A cartoon-attorney.

CAUCE (Coalition Against Unsolicited Commercial Email) (cauce.org) A volunteer organization dedicated to influencing legislation that fights spam.

ccTLD (country-code top-level domain) A two-character code that is part of a domain name associated with a particular country, such as .jp for Japan and .br for Brazil.

chickenboner An antispammer's derogatory reference intended to promote the stereotype of a lone spammer in a mobile home surrounded by take-out chicken boxes. Derived from the original phrase, "beer cans and chicken bones," claimed by newsgroup poster Ron Ritzman.

cracker A computer programmer who intentionally breaks computer encryption and other security hurdles, such as software copy protection. In

311

contrast to hackers, crackers commonly work toward stealing information or disrupting the systems they break into.

DNS (Domain Name Service)   A vast network of servers within the Internet infrastructure whose job includes matching domain names with IP addresses. Changes to the lookup tables propagate among DNS servers around the world. Each time an Internet request is made to a server by its domain name, a DNS server provides the IP address that the software uses to make the actual connection.

EHLO   Extended Hello command. (see *HELO)*

frea speach   An antispammer's way of referring to the commercial free speech argument of spammers. It derives from a misspelling in a spammer's forum posting, claiming "free speach." Antispammers picked up on the spelling error, and propagated it to both words.

gTLD (generic top-level domain)   One of the domains, such as .com, .org, .edu, and others that has no geographical location associated with it.

hacker   Originally, a clever engineer or programmer who discovered new applications or useful twists for existing technologies. Due to misuse of the term in popular media, "hacker" has gained the same connotation as "cracker," causing some former "hack"-related activities (such as the venerable MacHack Conference) to change their names. This book misuses the term in the same way popular media does.

ham   A euphemism for email that the recipient wants to receive. The opposite of spam.

HELO   The "hello" command that a sending SMTP server issues to a receiving SMTP server to initiate an email message transaction. A more modern version of the command, EHLO, signifies that the sending server is equipped to handle SMTP service extensions.

hexadecimal   A reference to base16 counting system, in which "digits" are indicated by 0 through 9 and continuing with A through F, for a total of 16 numbers that can be represented by a single digit. Hexadecimal values are used for URL-encoded characters (where %20 is equivalent to decimal 32, the ASCII value for a space character) and some forms of HTML color attribute values. Colors, represented by combinations of red, green, and blue intensities rated between 0 and 255 (0 and FF) are often notated by a sequence of all three values, such as #00FF00 (no red, full green, no blue). This notation is called a hexadecimal triplet.

honeypot An intentionally attractive target for spam or hacker activity designed to monitor such activity to assist in research. Presumably named after the honey container in the *Winnie the Pooh* stories, a honey pot is typically an open mail relay or proxy server awaiting discovery by automated IP address probes.

HTML (HyperText Markup Language) A system of document markup (with tags) that lets an author specify the context of a document's content. Modern Web browsers and HTML-equipped email programs apply visual styles to the context tags (such as italicizing text marked with an <em> tag to be emphasized text).

IP (Internet Protocol) The rules that Internet host computers follow to convey information packets from one to another.

IP address A number associated with an Internet host (computer or other networked device) that allows other hosts to connect with it. The format currently in use consists of four numbers separated by dots (a "dotted quad"), with each number in the range between 0 and 255, as in 192.168.0.1. IP addresses are assigned by ISPs, which parcel out individual numbers from blocks of contiguous IP addresses they control. A fixed IP address remains assigned to a host; a dynamic IP is assigned at random within a block of addresses at the time of each connection to a network.

ISP (Internet Service Provider) Large consumer services such as AOL, as well as organizations that resell Internet access and smaller IP address blocks to local Internet providers.

JavaScript A programming language built into most modern Web browsers. JavaScript code can be embedded within HTML documents to enhance interactivity with a page without requiring page refreshing. It can add user convenience to Web pages, but has no place in email messages.

Joe-job A tactic of a spammer to make a spam barrage appear to originate from the mail server of an enemy, or list the enemy's Web site as a spamvertiser in the hopes that thousands of bounce messages and complaints will land at the target's feet. Named after an attack on the joes.com domain.

LART (Luser Attitude Readjustment Tool) A report to an ISP or upstream provider about spam or other activity of one of its customers that violates the ISP's AUP or TOS. A LART is usually directed to an ISP's abuse desk.

listwash The act of removing a spam reporter's email address from a spammer's list database. The goal is to prevent the complainer from issuing more complaints to the spammer's ISP.

mail exchanger A computer server that sends, receives, or relays electronic mail. The address of a mail exchanger (MX) for a given Internet domain is retrieved via DNS each time an outgoing message is sent.

mainsleaze Usually, a provider of Internet connectivity or related services that tolerates or actively seeks the business of spammer operations. Also used to refer to the predominant spam gangs, such as those listed in Spamhaus' ROKSO list.

MAPS (Mail Abuse Prevention System, LLC) (mail-abuse.org) The first organization to offer a list of suspected spam IP sources, called the real-time blackhole list (RBL). The organization became an early lightning rod for lawsuits by spammers on grounds of commercial free speech and restraint of trade.

millionsCD A reference to the CD-ROM collections of millions of email addresses offered by spam facilitators to attract newbie spammers. Recent published analysis of one of these CDs showed the quality of the list to be very poor.

munge To remove or disguise a section of text to prevent its original content from being revealed. Spam reports to ISPs typically munge traces of the recipient's email address so as to prevent the spammer (who receives the report and copy of the suspected spam message) from listwashing the spam reporter's address.

MX Record A listing in DNS that reveals the domain and subdomain of the mail exchanger to which all email for an addressee's domain should be sent. Before each email message is sent, the outgoing SMTP server looks up the MX record for the addressee's domain and then queries DNS again for the IP address of the mail exchanger.

packet A small parcel of data, usually extracted from a larger collection, that is given its own header information before being sent on its way through the Internet. On the receiving end, packets from the same source are reassembled into their original form and sequence to recreate the original data (e.g., a file or email message).

proxy On the Internet, acts as an intermediary server between a client (e.g., a computer sending a request) and server (e.g., a computer responding to a request). In some forms, proxies intentionally modify the content from the server on its way to a client, such as a proxy server that formats Web content especially for small screens on Internet-capable cellular telephones. An open proxy server freely routes packets to their destination, disguising their true IP source.

relay In an email context, an open mail relay is an SMTP server configured to pass along email messages intended for other destinations. Originally a key component of the early ARPANET email system, open relays (which can be easily detected) are now discouraged because of the abusive way spammers have used them to hide their originating IP addresses from the recipient's incoming SMTP server.

RFC (Request for Comment) A document submitted to the Internet Engineering Task Force (IETF) as a way to present new ideas and proposed Internet standards for public discussion. The IETF has elevated numerous RFC to Internet standard status, including many that are responsible for the successful interoperability of the email system.

Rule #1 An informal antispam rule that states "Spammers lie." Rule #2 is, "If you think a spammer is telling the truth, see Rule #1."

Rule #3 An informal antispam rule that states "Spammers are stupid."

SMTP (Simple Mail Transfer Protocol) The Internet standard that describes how email servers communicate with each other during the exchange of an email message. The current specification is RFC 2821, which is separate from the message format standard, RFC 2822.

spam A bulk or automated message sent without the recipient's prior explicit consent. See Chapter 2 for other interpretations of this term.

SpamCop (spamcop.net) A volunteer and commercial service that provides spam reporting and blocklist services. Operated by Julian Haight and several deputies, the organization provides both free and paid services. It is now owned by Ironport Systems (ironport.com), maker of email server hardware and host of the Bonded Sender Program.

Spamhaus (spamhaus.org) An all-volunteer organization providing real-time blocklists (two types) and a database of information gathered on high-volume spammers, known as the ROKSO list (Register of Known Spam Operations).

spam trap A secret email address hidden from plain view on a Web page, but embedded within the page's source code. Email address harvesting software will find such an address and add it to a spammer's address list. Email messages sent to the address are deemed genuine unsolicited mail because the address is used for no other purpose and could have been gathered only by harvesting.

spamvertiser An advertiser that uses unsolicited bulk email (spam) to reach prospects. Links in such email messages lead to spamvertised Web sites. Spamvertisers regularly hire spammers to execute the mailing.

spim Unsolicited advertisements that are sent to recipients via Instant Messaging (IM), Internet Relay Chat (IRC), and Short Message Service (SMS) on cellular telephones. Spim messages have been known to spoof the sender's name to make the message appear to come from someone on the recipient's list of correspondents (e.g., a buddy list).

spoof In email, a forgery of any portion of an email header. Most commonly referring to the From: header field, which spam engines fill with false names and addresses or addresses culled from a worm-infected PC user's address book and other files.

TCP (Transaction Control Protocol) The rules that host computers follow during the exchange of data packets to detect errors and request retransmission of lost or garbled packets.

TCP/IP The combination of TCP and IP in a network system (like the Internet) that permits multiple flows of packets among hosts while keeping the packets flowing in the desired direction, obtaining corrected packets as needed, and occupying the same network "wire" without colliding with other packet streams.

tinlc Acronym for "there is no lumber cartel," a tongue-in-check remark that spammer's declare when they succeed in getting a spammer's service discontinued. The Lumber Cartel is a wholly fictional and mythic organization of companies dedicated to the publishing and mailing of paper catalogs and other physical advertising mail.

TLD (top-level domain) The final portion of an Internet domain name, such as .com and .org. Several TLDs are used worldwide, and are known as generic TLDs (gTLD); country-specific TLDs are called ccTLDs.

TOS (Terms Of Service) An ISP's written guidelines for acceptable behavior of its customers. Customers agree to the TOS as a condition of becoming a customer, and risk being kicked off the system for violations of the policy. Not all ISP TOSes prohibit spam. TOS and AUP are different names for essentially the same document.

Trojan horse A computer program that on the face of it the user finds desirable, but includes additional code that has entirely other (usually undesirable) purposes. A downloadable free program that installs a game, file-sharing utility, or humorous cursor designs may also install a keylogger program, which silently accumulates keyboard activity in Web page fields for user names and passwords before sending this security information back to the author. A Trojan horse is essentially a delivery vehicle for worms. The name is derived from the Trojan War myth, in which Greek solders hid inside a large wooden horse, which the Trojans welcomed into their walls as a peace offering.

UBE (unsolicited bulk email) Email with no restrictions as to content sent without prior consent to a large quantity of recipients through automated processes.

UCE (unsolicited commercial email) Email offering a product or service sent without prior consent to a large quantity of recipients through automated processes.

URL (Uniform Resource Locator) The address of a World Wide Web resource. Some pronounce it "earl," others spell it out (U-R-L). While a URL is a subtype of the Uniform Resource Identifier (URI), the distinction is of little consequence to most Web users.

USENET One of the first public electronic "bulletin board" systems, the network consists of numerous news servers containing thousands of individual newsgroups. Each newsgroup is aimed at a specific subject area. You can access newsgroups via your email program and ISP's news server (usually named nntp) or with your Web browser by visiting groups.google.com, where the archive is located.

virus A computer program that usually attaches itself to an existing program (such as an operating system) and uses a variety of techniques to spread itself to other systems by way of a network or (in the old days) disk swapping. A virus may do little or a catastrophic amount of damage to the system on which it runs, depending on the intentions of the virus writer.

worm A standalone computer program that performs whatever helpful or harmful activity its author desires, and also replicates and distributes copies of itself to other systems via network or disk. As a self-contained program, a worm can easily "call out" to other computers across the Internet to announce its infection (and IP address), ultimately to allow the machine to be taken over by external programmers. Worms reach computers as hidden payloads of Trojan horses and as attachments to email. They are responsible for the infection of PCs being used as slave SMTP servers for spam without the owners' knowledge.

zombie A computer that has been infected with a worm that opens a "backdoor" to external programmers, who then install additional software on the computer. The zombie machine becomes a slave, capable of issuing Distributed Denial of Service (DDoS) attacks and relaying vast quantities of spam without the user's knowledge. Full-time connection of PCs to the Internet via broadband connections facilitate both the initial infection and continued external control of the PC.

I N D E X